The
KNIGHTS TEMPLAR
in the New World

The KNIGHTS TEMPLAR *in the New World*

How Henry Sinclair Brought the Grail to Acadia

William F. Mann

Destiny Books
Rochester, Vermont

Destiny Books
One Park Street
Rochester, Vermont 05767
www.InnerTraditions.com

Destiny Books is a division of Inner Traditions International

Library of Congress Cataloging-in-Publication Data
Mann, William F., 1954-
  [Labyrinth of the Grail]
  The Knights Templar in the New World : how Henry Sinclair brought the
Grail to Acadia / William F. Mann.
      p. cm.
Previously published as: The labyrinth of the Grail.
Includes bibliographical references (p.) and index.
  ISBN 0-89281-185-4
  1. America—Discovery and exploration—Pre-Columbian. 2.
Acadia—Discovery and exploration. 3. Grail. 4. Tarot. 5. Sinclair,
Henry, Sir, 1345-ca. 1400. 6. Templars. I. Title.
E103.M35 2004
909—dc22
                                    2003024682

Printed and bound in the United States at Lake Book Manufacturing, Inc.

10 9 8 7 6 5 4 3 2 1

Text design and layout by Mary Anne Hurhula
This book was typeset in Sabon with Aquitaine Initials and Delphin as the
display typefaces

To my mother and father,
for their love
To the Mann family,
for their love of life
To Marie, William, and Thomas,
for my love

Contents

Foreword

by Michael Bradley

—————⮞◆⮜—————

In *Holy Grail Across the Atlantic* I presented evidence that an obscure group of European religious heretics had discovered Canada, established a settlement in Nova Scotia in A.D. 1398, and brought with them what they considered to be the Holy Grail.

In Europe, these religious heretics were known as Cathars, or "Albigensians." Their heresy was a stubborn belief in the ancient tradition that Jesus had been married, probably to Mary Magdalene, that they had one or more children, and that descendants of Jesus survived until the medieval era of the heretics. Indeed, these heretics, concentrated mainly in southern France, believed that the "Holy Bloodline" of Jesus lived among them and was represented by the de Bouillons, a notable family originating in the Pyrenees region.

Needless to say, this heresy threatened the Roman Catholic Church like no other. It was not a matter of religious hairsplitting. It challenged the basic legitimacy and validity of the Papacy. It encouraged a wry look at the heavily-edited Church version of the New Testament and it mocked the pomp and power of Rome. It appears that the Church had known of this heresy for years but, because many powerful noble houses also believed in it and some even claimed intermarriage with the Holy Bloodline, the Church could do little but watch the steady growth of Catharism. This growth of the heresy culminated in the year A.D. 1099 when Godfroi de Bouillon, who claimed descent from the Holy Blood and who apparently had plausible genealogies to prove it, was elected king of Jerusalem by a conclave of nobles and clerics who gathered in the city so recently conquered by the Crusaders. Very quickly, the dynasty of Godfroi de Bouillon took energetic steps to protect and establish itself on the most prestigious throne in Christendom.

In line with military thinking of the day, two elite orders of knighthood were formed to protect both the dynasty and the heresy that supported it. These knights were garrisoned in strong fortresses in Palestine and Europe. One of these orders was the Knights of the Temple of Solomon, better known to history as the Knights Templar. The other was the Order of the Knights of St. John of Jerusalem. They too became better known in history under another name: the Knights of Malta.

Despite the valor of these knights, the European Crusaders lost Jerusalem and much of the Holy Land in A.D. 1187, in a massive counterattack by the Saracens. Although later crusades were briefly able to retake some of the lost territory, the general pattern was a gradual expulsion of Europeans from Palestine. The Kingdom of Jerusalem became a construction of wishful thinking rather than Realpolitik.

With the loss of Jerusalem, the dynasty of Godfroi de Bouillon fell back to its natural constituency and origins in the southern French regime of Provence and Languedoc. But, along with the loss of Jerusalem as a prestigious geopolitical power base (as we would say today), the de Bouillon dynasty also lost its security and special aura of not-quite-so-secret sanctity. The pope called for a crusade against the Cathar heretics in A.D. 1209, and on March 16, 1244, the last Cathar fortress, the citadel of Montségur in the Pyrennes, was taken by the Vatican armies. By A.D. 1307, the Knights Templar had been officially disbanded by Pope Clement V and had been crushed in France by raids of King Philippe IV.

The most romantic and evocative aspect of the Cathar heresy was its connection with the Holy Grail. In medieval Europe, it was common knowledge that this Holy Grail was guarded by Templars and that it reposed in the castle of Munsalvaesch, which today's scholars accept as Montségur. What was this Holy Grail? It was long regarded as a cup or vessel of some sort, and most people today imagine it that way. The best guess was that the Grail was the cup from which Jesus drank at the Last Supper and that Joseph of Arimathea later held aloft to catch Christ's blood when Jesus's side was pierced by the spear of the Roman, Caius Longinus.

But it has now become clear, because of the work of many researchers and scholars, that this Holy Grail wasn't a physical cup or vessel of any sort. It was a code phrase describing the descendants of Jesus, the Holy Bloodline, that was a living vessel in which the Holy Blood was held, preserved, and perpetuated. Romances about the Holy Grail were attempts to tell the heretical beliefs without arousing the suspicion of the Catholic Church's terrible Inquisition.

What happened to the Holy Grail? It is said that it was spirited away from doomed Montségur by three knights just a few days before the citadel surrendered. The names of the three knights have been preserved in dozens of Grail romances, in many troubadour poems, and even in more or less plain history. If the Holy Grail is actually a bloodline descending from Jesus, then this can only mean that the three knights saved one or more representatives of the Holy Blood and took these people (children?) to safety, while the Templar defenders of Montségur fought and died.

History tells us that surviving Templars fled to Portugal, where they changed their name to the Knights of Christ and found such favor in high places that several kings and princes of Portugal became Grand Master of the new order. But history also tells us that many Templars fled to Scotland and eventually came under the protection and patronage of Henry Sinclair, earl of Orkney and baron of Rosslyn during the fourteenth century. So many Templars fled to Scotland that they actually formed the bulk of Scottish calvary at the Battle of Bannockburn (A.D. 1314), in which Robert the Bruce defeated the English.

Whatever happened to the Holy Grail? Conventional history is silent, and the silence has been so lengthy that few now even believe that the Holy Grail ever existed, much less survived to the present.

My only original contribution to this story was to realize the significance of one fact: this same Henry Sinclair, patron of refuge Templars, supposedly made a transatlantic voyage to a place called Estotiland and claimed to have established a settlement there. In *Holy Grail Across the Atlantic* I was able to show that many early maps of Nova Scotia refer to a hidden refuge, and that the strange ruins of a castle in midpeninsular Nova Scotia are of a style and type consistent with

Henry Sinclair's era and Scottish-Scandinavian character. The castle is shown on maps.

I realized one other thing and was able to argue it plausibly. Prince Henry Sinclair's domains in Orkney and Rosslyn were too insecure to permit him the luxury of a mere adventure of discovery across the ocean. Only some truly overwhelming motivation could have justified Sinclair's actions: he spent at least one year (and maybe two) across the Atlantic, and he took his entire fleet across the ocean, leaving Orkney and Rosslyn (and his wife and daughters) virtually unprotected during that time. Indeed, he arrived back in Scotland just in the nick of time to die fighting some invading British.

Because Henry Sinclair was a known patron of refugee Templars, and because the Templars had been created by the kings of Jerusalem and were guardians of the Holy Grail, the situation seemed clear enough. The Holy Grail had been evacuated from doomed Montségur. It was eventually taken to Scotland, a secure transatlantic haven for the Holy Grail, and some Templar guardians were established in Nova Scotia by Henry Sinclair in an urgent and risky enterprise. So much for *Holy Grail Across the Atlantic*. A North American chapter to an evocative and romantic story had been presented and supported with a surprising amount of hard evidence (when one learned how to look!), such as an early map of Nova Scotia (Caspar Vopell's map of 1545) decorated with a clearly labeled Templar knight drawn next to "Port Refuge."

In the years since *Holy Grail Across the Atlantic* was published many people have contacted me. Some have wanted to know where they could read about the entire Grail story, and I referred them to both older and very recent European books on the subject. Some people wrote to offer additional evidence regarding my own argument—a woman from Barrie, Ontario, a well-known and brilliant operatic soprano who is presently enthralling the European music critics, gave me a seventeenth-century drawing of an unknown "castle" that has been preserved in her Acadian family for many, many generations. Is this drawing a real representation of Sinclair's settlement before it fell to ruins and was abandoned?

Terry Punch, then president of the Royal Nova Scotia Historical Society, wrote that twenty-five miles east of the ruin that I had investigated he and a team from the society had found another, smaller and apparently secondary, construction. Gerard Leduc, a professor at Concordia University in Montreal, wrote to inform me of the old ruins he'd discovered near the Quebec-Vermont border. Were they evidence of Grail refugees gradually penetrating inland? Possibly. Don Eckler of Houghton, New York, wrote (and sent photos) of Templar symbols carved on boulders and ledges along the Allegheny River route in New York State and Pennsylvania. Old maps (sent by many correspondents) showed evidence of Europeans around Lake Ontario as early as 1546. A Concordia University core sample from the bottom of Aldophus Reach at the mouth of the Bay of Quinte in Lake Ontario seemed to prove a population concentration of at least 1,200 unknown Europeans lived in the area from 1580 until about 1620. Conventional history cannot explain these people's identity.

Altogether, because of my own research and information gathered by readers of my book, it seemed certain that Grail refugees pushed inland from their initial Nova Scotia haven. By about 1580 they had reached Niagara, and the evidence suggests that thereafter they simply melded into the frontier life of New France. This makes sense because most of Sinclair's original Templars had been French, even though they sojourned in Scotland, and may have retained much French culture and language. This sort of pattern seemed also to answer some perplexing questions about the Acadians, such as why some Acadian family genealogies are up to ten generations too long to fit in with known colonizations, or why one of the most common Acadian names is Gallant ("knight"). What happened to the Grail refugees after the initial 1398 Nova Scotia settlement is the subject of my most recent book, *Grail Knights of North America*.

But what happened to the Holy Grail itself?

If, as Cathar tradition suggests, the Holy Grail is actually a lineage of people descended from Jesus and Mary Magdalene, and if the scions of this Holy Bloodline were actually saved from Montségur, then these Holy Blood descendants, along with a fair number of Templar protectors, may well have ended up in Scotland with Henry Sinclair. According to Sir Walter Scott, the castle at Rosslyn was supposed to have held holy treasures. What could this mean?

The most probable explanation and scenario is that the actual scions of the Holy Blood were taken to the Nova Scotia haven, along with other religious and monetary treasures, and with many excess Templars, who constituted a real embarrassment and danger for Prince Henry. Since the Templars had been outlawed and excommunicated by the pope, they could form the excuse for a crusade against Rosslyn and Orkney. It would have been much more politic, and much safer, for Sinclair to have transported these Templars across the Atlantic, and that may be why he allocated his entire fleet of thirteen ships to the risky venture. Only by risking his entire fleet for one sailing season could he transport enough Templars across the ocean and away from Rome's notice. The actual record of Sinclair's voyage is a document known to historians as *The Zeno Narrative*. If carefully read, it infers that Sinclair arrived in Nova Scotia with several hundred armed men. The record states at one point that Sinclair was able to send "one hundred" soldiers off on a minor reconnaissance expedition. Surely he would not have sent his entire armed force away from his unprotected ships in an unknown land with unknown adversaries.

So it is very possible that the actual descendants of Jesus and Mary Magdalene (that is, according to the beliefs of this heresy) were also transported to Nova Scotia. Another possible idea is that a permanent record of the Holy Bloodline's genealogy was also transported across the Atlantic to the Nova Scotia refuge in addition to, or instead of, actual descendants of Jesus. There is also a third possibility. Enduring stories tell of a fifth gospel that can be attributed to someone directly involved with the life of Jesus, or perhaps even to Jesus himself.

This is where the most intriguing, fascinating, and tantalizing of all my correspondents comes into the picture. Bill Mann contacted me in early December 1991 to discuss the most fantastic possibility: the possibility of recovering the Holy Grail.

I was naturally skeptical at first, and I must admit, some skepticism lingers. On the other hand I could not, and cannot, dismiss Bill's ideas. As president of a planning and development firm, Bill holds professional accreditations in planning, landscape architecture, and forestry. To say that he's an expert in design and planning would be understating the case. He's been involved in some of the largest urban design projects in Canada and abroad.

In part because of this expertise, he claims to know *precisely* where Prince Henry Sinclair established his secret settlement in Nova Scotia and hid the Holy Grail. It still might be hidden there due to mischance and misfortune on the part of those few who once knew the secret of its location, unless it has been recovered by persons unknown.

But there is also another interesting aspect to Bill's background. He comes from a strong Masonic family connection. It was through a mysterious "secret" ring of his great-uncle, who was once Supreme Grand Master of the Knights Templar of Canada, that his personal quest began.

Briefly, Bill applied his eclectic knowledge of geometry, art history, the classics, and physical planning and surveying to the initial diagram shown to him by his great-uncle, and then applied that diagram to the real geography of Nova Scotia. Amazingly, it all fit better than he had hoped. Having established a pattern of sacred geometry, Bill was able to pinpoint a site that occupied the most significant position in a geometric figure known to be associated with both medieval Templar and modern-day Masonic "ultimate secrets."

The most disconcerting aspect of these manipulations, from my point of view, is that at the site that is identified there are apparent ruins clearly visible. But, more important, the land seems to have been purposely molded and transformed to present human and animal figures. These figures are those featured in the Gospel of John, the only gospel readily accepted by Cathar heretics and Templars, the only gospel that details the wedding at Cana with the clear indication that it is Jesus's own wedding. That is to say that John's gospel was the only one accepted by the heretics as being reasonably accurate, undistorted, and unedited. This is not to say that either I or Bill believe that the heretics' beliefs are the ultimate truth. It is only to say that certain mysterious organizations believed it to be true or may have used the belief to their advantage in their battles with the Church.

It should be emphasized here, because it is emphasized in both *Holy Grail Across the Atlantic* and now in Bill's book, that although the Templars always held the historical spotlight, another order of knighthood created by the Kingdom of Jerusalem was named in honor of Saint John—the Knights of St. John of Jerusalem, Hospitallers—better known as the Knights of Malta. And it was the Knights of Malta who played a mysteriously prominent part in the history of all transatlantic discoveries, but particularly in Canadian history.

Canada at one time was going to be ceded to the Knights of Malta; the citadel at Quebec City (the first known fortress in Canada) was a priory of the Knights of Malta. Sieur de Monts, one of Canada's premier early explorers, was even given a Knights of Malta castle as a retirement home. The list goes on and on. So it is not surprising that the landscape around Bill Mann's still pristine Nova Scotia site seems to feature figures symbolized in the Apocalypse of St. John. It is also not surprising that the site can be located through a combination of symbols relating to the Knights Templar, the Knights of Malta, and the House of Solomon.

I must confess that sometimes I'm more than a little skeptical of symbolic interpretations. Yes, at the Nova Scotia site I can make out representations of creatures mentioned significantly in Saint John's Apocalypse. But might they be the result of natural erosion or glacial action? On the other hand, aside from these landscaped figures Bill has shown me an aerial photo that reveals (to my eyes, at least) the remains of four circular agricultural fields beneath the present pattern of rectangular colonial and modern fields.

Circular fields were a Celtic feature, generally ancient (i.e., before the Christian era), but a system of land usage that persisted in fringe and remote areas into the medieval period. In addition to the circular agricultural fields, the aerial photo shows seven to ten square depressions in the ground near the fields that look to me like the foundations of Celtic mud-and-wattle huts.

Aside from this aerial photo, the same woman from Barrie, the operatic soprano, supplied a late Acadian map dated 1757 that gives a place-name to this site, although the map gives a name only and no indication of what was there and why it warranted a name.

To me, all of this is quite unnerving. Without ever seeing the geography in question, Bill locates a site by use of geometry and sacred symbols, and then an aerial photo and a late Acadian map indicate that *something* worthy of note is *precisely* there!

Bill believes that there was a castle or secure lodging at the site, which acted as the precise center of the New Jerusalem of the displaced de Bouillon dynasty. He also believes that indisputable proof of the alleged Holy Blood lineage was kept in this new Temple of Solomon. Even if the Holy Blood still exists, as is asserted by many researchers today, the Nova Scotia genealogy proving the lineage up to the medieval period may still be reposing at the undisturbed site. At the very least, the site may still contain some other Knights Templar or Knights of Malta treasure or religious relics that came from three centuries of crusades.

This may be a reasonable assumption. The secret of the Holy Blood lineage and treasure was shared between several knight-guardians because tortures of the Inquisition could, eventually, loosen any tongue. No one person knew the entire secret. Therefore, there is the real possibility that some parts of the secret as to the exact location of the Grail were lost through the untimely deaths of key knight-guardians. The exact location could not have been reconstructed from the information that was preserved at the time, but only by application of super-secret geometry and moral allegory to the geography of Nova Scotia. This may have been a task beyond the expertise of the knight-guardians who survived.

I cannot say if this book that you're about to read is true. But it may be true; if so, it unlocks one of the most important, evocative, and romantic spiritual realities of the Western world: the Holy Grail. If it is true, it also links some stories that we attribute to ancient myths with the so-called secret rituals of modern-day Freemasonry.

But even if Bill Mann's contentions cannot be proved (or disproved) except by excavation of the site he's pinpointed, what follows is utterly fascinating reading. Anyone who loves subtle detective stories will be enthralled by Bill Mann's research. Also, something more may gradually impinge upon a perceptive reader's sensibilities. The Grail is not just a belief or a heresy. It seems to be the alternative religion of the Western world. The Holy Grail is another perspective on the miraculous.

The Holy Grail isn't just a minor and mythic episode of medieval history. It emerges in this book (as in others) as a very complex and cohesive alternative view of Western history. Grail players have been active in most historical events covered in our conventional textbooks, from Arthur's Britain to the Age of Discovery. But the perspective of the Grail players lends new meaning and significance to the development of the West, from the smallest to the largest detail. After reading this book, you'll know why the Joker can trump any card; why, when you sit down to a game of chess, the knight is the only piece that can jump both his ally or his opponent; and why, when you play a friendly game of bridge, you're playing with symbols of the deadly confrontation between the Church and the Grail.

And you'll learn why the Fool is a major theme in Bill's book. The fool's errand is nothing less than the quest for the Grail, the truth brought about by knowledge. Immeasurably rich is the finder. And, in this case, immeasurably rich is the reader!

Foreword

by Reverend Lionel Fanthorpe

One of the mysteries overshadowing all mysteries is the way that authors and researchers in strange fields somehow manage to get together. One hears of another's work. They exchange information and discuss hypotheses. Data accumulates. Partial explanations abound; final solutions remain elusive. Strong coffee and mellow Scotch are put to good use; study clocks tick the night away. Conversations grow deeper and more complicated. Acquaintanceship matures into friendship and collaboration. It is as though some deliberate fate or higher destiny was manipulating unseen wires to make momentous, invisible things happen. Researching unexplained phenomena is definitely a team game.

It is almost twenty years since my wife, Patricia, and I first visited Rennes-le-Château and Glozel. During those twenty years we have made many fascinating and informative friends. They are Henri Buthion, who lived in Saunière's mysterious old house at Rennes; and Monsieur Rousset, who showed us the grave of old Father Gelis, so brutally and mysteriously butchered in his own presbytery at Coustaussa during Saunière's days at Rennes. There is also Marcel Captier, the artist, who is a direct descendant of Saunière's bell-ringer; Monsieur Fatin, the gifted sculptor, who lives in the crumbling ruins of the once magnificent Château Hautpoul that gives Rennes-le-Château its name; and Emile Fradin, who discovered the amazing alphabet and weird artifacts at Glozel when he was a young farm-boy in 1924. I must also mention Dan Blankenship, the toughest and most determined of all the Oak Island pioneers; bluff, jovial Nova Scotian engineer-adventurer George Young, with his deep knowledge of the South Shore and his intuitive grasp of highly significant but unexpected links between hitherto unrelated data; and Dr. Bob Hieronimus of Maryland, whose brilliant radio show has shed clear investigative light on many unsolved mysteries.

Bill Mann is the newest name on that list. The author of this wide-ranging and intriguing study, Bill contacted us in the course of his own extensive research. He is a thoughtful and knowledgeable writer whose considerable talents are currently being directed toward some of those arenas of study that have taken our attention over the past twenty years.

Bill's new book, *The Knights Templar in the New World,* is well worth reading and rereading. The breadth of his research does not detract from its depth. He has combined close studies of Freemasonry and Templar history with Grail legends, classical mythology, and Egyptology. He has examined the relevance of Prince Henry Sinclair's epic voyage from Orkney and explored Francis Bacon's controversial contribution to the mystery.

Bill has realized the massive importance of the Rennes-le-Château enigma and its strange links with the intriguing Nova Scotian phenomena that he has just unearthed. All in all, it is a powerful and perceptive survey of the field that he has made.

Experts inevitably draw different conclusions from the same data, and it is only to be expected that Bill's conclusions do not always run parallel to ours, to Jean Robin's, to George Young's, to Andrew Sinclair's, or to Henry Lincoln's. Patricia and I are convinced that the heart of the Arcadian treasure mystery that links Rennes-le-Château to Oak Island and Nova Scotia is something far older and stranger than the legend of the Merovingian monarchy and its supposed connection with Jesus and Mary Magdalene. (See Fanthorpe, *The Oak Island Mystery: The Secret of the World's Greatest Treasure Hunt*) But free, frank, honest, and open argument and discussion is one God-given road to ultimate truth, and I warmly welcome Bill's excellent contribution.

Acknowledgments

————◆◆◆————

This book is but one stone in a multistoried building that may never be completed. It stands upon a multitude of concepts and research by authors too numerous to acknowledge, although J. R. R. Tolkien, C. S. Lewis, James George Frazer, Joesph Campbell, Homer, and Robertson Davies immediately come to mind. There are, however, specific individuals to whom I wish to express my heartfelt thanks.

First and foremost, I would like to acknowledge the loving support provided by my wife, Marie, without whose encouragement, during a time when I lost both of my parents, this book would not be a reality.

Second, I would like to thank my sister-in-law's husband, Daniel MacCormack, who became my eyes and ears in Nova Scotia and introduced me to many of the local historians.

I would also like to thank another sister-in-law's husband, David Fowlie, who unknowingly spurred me on every time he claimed, "Mann, there ain't no gold in them thar hills." David was right. There isn't any gold, but there is something of far greater value. John Coleman of Waverley, Nova Scotia, must also receive thanks for providing clues derived from his own explorations of Nova Scotia.

A great deal of thanks must also go to my dear friend George Karski of Fort Lauderdale, Florida. He not only acted as the devil's advocate throughout this story but also traveled with me to Nova Scotia several times. He provided me with the kind of encouragement that could only come from someone who had also just recently lost his father.

On another level, Henry Lincoln, coauthor of *Holy Blood, Holy Grail* and author of *The Holy Place,* must receive a large amount of credit for this book. It was only through our ongoing correspondence and his encouragement that I realized that only I understood the full depth of my research.

Michael Bradley, author of *Holy Grail Across the Atlantic,* must also receive a considerable amount of acknowledgment, for it was the reading of his book that first helped me make the connection between the Knights Templars' pre-Columbian exploration of Nova Scotia and my great-uncle.

Andrew Sinclair, author of *The Sword and The Grail,* and Lionel and Patricia Fanthorpe, coauthors of *The Oak Island Mystery,* also provided stimulating and insightful direction.

Thanks must go to the Champlain Society, the Louvre Museum in Paris, the trustees of the Chatsworth Settlement, the trustees of the Dulwich Picture Gallery, the National Gallery of Scotland, the Metropolitan Museum of Art, the University of Toronto Press, the Staatliche Museum in Berlin, the trustees of the Helen Creighton estate, and the Helen Creighton Folklore Society, Inc., for their kind and generous use of copyrighted materials.

I also wish to acknowledge the professionalism and interest of the people at Digital Imaging Incorporated of Oakville, Ontario. Their work has added a dimensional quality to this book that would have otherwise been lacking.

Returning to a more personal note are those individuals who first shared an interest and who later became lifelong friends. To me, this is the greatest treasure that anyone could hope to find.

Among these special friends, are Niven Sinclair and John Ross Matheson, two gentlemen in the truest sense of the word. There is also Bill Sinclair, Bill MacLennan, and Dr. Paul Fleming, the late Pete Cummings, the ever-stimulating Bill Beuhler, and, last but not least, E. David Warren and Thomas D. Carey of Oakville Lodge #400.

Finally, I wish to thank two special groups of people. Aleta and Hamilton Boudreaux and all those at Laughing Owl Publishing for their thoughtful guidance and support. Without their belief in this book, it would have remained but a concept in my mind. And, to those at Inner Traditions International, I wish to extend a heartfelt thanks for their ongoing support in taking *The Knights Templar in the New World* to the next level.

The fear of the Lord is the beginning

of wisdom: and the knowledge of the

holy is understanding.

Proverbs 9:10

Introduction

◆◆◆

T*he Knights Templar in the New World* is the recounting of a journey of discovery that started in October 1991, following my reading of the book *Holy Grail Across the Atlantic*. That book's basic premise is that, in the late fourteenth century, a group of outlaw knights/heretics led by a Prince Henry Sinclair established a pre-Columbian settlement in Nova Scotia, Canada.

The Knights Templar in the New World is based upon the story of Prince Henry Sinclair and his Knights Templar and how they hid the Holy Grail treasure—at what they considered a "New Jerusalem"—through a series of ingenious geometric surveys and esoteric keys.

Since 1955, the background to this story has evolved by facts so mysterious and inexplicable that a far greater mystery confronts us. Starting about 1950, curious material was deposited in France's famed Bibliothèque Nationale: genealogies of little-known families in the Pyrenees region of France; long dissertations about the history of the Knights Templar and Knights of St. John and Malta; discourse on "Catharism" of southern France; and many more items. These depositions made little sense individually. Yet when taken together, they told an amazing story. Strangely, most of this material was deposited within France's supreme cultural establishment minus the necessary author-publisher data.

When author-publication data was given, the information turned out to be false. Nonetheless, in spite of Bibliothèque Nationale regulations, this material was accepted into the national collection and transferred onto microfiche to make it easier for researchers to find. Researchers know this vast body of material as the *Dossiers secrets,* the Secret Files.

The most startling body of work is entitled *Le serpent rouge* (the Red Serpent). It contains a Merovingian genealogy, two maps of France in Merovingian times, and a ground plan of the Church of St. Sulpice in Paris. But the bulk of the text consists of thirteen short prose poems, each corresponding to a sign of the zodiac, a zodiac of thirteen signs. The thirteenth, Ophiuchus, the serpent holder, is inserted between Scorpio and Sagittarius. According to most articles on the subject, *Le serpent rouge* presents a pathway through astrological signs to the Holy Grail.

As *The Knights Templar in the New World* unfolds, the reader will sense that over the past six hundred years a myriad of clues have been distributed. It would appear that a mysterious world body that either possesses the true secret of the treasure, or enough information to attract all inquiries so that the true secret may be deciphered, has distributed these clues. As a result of several recent bestsellers, this world body is now known as the Priory of Sion. According to stated claims made by a past leader of the Priory, its aim is to reunite Europe.

Throughout the centuries, other clues have centered around what has become a circle of esoteric knowledge, including the use of Tarot cards, alchemy, and chess. These media of communication once had totally different meanings than they do today. Only lately have their earliest use and distribution been attributed to the medieval Knights Templar.

Readers will also realize that the medieval Knights Templar relished their sense of purpose and "black" humor and consequently left many a false clue or blind path. Legend maintains that only the truly initiated and pure of heart will discover the true secret. Yet inklings of a secret of this nature were bound to circulate over the years—especially, as many authors have conjectured, if a mechanism had been established by the Knights Templar themselves whereby one-sixth of the total secret was to come together every 120 years.

But it is Masonic ritual that has supported the largest number of clues during its approximately three-hundred-year official history. Unknowingly, Masons have maintained a secrecy that was initiated by the medieval Knights Templar to hide a treasure—a treasure that could, in all possibilities, shake the Roman Catholic Church to its very foundations. As such, the philosophical moral to be found within this book, if there is one, is that only by digging to the very foundations of ancient civilization will the true Grail be found.

Many of these foundations will be elaborated upon as one reads this book. Yet so many relationships, associations, and false leads are given that some readers will be tempted to throw this book away before its conclusion is reached. Just remember, the infamous fictional detective Sherlock Holmes would make no deduction until he accumulated all the facts. In Holmes's mind, one piece of evidence was just one piece of a larger puzzle; yet many pieces that fit together presented a mosaic, a virtual story within a story.

Sir Arthur Conan Doyle's adventures of Sherlock Holmes confirm that the first attribute a good detective must possess is general background knowledge, knowledge that only comes from a combination of reading and experience. Therefore, this book's first four chapters concentrate on the current information available through recent works on the subject. The subsequent chapters piece together the many seemingly unrelated clues that can be found within all of this background information. And only by following the unraveled thread through the immense labyrinth of "Grail" information can the reader hope to find the answer.

Some will find the style of this book too eclectic and far ranging to make much sense. To those I can only apologize and suggest that every line and clue should not be interpreted individually. What I recommend, if this is the case, is that the reader lightly read the book from beginning to end to understand the general direction. Then go back and try to identify the various levels of meaning that can be found on every page, if desired.

A further suggestion might be for the reader to relate the development of the clues to the continuous turning of a set of wheels within a clock. Although all the wheels stop at different stages of their journey, eventually they all come around to where they started. *The Knights Templar in the New World* can be viewed similarly.

Another interesting analogy is to view the first clue as a pebble thrown into a calm pool of water. Depending upon the obstacles that lie in the water, a single circle of ripples first appears, and then many more intertwining circles or patterns form. When another pebble and then another pebble is thrown, layers of ripples or circles interact and play against one other. The key is to always remember where the original pebble fell.

1

A Fool's Quest

There is a faint whisper among traditional historians that North America—the New World—was regularly visited not only by the Vikings and Irish, but by pre-Christian mariners such as the Egyptians, Greeks, Phoenicians, Carthaginians, and the Celts. Hints of these visits now appear to be revealing themselves through a variety of sources, including classic mythology, Indian legend, and maritime folklore.

If true, one would expect a wealth of solid evidence to have been found suggesting at the very least temporary settlement, specifically along the eastern seaboard of North America. But hard physical evidence has yet to be found in any great detail. Could it be that those who came before Columbus and Champlain, men like the enlightened fourteenth century Prince Henry Sinclair, were agents of the secret Order of the Knights of the Temple of Solomon and other earlier secret societies? And could it be that these same Knights Templar, whose secrets and mysteries provided the basis of Freemasonry in Scotland, purposely covered their tracks throughout the New World?

This "New World secret" may have been part of a more ancient mystery that involved the royal Merovingian bloodline of France, the suggested "Grail family" of Jesus Christ, and the royal House of David and King Solomon. These unanswered questions have followed me for many years, and as I searched for the answers I began to unravel the thick tapestry of intrigue that hides the keys to these and many other secrets of the Knights Templar in Nova Scotia.

My story begins with my own bloodline and its peculiar interests.

The Mann family is steeped in military and Masonic history. From my earliest times I can remember my great-uncles and father confusing me with little stories of intrigue and honor, both on the battlefield and among the shadows. They constantly enthralled me with unusual puzzles and games. It was as though I was being challenged, yet to what purpose I did not know.

Unfortunately, every time it appeared that I was starting to understand the symbolism behind their stories, the philosophy of love and harmony that was being radiated toward me, someone would die before I could ask the right questions. I soon learned that to discover the answers to these secrets I would have to follow my own course.

As a career path I chose forestry and landscape architecture over the more conventional occupations, and as fate would have it, my wife is from Nova Scotia. It was as though I was being drawn to some inexplicable conclusion: to interpret the Grail landscape across Nova Scotia. That conclusion came in May 1992. Shortly after my mother's death from cancer, I took a trip to Nova Scotia. My objective was twofold. First of all, I needed to get away and to gather my thoughts following such a personal ordeal. Second, it gave me an excuse to explore an area that I had identified in relation to the pre-Columbian explorations of Prince Henry Sinclair.

Although not in the best frame of mind, when I finally came to stand on the very point that I had developed two-dimensionally, I knew that I had arrived at a higher level. It was on top of a hill in Nova Scotia that, for the first time since my childhood, I experienced a sense of peace.

The setting was idyllic. With the sun shining and a slight breeze rippling through the trees, I had a profound sense of security and comfort. It was as though I had discovered the mythical land of the Greek Arcadia.

Some may say this was a subconscious release from all of the tension and anxieties I had been experiencing during a particularly troubling time. This was partly true, but there was more. There was the sudden realization that the landscape had been altered. Majestic white oaks were growing on the south-facing hillside where the natural cover is spruce and birch. But this was not all. The tidal stream that ran through the adjacent valley appeared to have had its natural course altered to faintly depict the heads of certain animals. As I descended into the valley, a huge limestone outcrop took on the form of a bear that appeared to be drinking from a waterfall. Later, back on top of the "bear's" head, amid a rich cover of hemlock and cedar, I discovered the stone remains of what appeared to be a man-made structure, a "crown" of some sort. What was even more amazing at the time was that the stream into which the waterfall emptied appeared to disappear underground, where it enters the larger Shubenacadie River.

Completing a natural circuit, deep on the valley floor I experienced the same sense of inner harmony and peacefulness as I had on the highest hill. It was as if I had stepped back in time, to the earliest times of the Neolithic hunter, when life was ruled by the elements of nature. The site is a natural refuge from the elements and is positioned so that it is invisible from any point on the Shubenacadie River. Even to this day, to an anxious explorer traveling by boat there would appear to be no access by water into the valley, because the stream disappears underground. I now realize that it was at this very moment that I pinpointed the mysterious lost settlement of Prince Henry Sinclair: a settlement that was established as the center of a New Jerusalem of the displaced Bouillon dynasty, but also a settlement that had an unbroken connection to earlier Celtic, Bronze Age, and even Neolithic origins.

Without ever sensing so, I had been preparing for this moment all my life. Even when I was thirteen years old I was experiencing life's little ironies. Thinking that I could impress an older girl, I got into a fight at a Halloween party and broke a plate over a rival's head. Unfortunately, a piece of glass from the plate flew and struck me in the eye, blinding me. Luckily it was only temporary, but for a month I lay in the hospital with patches over both eyes, unable to see. It was terrifying, not knowing whether the sight in my right eye would be saved.

At that moment I felt that I had become a complete and utter failure. Yet two things saved my spirit. Most important, both my mother and father, every day, rain or shine, made the effort to come visit me. Also, I received a visit from my great-uncle George who, along with his brother Frank, was as close to me as the grandfather I never knew.

My great-uncle was a gentle and understanding man. He explained to me that everyone possesses the ability for good and evil. In this way, all individuals have to search for their own balance of human nature, a balance between good and evil. I never questioned why he always talked in a moral, philosophical manner. I was exposed so often to the spiritual level of thinking that I considered it to be second nature. What my great-uncle did to raise my spirits was to ask me if I wanted to know a secret, a secret that no one knew except him. With patches over my eyes I could not see what he was describing, so I made him promise that if I regained my eyesight he would show me, and this he did. What he described, and ultimately showed me, was his Masonic ring, a ring that to a thirteen-year-old appeared magical and secretive. I knew nothing at this age of the Masons or Knights Templar. I only discovered afterward, during the sorting of my mother's personal things following her death, that Frederic George Mann had shown me a ring of the Supreme Grand Master of the Knights Templar of Canada. I now know that it

Most Eminent Knight Frederic George Mann
Supreme Grand Master of the Sovereign Great Priory of Canada, Knights Templar. Licentate in Music, 1927. Honourary Fellowship in the McGill Conservatorium of Music, 1952. Knight Grand Cross of the Temple, 1959. Photo property of the author.

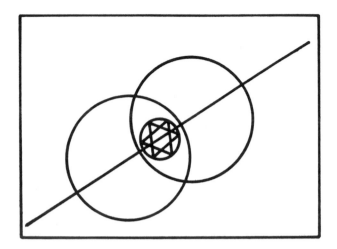

A diagram of the symbol in my great-uncle's Masonic ring
Note how the intertwining rings are centered on the bar running from the upper right-hand corner to the lower left, bisecting the jewel.

was my great-uncle's instilling in me the notion of good and evil and the balance of nature that started me on my quest—a quest that ended at a secret Templar refuge in Nova Scotia.

What intrigued me and set me on a mosaic of fascinating geometric patterns was a map within the book *Holy Grail Across the Atlantic* by Michael Bradley. This book illustrated what was thought to be Prince Henry Sinclair's travels and exploration throughout Nova Scotia. Somehow, I traveled back to the ring of my great-uncle. The ring had a secret compartment. The setting was the standard Masonic emblem of a set-square and compass. But when manipulated and opened on hinges, underneath, set on a pale blue jeweled background, was the intertwining of two golden rings centered on a gold bar with a round purple stone (amethyst) set in the middle.

Don't ask me how I made the mental connection, but what was truly startling was that I could apply this configuration to the mainland portion of a map of Nova Scotia, with the center of the jewel falling precisely on Nova Scotia's geographical center at a place called Mt. Uniacke. In my mind I turned over the name Uniacke, "one axis." Was it possible that this symbol related specifically to Nova Scotia?

I was hooked! I rushed to the local library and gathered as much reading material as I could. The primary trail was through the many references to the Freemasons. However, I was unaware of my great-uncle's position within the Freemasons/Knights Templar at that time. I was like a blind man in a train station, not knowing which way to turn. Still, a nagging feeling made me sense that someone was guiding my hand. It was as though my great-uncle had planted a seed, and I had to feed and nourish and tend to the plant and follow its growth.

At the library I zeroed in on two books. One was the *Royal Masonic Cyclopedia* by Kenneth MacKenzie; the other was the more recent *Holy Blood, Holy Grail* by the British authors Michael Baigent, Richard Leigh, and Henry Lincoln. Whereas *The Royal Masonic Cyclopedia* is the reference book to this story and *Holy Grail Across the Atlantic* provides the compulsory background, *Holy Blood, Holy Grail* must be considered the "ultimate travel guide." *Holy Blood, Holy Grail* implies that the mother goddess of Christianity would not appear to be the Virgin Mary but Mary Magdalene, and that the Grail is not an object but direct descendants of the House of David through Jesus Christ and a French Merovingian lineage. The funny thing is, however, that the authors of *Holy Blood, Holy Grail* failed to recognize the journeys of Prince Henry Sinclair and the possibility that the Holy Grail was brought to the New World.

This is the beauty of the notion: Where else would you hide the world's greatest treasure but at a place that was thought to be the end of the Earth? And where else would you hide what you considered to be a direct connection to God and heaven but in a place you considered to be a paradise on earth, a Garden of Eden, or more simply put, a refuge or sanctuary?

It is quite conceivable, as this book will demonstrate, that Prince Henry Sinclair knew exactly where he was going and that there were signposts along the way directing him.[1] Indeed, the mysterious Oak Island, which is located on the South Shore of Nova Scotia, acted as one of the signposts.

THE HOLY BLOODLINE

Quickly becoming an international bestseller, *Holy Blood, Holy Grail* is centered on a "treasure story" that is linked to a part of southern France, the small village of Rennes-le-Château, that has attracted considerable interest over the last century.[2] However, Rennes-le-Château did not receive any great amount of interest until Baigent, Leigh, and Lincoln first pieced together a number of varying factors and related it to the present-day activities of the rather mysterious European fraternity known as the Priory of Sion.[3]

Part of the story begins on June 1, 1885, when the village received a new parish priest, Abbé (Father) Bérenger Saunière. In 1891, Saunière started a modest restoration of the village church that was consecrated to the Magdalene in 1059. Then the first of many strange events occurred. During renovations Saunière discovered that one of the two archaic Visigoth columns that supported the altar stone was hollow; inside were supposedly four parchments preserved in sealed wooden tubes. Two parchments were comprised genealogies; the other two parchments had apparently been composed in the 1780s by an earlier priest of Rennes-le-Château, the Abbé Antoine Bigou. One genealogy dated from 1244, the year that Montségur, the last heretical fortress, surrendered to northern forces; the other was from 1644.

The two parchments appear to be encoded Latin texts. Both have been deciphered and the following interpretation has appeared in many books devoted to Rennes-le-Château:

BERGERE PAS DE TENTATION QUE POUSSIN TENIERS GARDENT
LA CLEF PAX DCLXXXI PAR LA CROIX ET CE CHEVAL DE DIEU
J'ACHEVE CE DAEMON DE GARDIEN A MIDI POMMES BLUES
(SHEPHERDESS, NO TEMPTATION, THAT POUSSIN, TENIERS,
HOLD THE KEY; PEACE 681, BY THE CROSS AND THIS HORSE OF
GOD, I COMPLETE—OR DESTROY—THIS DAEMON OF THE
GUARDIAN AT MIDDAY. BLUE APPLES.)[4]

Another interpretation from the second parchment reads:

A DAGOBERT II ROI ET A SION EST CE TRESOR ET IL EST LA MORT.
(TO DAGOBERT II, KING, AND TO SION BELONGS THIS TREASURE
AND HE IS THERE DEAD.)[5]

Following his discovery, the story goes that Saunière was sent to Paris by his superior, the bishop of Carcassone, with instructions to seek out the Abbé Bieil, director general of the Seminary of Saint Sulpice. Having presented himself to Bieil, Saunière spent three weeks in Paris in the company of Bieil's nephew, Emile Hoffet. He also spent time in the Louvre, where he purchased reproductions of three paintings. One was a portrait, by an unidentified artist, of Pope Cèléstin V. The second was an unknown work by David Teniers, and the third was the most famous painting of the artist Nicolas Poussin, his second version of a painting based on the theme of *Et in Arcadia Ego*.

Upon his return to Rennes-le-Château, Saunière undertook rather mysterious projects; he appeared to have acquired a great deal of money and a newly defiant attitude toward the Roman Catholic Church. In the churchyard, for example, Saunière erased the headstone inscription found on the sepulchre of Marie de Blanchefort, the Marquise d'Hautpoul, not knowing that the inscriptions on the tomb had already been copied.

Some of Saunière's unexplained wealth was devoted to curious constructions and practices. A replica of a medieval tower, the Tour Magdala, was built to house Saunière's ever-growing library. As well, a rather grand country house was constructed, called the Villa Bethania, which Saunière himself never occupied. In addition, the village church was restored in a most unusual fashion, including this Latin inscription that was carved in the arch above the entrance:

TERRIBILIS EST LOCUS ISTE
(TERRIBLE IS THIS PLACE)

Inside the church reliefs were installed depicting the Stations of the Cross, but they deviated from accepted scriptural account in some manner. Just as odd, on January 22, 1917, Saunière died after unexplainably falling ill on the 17th. Somewhat more mysterious, the morning following his death his body was placed upright in an armchair on the terrace of the Tour Magdala, clad in an ornate robe adorned with scarlet tassels. As mourners filed past, many of them plucked a tassel from the garment.[6]

Holy Blood, Holy Grail's conclusion is as unorthodox, yet as fascinating as the Rennes-le-Château mystery itself. Baigent, Leigh, and Lincoln's theory supports the old Cathar belief that Mary Magdalene was the wife of Jesus and that offspring were produced. It continues to hypothesize that after Jesus was crucified, Magdalene, either pregnant or accompanied by at least one child, was smuggled to an oversea refuge by her uncle, Joseph of Arimathea. This would mean that there exists a hereditary bloodline descended directly from Jesus and that this "Holy Blood" may have perpetuated itself to this very day. One recent result of this theory is the spawning of a rash of books on this very subject, including Laurence Gardner's *Bloodline of the Holy Grail*, Keith Laidler's *The Head of God*, and many more.

If this theory is in any sense true, then it serves to explain a great many elements in the Rennes-le-Château mystery. It would explain the cultlike significance that Mary Magdalene attained during the Crusades, as well as the "Grail family" in the Grail romances.[7] It would also explain the status accorded the Merovingians by the present-day Priory of Sion and their neopolitical activities in Europe.

Unfortunately, as the authors themselves noted, the Jesus material tended to outweigh all of the other information presented in *Holy Blood, Holy Grail*. For this reason, *The Messianic Legacy*—Baigent, Leigh, and Lincoln's follow-up to *Holy Blood, Holy Grail*—concentrates primarily on the concept of Jesus as the Messiah, and how any messiahship concept could be relevant to the twentieth century.

Through a gradual process of shifting through a labyrinth of deliberately disseminated disinformation, the authors have discerned another possibility: that Jesus survived his crucifixion and was nursed back to health by Joseph of Arimathea. Yet, as the authors have also noted, as soon as any such claim is made it is as if each new possibility is singularly dismissed by the church.

For Baigent, Leigh, and Lincoln, the Jesus theory was not the only aspect of their research, nor was it the most important one. Their attention was ultimately focused upon the Priory of Sion's true aim. But if restoration of the Merovingian bloodline was the ultimate end, what were the means to be?[8] In any case, the authors are convinced that the Priory of Sion can substantiate a claim on behalf of the families it represents, i.e., that there exists to this day a dynastic succession extending back to the Old Testament House of David.

Another book by Henry Lincoln, *The Holy Place,* continues the notion of a hidden, forbidden secret by suggesting that there is an underlying geometric layout to one of the parchments that Saunière purportedly found. The geometry that he found is pentagonal, an irregular five-pointed star, and when Lincoln later uncovered a complex hidden geometry in Poussin's *The Shepherds of Arcadia,* this, too, proved to be pentagonal. Furthermore, this work led Lincoln to the discovery of a natural pentagon of mountains within the landscape surrounding Rennes-le-Château. And amazingly, this led Lincoln to the identification of a tomb near Rennes-le-Château which, in its construction and mountain setting, is identical to the tomb depicted in Poussin's most famous painting. Thus, the circle was complete. Or was it?

When the geometric design was first found by Lincoln in 1971, he considered that the circle and crescent were meant to represent the astrological and alchemical signs for the sun and the moon—gold and silver. Yet in his mind there was also the fact that the five-pointed star was breaking through its surrounding circle.[9] He realized that this too had implications in the realm of magic, the occult, and secret societies.[10]

Following this train of thought for a moment, another recent book, *The Temple and The Lodge* by Michael Baigent and Richard Leigh is an investigation into Freemasonry from its Templar beginnings to the modern day. In *The Temple and The Lodge,* the authors indeed attempt to make a definitive connection between the Knights Templar of the First Crusade and Robert the Bruce's reign in Scotland to the emergence of Masonic lodges and ritual in the latter part of the seventeenth century.

Using the discovery of what appeared to be a coherent pattern linking the earliest Templar graves throughout France, Spain, and the Middle East with later ones found throughout England and Scotland,[11] Baigent and Leigh weave an intricate mosaic of Templar/Freemason influence on British politics, military campaigns, and royal intrigue.[12] Of special note is the Masonic history that leads up to the American Revolution and the way in which the Ancient and Scottish Rites (Jacobite) branch of the Freemason movement was absorbed by the much smaller, outwardly Protestant, Grand Lodge of England, to become the United Grand Lodge of Freemasonry on June 24, 1717.

Unfortunately, most Masonic history that exists today has been written by scholars working under the influence of United Grand Lodge, who present Jacobite Freemasonry and the proliferation of "higher degrees" as deviations from the mainstream they claim to represent.

However, according to the authors of *The Temple and The Lodge,* this would appear to be precisely the opposite of what actually occurred, with Jacobite Freemasonry apparently forming the original mainstream and United Grand Lodge the deviation that eventually became the mainstream itself.[13]

This is an important concept that should be kept in mind, as *The Knights Templar in the New World* explores many instances where one group's ideals are absorbed by another. For instance, the Priory of Sion seems to have begun as a deviation of the mainstream, although it has (recently?) displaced the Knights Templar and become the central body itself.[14] It is for this very reason that, by seeking a direct connection with the Knights Templar of the Holy Crusades, the Grand Lodge has tried so hard over the years to assert its claim, much like the Priory of Sion is attempting to do in Europe through its many activities.[15]

Another book that tries to make the connection between the Knights Templar and modern-day Freemasonry is *The Sword and The Grail* by Andrew Sinclair. *The Sword and The Grail* theorizes that if not since the Battle of Bannockburn then from the fifteenth century, the Saint Clairs of Rosslyn became the hereditary Grand Master Masons of Scotland. More importantly from *The Knights Templar in the New World*'s perspective, Sinclair explains that Nordic and Celtic influences as well as Templar and Masonic symbols decorate the magnificent Rosslyn Chapel.[16] And in the chapel can be found the famous "Apprentice Pillar," a carving that is rich in both pagan and Masonic symbolism, reflective of ancient teachings and beliefs.

In Masonic tradition it is believed that the secret of the Shamir, a worm or serpent of wisdom whose touch slit and shaped stone, was the secret that the martyr Hiram, the architect of the temple, refused to surrender.[17] Therefore, as Masonic tradition dictates, eight worms or serpents are grouped in a rough octagon around the base of the Apprentice Pillar.[18] According to Andrew Sinclair, these comprise the number of points and the shape of the Maltese Cross of the Knights of the Order of the Temple of Solomon.[19]

The Sword and The Grail attempts to answer all of the following questions: What happened to the Templars and their treasure after their suppression and official disbanding following the execution of their Grand Master? What were the Templar's secret rituals and upon what were they based? Were these ceremonies passed on to the Freemasons as they developed in the seventeenth century? What is the meaning of the symbol of the grail on the Saint Clair tombstone and are further clues in stone to be found?[20] Why is Rosslyn viewed specifically as a chapel of the Holy Grail, with its dedication to the mystic quest written in stone within its walls?[21]

These are just some of the questions that prompted me to pursue my quest. But first, credit must go to Michael Bradley, since it is his book that transports Prince Henry Sinclair across the Atlantic to a refuge in Nova Scotia, Canada.[22] In turn, Bradley's book is based in part on Fredrick Pohl's *Prince Henry Sinclair: His Expedition to the New World in 1398.*

Bradley's own story starts in 1982, when he first saw "castle ruins" at what he identifies as "The Cross" (New Ross), Nova Scotia. Although he has not said for certain, it appears Bradley is convinced that the ruins

The west entrance of Rosslyn Chapel
Note the "engrailed cross" in the circular window above the west entrance door. Photo by William F. Mann.

The Apprentice Pillar in Rosslyn Chapel
Legend has it that the architect of the pillar, an Apprentice Mason, was murdered by his master who flew into a jealous rage upon arriving back from a pilgrimage to the Holy Land and witnessing the beauty of the finished carving. Photo by William F. Mann.

hint at a hidden pattern of historical relationships.[23] He suggests that the royal Stuarts were intimately connected with the early history of Nova Scotia and North America.

The Stuarts were originally Scottish and had a great deal of contact with the Norse, who controlled much of Scotland and the Isles from the eighth to the thirteenth century. The Stuarts also spent an immense amount of gold on doomed military adventures. In support of this, Bradley notes that the Gold River in Nova Scotia flows from the castle ruins down to the Atlantic Ocean at Mahone Bay. (And located at the mouth of the Gold River in Mahone Bay is the most famous treasure mystery of all time, the infamous "Money Pit" of Oak Island.)

Bradley also makes the connection that Prince Henry Sinclair acted as an agent to the so-called Holy Bloodline and, along with approximately five hundred Knights Templar, occupied in Nova Scotia (New Scotland) an agricultural settlement of possibly unbelievable importance during the late 1300s. Bradley supports this claim with a study of early Maritime and North American maps that make reference to a certain "refuge" in the vicinity of Mahone Bay and that, rather cryptically, spell out sentences or secret messages.

Since maps exist as physical artifacts to vast explorations, I consider Michael Bradley's work in his chapter "Map Memorials" to be his most crucial in relation to identifying Nova Scotia as the New Jerusalem. Indeed, as Bradley surmises, it appears that some of the early cartographers were "in on the secret."

Bradley suggests that an example of a map that provides this connection is the Caspar Vopell map of 1545, which illustrates the coast of Nova Scotia with a drawing of the bust of a Templar knight and the legend *"Agricolae pro Seu. C. d. labrador,"* which could be interpreted literally as "farms (or farmers) for the Lord of the Cape of Laborers." According to Bradley, we are stuck with the idea of some lord who controlled a Cape of Laborers, and who had some farms.[24]

Bradley highlights the fact that two levels of mapping existed at this time and possibly before. There were the conventional Ptolemaic maps of the 1500s and 1600s, which appeared crude and distorted; and there were the more accurate, and therefore more mysterious, maps called *portolans*. Most of the portolans covered the area of the Mediterranean and the European Atlantic Coast.[25]

The main problem demonstrated by the Ptolemaic maps was finding longitude (the vertical lines on a map denoting how far east or west one is). Latitude could be fixed according to the relative position of the stars, but longitude needed the invention of an accurate method for telling the time.

Some medieval sailors had used reasonably accurate maps based on grids that radiated like spokes on a wheel. For example, the Piri Re'is portolan map of 1513 illustrates a shape of North America and South America that is based on an "azimuthal equidistant projection" of the world.[26] Remarkably, the American coastline is similar to the same coastline shown in a modern Strategic Air Command azimuthal equidistant projection of the world.[27]

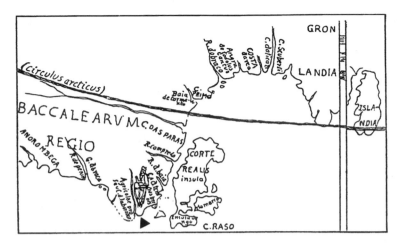

Copy of Caspar Vopell map of 1545
Note the illustration of the Templar knight only from the waist up, with his shield positioned to the east of what appears to be a major river. Notice the inscription: "Agricolae pro Seu. C. d. labrador." Reproduced from Crucial Maps in the Early Cartography *and* Place Nomenclature of the Atlantic Coast of Canada *by W. F. Ganong, by permission of the University of Toronto Press.*

Whatever the source, Bradley makes a strong argument that the Templars obtained such maps in the Holy Lands during the Crusades, and that the maps led them to the Americas and Oak Island, Nova Scotia at least one hundred years before Columbus, if not earlier.[28]

OAK ISLAND AND THE MONEY PIT

The longest and likely most famous treasure hunt in history deals with Oak Island and the Money Pit. Incredibly, for more than two hundred years since its initial discovery in 1795, the Money Pit has become the center of speculation for untold riches, including pirate booty, Marie Antoinette's jewels, the treasures of lost civilizations, and even the original Shakespeare manuscripts allegedly written by Francis Bacon. Although numerous artifacts have been recovered on the island, none of these finds provides the identity of those who originally constructed the Money Pit or the nature of their treasure. In fact, the only profit recognized to date is by those who have bought and resold the island, published numerous books or articles on the subject, or by those local residents who reside on the South Shore and who have capitalized on its intriguing history.

The official story of Oak Island begins in 1795, when three boys from the small town of Chester, on the eastern shore of Mahone Bay, paddled across the bay to a small island where a large number of red oak trees grew. By following a path, they found themselves at an old oak tree in the center of a clearing. Inspecting the tree, they saw that a severed branch overhung a depression in the ground and from this limb dangled a ship's block. Excited by stories that the island was the legendary haunt of pirates, it did not take the boys long to begin digging beneath the tree. Shoveling out the loose earth, they found a thirteen-foot-wide, well-defined circular shaft, and at four feet they unearthed a layer of flagstones uncommon to the island.

At a depth of ten feet they found a platform made of oak logs extending across the shaft. Finally realizing that the task was too much for them, the three boys returned to the mainland to seek help—a task that took them nine years to find backers to provide the equipment they required.

Work on the site resumed in 1804 when a company was formed to assist the boys in the search for the treasure. The newly formed company had only just begun when they struck a second tier of oak logs similar to the first. Ten feet lower they supposedly found a layer of charcoal on top of the next tier of logs, and ten feet below that a layer of putty. Another version states that a layer of coconut fiber was found at the forty-foot oak platform. At a depth of ninety feet the searchers uncovered a flat stone three feet long and one foot wide; crude letters and figures had been cut into the stone on the reverse side. According to tradition, the syndicate had hopes that this inscription would throw some valuable light on their search, but unfortunately they could not decipher it. Eventually, in 1864, the stone was interpreted to read:

TEN FEET BELOW TWO MILLION POUNDS

In 1804, when the searchers returned the next morning they found that the Money Pit was flooded to within thirty-three feet of the top. (Coincidentally, the highest level in the Masonic Scottish Rite is the 33rd degree.) Despite all their efforts, the water level remained at the same height. As a result, their work was abandoned for the year.

The story continues that, in the spring of 1805, with the idea of draining the Money Pit, the treasure hunters dug another shaft alongside the original. Overnight the second shaft also filled with water, again to within thirty-three feet of the top, and that was the end of the first organized treasure hunt on Oak Island.

In 1897, the probe drill of another company of treasure seekers apparently encountered two oak chests at the 150–160-foot level. It was from this depth that a scrap of parchment was brought to the surface with writing on it that looked like the letters *vi* in an Elizabethan script. At the 171-foot level, the same drill supposedly encountered an iron plate or hard-cast cement, which seemed to be a floor or ceiling.

In 1909, a young Franklin D. Roosevelt bought shares in the Old Gold Salvage and Wrecking Company, whose subsequent effort was no more successful than any of the others. What fascinated the young Roosevelt most was the idea that someone had constructed such an ingenious and deadly labyrinth. FDR retained a lifelong interest in the Money Pit, and even during the activities of World War II, Roosevelt wrote letters of inquiry concerning the latest attempt to recover the presumed treasure.[29]

In *The Money Pit Mystery,* author Rupert Furneaux presents a very interesting theory as to who created the money pit—an "evil genius" Furneaux refers to as "Mr. X who seems to have enjoyed the thought that the Money Pit might be found.[30] Still, nobody has been able to confirm the two clues that Furneaux relies most heavily upon to establish Mr. X's year of endeavor. It has never been verified, first, that one or all of the flood tunnels run precisely fourteen degrees south of east from Smith's Cove to the Money Pit, and second, that the angle of declination demonstrated by a stone triangle found on the island was exactly seven degrees, not six and one half or six degrees, or even seven and one-half degrees.

What Furneaux fails to realize, although he does inadvertently hint at it in several places, is that the stone triangle may have been built by someone other than Mr. X, and that military engineers of the highest rank were not the only ones who possessed the necessary skills to develop such an intricate system of floodworks. It is even possible that the original builders of the Money Pit left their ground markings—the stone triangle and drilled rocks—for later groups either so that they could recover the treasure or to tantalize them beyond frustration. It is also possible that the original works have been elaborated upon by subsequent groups who were also "in on the secret."

It is not for lack of investment in time or money that the mystery of Oak Island has not been solved, which is rather ironic when you think about it. Unfortunately, due to the foolishness of many of the treasure seekers during the past two hundred years, the site has been disturbed to such an extent that most of the evidence that could have led to the identity of the original architects of the Money Pit has been lost.

On another level, other hidden clues that hint at the true purpose of the greatest ruse on earth (which now appears to have been perpetrated by, among others, the Knights Templar) can still be found on Oak Island, as well as in such diverse sources as the Bible and ancient myth and through some of the oldest imagery and symbols known to man.

2
A Balance of Nature

To understand the actions of the Knights Templar, one must first understand the origins of their beliefs. Of course, many historians claim that the primary source of the Templar beliefs was the Bible. But recent investigation has revealed the New Testament to be at least a third-generation document that was altered and censored for specific reasons. Just as confusing, the Dead Sea Scrolls found at Qumran consistently predate the birth of Christ, yet apparently speak of a messiah who performs deeds later attributed to Jesus Christ. The suggestion is, therefore, to look beyond the accepted tenet to earlier times in order to truly understand the beliefs of the Templars.

In the earliest times the female was worshipped in a fashion similar to worship of the earth. Both Earth and Woman were considered life-givers and symbols of fertility. Even now many people do not comprehend that past societies placed women on a higher plane than men. In present-day matriarchal societies, such as the First Nations, women are still judged to be wisest, while the men maintain their roles as guardian and provider. Thus a balance between man and woman, between Earth and its people, is maintained. History tells us that the Templars believed in this balance.

The Templars also believed that whatever evil was committed, especially to women and children, would be redeemed over time. ("What goes around, comes around!") This type of thought is usually associated with the Greek philosopher Pythagoras (569–500 B.C.), and his assumption that the universe and its matter is nonaccidental, ordered, and coherent, and is therefore open to interpretation and susceptible to balance.[1]

Significantly, astrology has always been considered one "key" toward such interpretation and was employed by the Knights Templar on a variety of levels.[2] The reasoning behind the use of astrology is again a balancing of matter, perhaps best and most commonly expressed in the saying adopted by the Templars: "As above, so below." The Knights Templar believed that the solar system was a balance of the earth and of man, and that everything on earth related to man. As such, the Knights Templar were inclined to view the zodiac as the "symbolic" chart upon which all the earth's forces interact.

The word *symbol* is derived from the Greek word *symbolon*.[3] In ancient Greece it was a custom to break a slate of burned clay into several pieces and give each individual in a group one piece as a mark of identification. When, at a later date, the individuals met and fitted the pieces together, it was confirmed that the persons were the same ones, or representatives of those who had received the pieces of clay in the first place. (Those who enjoy a good pirate story will recognize the analogy of the torn map, with the pieces being divided among the partners.)

In the Celtic world, the Holy Grail itself is only one of many symbols that fit together. For example, the concept of the "four hallows" encompasses several symbols, or talismans: the sword, the spear, the cauldron, and the Lia Fail.[4] When pieced together they create a fine tapestry of mystery. In turn, each of these Celtic hallows has its equivalent in the Grail romances and Arthurian legends.[5]

Another enduring image is that of the salmon. In Celtic tradition, it is a symbol of everlastingness and of the greatest wisdom, and it figures in many myths as the oldest animal who remembers things from the beginning of time. Similarly, one of its richest symbols of medieval alchemy, aside from the sun, which signifies gold, is the hermetic "breaking of the water." This is reflective of an aging salmon struggling upstream to lay its eggs before dying. In alchemy, the salmon symbolizes the alchemist's revival of the unconscious imprints of the birth trauma, experienced in reverse as a trauma of rebirth. More simply put: in death there is life, in life there is death.

Christ the King is also represented by the symbol of the fish, the *vesica pisces*. In alchemy, Pisces is associated with the image of reflection: one fish stands for death, or the end, the other for primal birth, or the beginning. Pisces extends from February 20 to March 20, or the winter period in which the old cycle comes to an end at the same time as the new cycle is prepared. It is natural, therefore, that the intertwining of two circles or rings represents Christ.

The Templars are known to have utilized a similar symbol in their secret messages; to come full circle for the first time, it was a modification of this symbol that was hidden within my great-uncle's Masonic ring. The only difference is that in the center of the rings lay a jewel: a purplish, many-sided stone that sparkles like the eye of a fish.

To me, this confirms the notion that Prince Henry Sinclair established a Templar settlement in pre-Columbian Nova Scotia that paid homage to a trinity of Earth, Christ (Man), and Woman. It also supports the notion that the settlement can be rediscovered through the proper application of the two main principles of Masonry—sacred geometry and moral allegory.

In his book about Prince Henry Sinclair, Frederick Pohl reconstructs Sinclair's explorations around Nova Scotia.[6] If Sinclair had

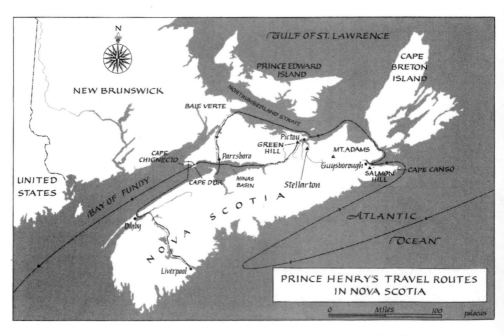

Pohl's map of Prince Henry's travel routes in Nova Scotia

Note how Pohl fails to consider the Shubenacadie River as a viable route across Nova Scotia, even though it is one of the largest navigable rivers in Nova Scotia.

taken the route as shown by Pohl, he would have in essence completed a "circuit." But what was the reason for this circuit? If he wanted to explore this vast new land, why didn't he just go with the flow, so to speak? Was it possible that he wanted to map the countryside as he went? And why does it appear that he "slammed on the brakes" in the mid-Atlantic and reversed his direction to make land at the eastern-most tip of Nova Scotia?

These were the questions that tumbled about in my mind when I first read Bradley's *Holy Grail Across the Atlantic.* Given my back-ground and knowledge of surveying, I wondered if it was possible that Sinclair was conducting a ground-controlled survey as he went, based on his knowledge of sacred geometry? To my amazement, I was able to fit the image of my great-uncle's ring exactly to the mainland of Nova Scotia and, as I already confirmed, the center of the jewel fell exactly on the center of mainland Nova Scotia—Mt. Uniacke.

Then I realized that if one projected, axislike, the spokes of a wheel

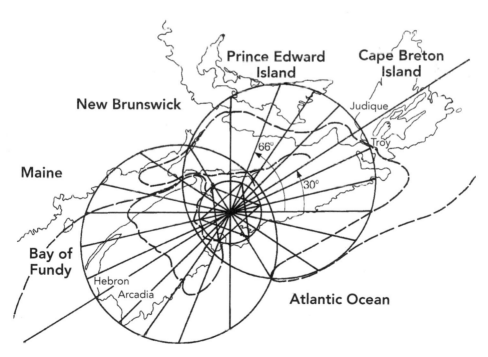

Application of sacred geometry to mainland Nova Scotia
Note how the central axis through Nova Scotia splits the mainland exactly in half.

from the center of the diagram (similar to the portolan maps), certain relationships came to light—relationships that I realized reflected the sense of opposites, or balance of nature, so prevalent in Templar belief. At the western tip of one axis there lay the community of Hebron, where at the eastern tip lay the small village of Judique. A similar relationship appeared between Arcadia and Troy.

But how could there be any relationship with place names that originated during the eighteenth century and an exploration that supposedly occurred in the fourteenth century? Furthermore, how did I come to draw the inner jewel as a Star of David, unless subconsciously (or consciously) the carving of the amethyst in my great-uncle's ring was based upon the pattern of the Seal of Solomon/Star of David? One can only imagine the confusion that raged through my mind at this point. So many clues and not enough time in the day!

ANCIENT SECRETS

Over the centuries, clues suggesting ancient secrets shared by a variety of so-called secret societies have been slowly revealed, clues that I believe eventually became intertwined with the rituals of the modern-day Freemasons and Knights Templar. These ancient secrets apparently all have a common origin among what is known as "sacred geometry," which raises the immediate question as to what exactly is sacred geometry and why it was considered sacred? To answer this, one must explore both the origin of geometry and the secret societies.

The origin of geometry has been attributed to the Babylonians; based upon the earliest Babylonian system, the ancient Egyptians built up a considerable body of knowledge of arithmetic, simple algebra, and measurement.[7] About 1700 B.C., an Egyptian priest named Ahmes wrote the oldest of these ancient Egyptian manuscripts that has so far been discovered. The original manuscript is now in the British Museum; the title of the treatise is *Directions for Knowing All Dark Things*.[8]

The system of land measure used by the ancient Egyptians was purely practical, whereas the early Greek philosophers were interested in the knowledge of geometry purely for its own sake, regardless of utility.[9] Greek scholars studied the properties of the geometrical figures, the relations among these properties, and the proof by pure logic of new geometrical truths from those already known. In this way they knew far more about the subject than the Egyptians did and wrote papers and books dealing with various parts of the science of geometry.

Greek surveyors, builders, mariners, and astronomers, in turn, made use of the practical parts of the philosophers' pure science of geometry. From these applications the Greeks developed the fine arts and sciences, and from this combination of sciences and geometry came the new sciences of trigonometry and of geodesy, which deals with the size and shape of the earth as a whole.[10]

The first to investigate the principles upon which the science of geometry is based and to apply the methods of logic to its systematic development was Pythagoras. After some years in Egypt he settled in a Greek colony in the south of Italy and taught geometry, philosophy, and religion, attempting to base the last two subjects on mathematical principles.

His school grew into a sort of brotherhood that finally developed into a secret society or fraternity. The society's emblem was the five-pointed star, drawn by continued motion of the pen without lifting it from the paper. In the study of the properties of this figure the Pythagoreans also discovered many of the properties of triangles (three-sided figures) and pentagons (five-side figures).

Pythagoras taught other branches of mathematics besides geometry, but it was in geometry that he discovered several important new rules and propositions. He is said to be the first to prove that the square constructed with a side equal to the longest side of a triangle with one right angle (square corner) has an area equal to the sum of the areas of the squares whose sides are the other two (shorter) sides of the triangle. In his honor this proposition is still known as the Pythagorean theorem.

Another of the famous early Greek geometers was Archytas, born about 400 B.C., who was a follower of Pythagoras. He was the first to solve the famous problem of determining by geometry the dimensions of a cube that should have twice the volume of any specified cube, called the "duplication of the cube." Archytas is said also to be the first to make use of the principles of geometry in the study of mechanics.

Hippias of Elis, who lived at about the same time as Archytas, was the first to solve the theoretical problems of dividing an angle into three equal parts ("trisection of an angle") and of "squaring the circle," or finding a square that has the same area as any specified circle.

Two of the greatest of the ancient Greek philosophers were Plato (429–328 B.C.) and his pupil Aristotle (384–322 B.C.), both of whom lived and taught in Athens, the capital and center of Greek culture. Plato conducted a school that was located in a grove near the city of Athens. He is said to have placed over the entrance a notice that warned away those who knew no geometry. (Remember the use of the sign by Saunière over the entrance to the chapel of Rennes-le-Château.)

After Aristotle's time the center of geometrical and other Greek learning returned to Egypt, which had by then been conquered and

The squaring of the circle

In alchemical terms, "squaring the circle" represents the coming together of male and female elements in perfect harmony and dimension. From Michael Maier, Atalanta fugiens, Frankfurt, 1617.

colonized by the Greeks under Alexander the Great. He built on the delta of the Nile a great city, which he named Alexandria after himself, and there founded a great university and library. Scholars and students of the entire world flocked to the university at Alexandria, and for hundreds of years, until its destruction, it was the center and headquarters of the study and development of geometry, trigonometry, and astronomy.

After the destruction of Alexandria, in A.D. 396, many of the scholars went to Byzantium (later called Constantinople, after the Roman emperor Constantine) and established there a center of learning that in the Middle Ages spread its influence into Europe. Others went from Alexandria to Arabia, chiefly to the city of Baghdad, and became teachers and physicians to the Arabs. In this way geometry became known to the Arabs. The Arab conquerors of Alexandria also preserved some of the scientific works from the Alexandrian library. Among these were Euclid's *Elements* and Ptolemy's *Almagest,* which were translated into Arabic and became the standard works on geometry, trigonometry, and astronomy.[11]

Contrary to general belief, the Arab scholars did not contribute a great deal to the development of geometry and trigonometry. Their greatest contribution to the cause of science and the history of geometry was the preservation of scientific knowledge during the Dark Ages. They translated and published the learned works, and established schools over all of the Arabian Empire that at times spread as far into Europe as Spain. Only through them was the science of geometry finally reintroduced into Europe at the time of the great revival of learning— the Renaissance.

Even today many scholars use the preserved classical writings to confirm their theories. For example, works such as Plato's *Timaeus* and Aristotle's *America* are still used to illustrate that North America was regularly visited in early times. Unfortunately, the burning of the library at Alexandria destroyed much of the potential knowledge of the ancient world, including fascinating sea maps, maps that may have provided the basis for the portolans.

The earliest existing reference to land beyond the Strait of Gibraltar comes from Herodotus, the fifth century B.C. Greek historian. He speaks of the trading methods adopted by Celtic and Phoenician merchants who did not speak the language of their customers. The most quoted and fascinating reference comes from Diodorus Siculus who, writing in the first century B.C., describes an intriguing island beyond the Pillars of Hercules (Strait of Gibraltar) that the Phoenicians apparently discovered after being driven a great distance into the ocean during a violent storm.[12]

Another Greek writer, Hecataeus, in his account of the same mysterious island and its temple, supplies the first hint as to its residents. It is generally accepted that he is writing about the Britons or Celts, specifically devotees of the god he calls "Apollo." But his word for them is Hyperboreans.[13]

People called Hyperboreans figure a number of times within Greek myths. Their name has been explained as meaning "dwellers at the back of the north wind," but strictly interpreted it means "dwellers beyond Boreas." According to Geoffrey Ashe, the translation of Boreas as "the north wind" is a sophistication that came only with the invention of exact compass points.[14] It was said that one consequence of these people living beyond the fierce northwest wind was that they enjoyed a calm, welcoming climate. Hecataeus described their island as "both fertile and productive of every crop, and since it has an unusually temperate climate it produces two harvests each year."

What is striking about this description is that the same notion resurfaces, with modifications, in Avalonian legend and Celtic lore, concerning the mystical island-valley of the otherworld—Avalon. Many a reader will automatically relate Avalon with Arthur and the Glastonbury Tor. However, the Hyperborean description suggests why Hecataeus concentrated on the Briton god identified with Apollo. Wherever the Hyperboreans were imagined to be, they always were associated with Apollo, the archer-god.

Apollo's principal home was at Delphi, which, according to the Greeks, was the "navel," the center of the earth. There he was known to have his chief oracle, but it was said that he left Delphi for three months of every year, in a flying chariot drawn by swans, to visit his Hyperborean friends.[15]

Therefore, it has been suggested that Boreas, or Avalon, was seen as the opposite focal point, or center of the earth, to the Greek Delphi/Arcadia. In other words, the island was considered to be the Arcadia of the Western Hemisphere, thus achieving the necessary balance of the world. It equally makes sense that this "other world" was to be found in what was known as the boreal forest, or the winter forest.

In reality, by the fourth century B.C., the Celts were considered one of the four peripheral nations of the known world, beside the Scythians, the Indians, and the Ethiopians. From their original homeland in southern Eurasia they moved with relentless energy to the eastern and western limits of the European continent and threatened the spreading "civilization" of Rome. By the end of the fifth century the area of Celtic settlement extended well beyond its original limits. In Spain, for instance, it is assumed that Celtic peoples were established over much of the country following successive immigrations.[16]

Yet nothing about the Celts is more certain than that they believed in a life after death among the bliss of the otherworld. The grave furniture that has been found among Celtic burials reaffirms such a belief. Classical authors make explicit reference to it, and even later storytellers have woven it imaginatively into the fabric of their literature.[17]

The Celtic Otherworld, the Elysian Fields of the Greeks, and the Roman's Realm of the Dead, are ultimately the same. And supporting the Irish tradition that the dead went to the Kingdom of Donn, the otherworld was frequently conceived as a number of coexisting regions representing so many different aspects.

The evidence for this view is exemplified by an Old Welsh poem entitled *The Spoils of Annwn (Preiddeu Annwn)*, which tells of a disastrous expedition to the otherworld, commonly known as Annwn, by Arthur and his men.[18] The general structure of the poem supports the common notion of the otherworld as an island, but it is named by several different titles and described in terms that imply several different concepts.

In one stanza it appears as a kind of twilight underworld, and once it is even referred to as *uffern*, "hell"; whereas, in another stanza it becomes Caer Wydyr, the "Fortress of Glass" from which Arthur and his company find it difficult to obtain response.[19]

In contrast, *The Royal Masonic Cyclopedia* traces the Elysian Fields back to a far more ancient world, when the people of the hamlet of Eleusis, near Athens, celebrated a series of rituals known as the Eleusinian mysteries.[20]

At first none but natives of Greece were eligible for initiation, but as time wore on this rule was relaxed, and citizens of all countries were admitted. Later, in the days of the Roman Empire, these mysteries became highly popular throughout the known world.

Therefore, it is impossible to avoid the conclusion that the Eleusinian mysteries exercised a powerful influence in perpetuating a desire for mysterious unions and the quest for mystical places. Hence, modern Freemasonry must be considered indebted to them for the maintenance of the leading idea of a secret bond of union between men of pure lives and conduct. And, as the wheel turns, it is also impossible not to associate this perpetuation of the secret mysteries with all that is considered to be included within the mystery of sacred geometry.

Two other connections come to mind when examining the movement and development of geometry and its related mysteries throughout the Far East and Europe. First of all, could a people such as the Celts and their holy men, the Druids, have developed their own form of geometry independent of the Greeks? It would seem unlikely, but through their wanderings and conquests the Celtic tribes would surely have been exposed to the teachings from the university at Alexandria. As mercenaries they may even have taken part in the sacking of the great library. The Knights Templar, during their time of occupation of Jerusalem and their tentative alliances with the Arabs and Jews, would similarly have been party to all types of learning and thought, as would have the monks who accompanied them on their crusades.

Is it any wonder that both church and state envied not only the riches of the Templars but the knowledge that had been gained through their alliances with the Arabs and Jews? The Church certainly recognized power in knowledge. And is it any wonder that the Church, during the period between the fall of Rome (A.D. 476) and the revival of learning (about A.D. 1200–1300), considered the high priests and high priestesses of nonorthodox thought, such as those of the Cathars, to be the "very essence of evil"?

TEMPLAR TREASURE

The earliest historical information on the Templars is provided during the first crusades, following the conquest of the Holy Land and establishment of the Kingdom of Jerusalem.[21] According to most books on the subject, including *Holy Blood, Holy Grail,* the Order of the Poor Knights of Christ and the Temple of Solomon was founded in A.D. 1118, nineteen years after the capture of Jerusalem. The declared objective of the original nine Templars was to keep the roads and highways safe for pilgrims. However, there is little evidence of their doing so, and the true objective of these first Knights Templar may never be known. Many historians do suggest that these knights discovered something hidden beneath the Temple of Solomon confirming, among other things, the very existence of Jesus Christ.

In 1127, after nine years in the Holy Land, most of the nine knights returned to Europe (notice the repeated number 9) and, in January 1128, at a Church council in Troyes, the Templars were officially recognized as a religious-military order. This was mainly due to their patron, Bernard of Clairvaux. This indeed suggests that the knights had discovered something of tremendous religious and historical value.

The Templars were sworn to poverty, chastity, and obedience. They enjoyed virtual anonymity due to a papal bull issued by Pope Innocent II in 1139. It stated that the Templars would owe allegiance to no one other than the pope himself. One result was that, over the next two decades, younger sons of noble families throughout Europe flocked to join the Order's ranks. And since on admission to the Order a man forfeited all his possessions, including his land, Templar holdings proliferated.[22]

Within a mere twenty-four years of the Council of Troyes, the Order held substantial estates throughout most of Europe, the Holy Land, and points east. By the mid-thirteenth century the Templars had become powerful enough to be involved in high-level diplomacy between nobles and monarchs throughout the Western world and the Holy Land. The Orders' political activities were not confined to the Christian world. Close links were forged with the Muslims. Moreover, the Templars commanded a respect from Saracen leaders far exceeding that accorded any other Europeans.

At the same time, the Templars created and established the institution of modern banking and, in effect, became the bankers for every throne in Europe and for various Muslim potentates as well.[23] But the Templars did not only trade in money. Through their ongoing relations with Islamic and Judaic culture, they came to learn and to accept new areas of knowledge and new sciences. The Templars controlled a veritable monopoly on the best and most advanced technology of their age, and contributed to the development of surveying, map making, road building, and navigation.

They possessed their own seaports, shipyards, and fleet, both commercial and military, with their major fleet based in La Rochelle, France. The Order also maintained its own hospitals with its own physicians and surgeons, who apparently understood, among many other things, the properties of antibiotics.[24] But during this time of advancement, in 1185, King Baudouin IV of Jerusalem died. One immediate consequence was that in July 1187, Gerard de Ridefort, Grand Master of the Temple, through certain folly, lost Jerusalem and most of the Holy Land to the Saracens. In addition, another religious-military order, the Teutonic Knights, had established an independent state for themselves, the "Ordenstaat" or "Ordensland," where they enjoyed a virtually unchallenged sovereignty.[25]

Not surprisingly, from the very inception of the Ordenstaat the Templars envied the "Knights of the Sword," as they were known, and after the fall of the Holy Land they thought increasingly of a similar state of their own. It was at about this time that the broad concept of a New Jerusalem, somewhere outside of the Holy Land, began to take shape.

The Templars thus retreated to the south of France and, more specifically, to Languedoc, the principality of the heretical Cathars. There they felt that perhaps the Languedoc could become their New Jerusalem because many wealthy landowners, who were Cathars themselves or sympathetic to the Cathar beliefs, had also donated vast tracts of land to the Order.[26]

Generally, the Cathars adhered to a life of simple devotion and conducted their rituals and services in the open air or in any readily available building, such as a barn. The Cathars believed in reincarnation and recognition of the feminine principle in religion. Indeed, the preachers and teachers of Cathar congregations, who were of both sexes, insisted on a religious or mystical experience acquired by direct knowledge.[27] This experience was called *gnosis,* from the Greek word for knowledge.

In the early 1200s, the independent principality of Languedoc extolled the four virtues of learning, philosophy, poetry, and courtly love. In fact, within the boundaries of this principality, a culture that was the most advanced and sophisticated in all of Christendom flourished.

The Languedoc promoted religious tolerance. As a result, Greek, Arabic, and Hebrew, along with the "Kabbalah," the ancient esoteric tradition, were enthusiastically studied. However, not unlike the Roman Empire, complacency and decadence set in, and by A.D. 1208 the Roman Catholic Church had become increasingly threatened by the Cathar heresy.

Under direct orders of Pope Innocent II, a Holy Crusade was waged against the Cathars. In 1209, a northern army led by Simon de Montfort invaded the Languedoc; during the next forty years, approximately thirty thousand people were killed.[28] This genocide, for it is the only truthful way to describe it, is now known as the Albigensian Crusade. And although the Pope initiated the Crusade, it is best remembered for the fanaticism of a Spanish monk named Dominic Guzmán, who created the tortures of the "Holy Inquisition."

By 1243 the Crusade had leveled all major Cathar towns and forts, except for a handful of isolated strongholds. Chief among the holdouts was the remote mountain citadel of Montségur. Fighting against all odds, in March 1244 the fortress finally surrendered, and the Cathar heresy, at least officially, ceased to exist in the south of France. What is known is that the Cathars were wealthy, and rumors of a fantastic Cathar treasure spread. This treasure was supposedly kept at Montségur, but when the fortress fell nothing of consequence was found beyond the normal material wealth.

A lull existed for another sixty-three years, but at dawn on Friday, October 13, 1307, King Philip IV of France ordered that all Templars in France be placed under arrest and their possessions seized.[29] However, Philip's primary interest, the Order's immense wealth, was never found, and what became of the fabulous treasure of the Templars has remained a mystery to this day. Rumors that still persist tell of the treasure being smuggled to the Order's naval base at La Rochelle and loaded into eighteen galleys, which were never heard of again. According to tradition, many English and French Templars found a Scottish refuge and are said to have fought at Robert the Bruce's side at the Battle of Bannockburn, in 1314, while many others apparently fled to Portugal, and maybe even to Denmark and Norway.

Could the Cathar treasure, so sought after by both church and state, be the same treasure that disappeared with the Templar fleet from the port of La Rochelle? And where could it have gone? Would the eighteen galleys of the Templar fleet have gone to Scotland or Portugal, or would they have just disappeared off the face of the earth to the west?

Nothing is ever said about the west because few believe that the Europeans possessed any knowledge of the Americas until the late fifteenth century. Yet historical evidence confirms that, centuries before Columbus's famous discovery, the shores of North America were being visited not only by the Vikings of the tenth and eleventh centuries, but by the Celts, Phoenicians, Greeks, Egyptians, and Carthaginians, a virtual who's who of ancient maritime traders and explorers.

One of the first recorded voyages to the West is by Pliny the Elder, who reported briefly the four-month journey of Himilco, son of Hamilcar, about 525 B.C.[30] Around the same time Pytheas made a voyage that is reasonably well documented. According to the accounts, Pytheas and his crew sailed to southern England, Ireland, Scotland, the Hebrides, the Orkneys, and ultimately to Thule, the outermost of all countries. On his return to Massilia (Marseilles, France), Pytheas tried to convince the Greek world of the relationship between the moon and the tides, but no one would listen. He is now credited, though, with being the first known navigator to apply astronomy to geography as a means of fixing specific locations.

The next figure to emerge from the shadows is an Irish monk, Saint Brendan of Clonfert.[31] The tales of Brendan's exploits in the sixth century were handed down for several centuries and were then drawn together in the Middle Ages into the *Imrama,* one of Ireland's most popular sagas.

The next noted explorer was a Viking, Ari Marsson. It is told in the Norse saga known as the *Landnamabok* that Ari, about A.D. 970, was driven by storm for several days past his intended port of Reykjavík, Iceland, until he reached Albania and Hvitramannaland ("White Man's Land"). It was reported as lying "westward in the ocean adjacent to Vinland the Good."[32] Then in 982, Erik (the Red) Thorvaldsson was banished from Iceland for three years for murder. Crossing Denmark Strait to Greenland, he is known to have rounded Cape Farewell and explored the fjord area of Julianehaab, which he named Osterbygden

("Eastern Settlement") and coasted further along the western coast to the Godthaab district, where he placed Vesterbygden ("Western Settlement").[33] He chose the name Greenland for the huge ice-capped island, for he felt that "men would be more readily persuaded to go there if the land had a good name," and in the spring of 986, he returned with his own colonizing expedition. According to the sagas, Leif, son of Erik the Red, is reputed to have made his first voyage to Vinland from Greenland in the spring of 1001.[34]

Recently, competing experts have jousted to claim Vinland for their chosen "sound which lay between the island and the cape" where "a river flowed out of a lake." Many have claimed that L'Anse aux Meadows in Newfoundland is the site of Leif's brief settlement. On the other hand, several American scholars have "located" Leif's winter home in Plymouth, Massachusetts or on the Bass River off Nantucket.[35] But, as we shall see, there also lies in Nova Scotia an area that remarkably fits Leif's saga and his description of the *promontorium vinlandiae*: where "tales of grape clusters and warm winters enriched the Norse tradition of Vinland"; where "a river flowed out of a lake"; and, where "there were big shallows there at low water."[36]

Tragically, from the eleventh century onward, the Vikings' contact with the northeastern mainland began to slip away because of their inability to make peace with the natives. In 1121, Icelandic histories report that Bishop Erik Gnupsson of Greenland went in search of Vinland, and King Magnus of Norway sent forth Paul Knutsson in 1354. Other vague references dot the medieval histories, but following the Black Plague in Europe, few ships sailed westward. There has now come to light, however, historical documentation known as *The Zeno Narrative* that strongly suggests Prince Henry Sinclair found and established across the Atlantic a secure haven—a refuge where the Holy Bloodline could await the dawning of a more modern and more tolerant age.

3

The Legend of Glooscap

The idea of a holy refuge or settlement in pre-Columbian North America centers on a plot that even fiction writers would abandon with a sigh. Still, many years of investigation have pieced together one of the world's most intriguing might-have-been accounts of exploration and discovery.

In the early sixteenth century, in Venice, Italy, a young boy named Nicolo Zeno came upon letters apparently written 140 years earlier by his great-great-grandfather, also named a Nicolo Zeno, and by his brother Antonio. Unfortunately, the boy tore up most of the letters. But as a young man Nicolo, regretting his past actions, pasted together what remained of the letters and in 1558 he published the narrative *The Discovery of the Islands of Frislandia, Eslanda, Engronelands, Estotilanda, and Icaria; Made by Two Brothers of the Zeno Family, Namely, Messire Nicolo, the Chevalier, and Messire Antonio. With a Map of the Said Islands.*

This rather mysterious account is now known as *The Zeno Narrative.*[1]

The book tells of voyages reportedly made by the Zenos in the North Atlantic, both to Greenland (Engronelanda) and to Drogio (America) under the command of a Prince Henry Sinclair. Several contemporary believers, most notably Frederick J. Pohl, have shown how the narrative can be translated into a recognizable journey from the Orkneys to Newfoundland to Nova Scotia and New England, and back again. Pohl has even confirmed the date and place for the arrival on Canadian soil: Sunday, June 2, 1398, at Guysborough Harbour, Nova Scotia.[2]

Frederick Pohl carefully weighed each of the related points of *The Zeno Narrative* and concluded that the hill of fire that Sinclair spotted upon his arrival was at the burning coalfields of Stellarton, close by present-day New Glasgow, Nova Scotia. The narrative tells that after several days of exploring the countryside and making contact with the local Indians, the Mi'kmaq, Prince Henry sent Admiral Zeno back to the Orkneys with part of his fleet. Sinclair then led the remainder through the Strait of Canso into the naturally protected harbor of Pictou, Nova Scotia.

What is curious about this whole episode is that Sinclair sent Antonio, his best navigator, along with many of his people back to Scotland, and only retained small boats capable of portages. This would suggest that Prince Henry knew of his travel requirements beforehand.

Exactly what did Prince Henry do after the departure of Antonio Zeno? Unfortunately, the narrative does not tell us what happened to Prince Henry and who stayed with him. The most intriguing theory is that Sinclair became Glooscap, the man-god of Mi'kmaq legend.[3]

The tradition, or legend, of Glooscap is in the form of songs or chants preserved in tribal memory and handed down by oral transmission. Several passages in the Mi'kmaq chants, however, are of a higher order of poetry or allegory than one can generally attribute to the Mi'kmaq.[4]

To my mind the finest of these poems is "The Legend of the Shubenacadie":[5]

> *Stranger, beneath this willow's shade*
> *For many years a rose tree bloomed*
> *Where Acadie the Indian lad*
> *By Shuben, his love, was sadly tombed.*

> *Shuben was lovely as the moon*
> *At evening coming from the sea,*
> *And glorious as the summer's sun*
> *Ere twilight comes, was Acadie.*

When he was but a small papoose
And she was very young
He brought the skins of rabbits white
And round her father's wigwam hung.

When he had seen a few more moons
He smiled on danger's sternest form
And left the fur from fierce grey lynx
To wrap his Shuben from the storm.

Stranger, he loved as Indians love,
And strangely wild and jealous grew,
And night and day he watched the grove
Where Shuben hunted caribou.

One twilight many moons ago
As he was hunting porcupine
He slew a deer as white as snow
And round him wrapped its ample skin.

As foxes frisk with wanton glee
And frolic in the copsewood dell
So frisked and frolicked Acadie
Till evening shades around him fell.

He thought (alas his thought was vain)
To meet with Hooran in the dale,
Hooran was chief of Avon's plain
And milder than the summer's gale.

Shade darkened shade till many a star
Shot through the wood its tepid gleams,
When Shuben something eyed afar,
A vagrant deer to her it seems.

She steals along the mountain brow
And wanders softly through the wood
Until at last a form of snow
The lovely deer before her stood.

She brought the arrow to her eye,
A sudden trembling seized her frame,
She sighed, she wept, she knew not why,
Again she took the deadly aim.

The aim was sure, the string she drew,
Alas too well she knew the art,
Twas done, the fated arrow flew,
It struck, it pierced him to the heart.

Stranger, I cannot tell my woes
But the Great Spirit knows the whole
That Acadie was my papoose
And Shuben died of troubled soul.

Where yonder weeping willow grows
Was Acadie in sorrow laid
And there the band of Indian braves
Their warlike homage to him paid.

Not distant far is Shuben's bed
Amid a baleful hemlock bower,
And when the summer mantles spread
Her tomb is graced with many a flower.

For them still flows in stream of tears
The troubled waters that you see,
Their memory still the river bears,
the river Shubenacadie.

—HELEN CREIGHTON[6]

Mi'kmaq lore tells that Glooscap wintered on Cape d'Or in the Bay of Fundy at a site known as Owokun.[7] Yet it is unreasonable to assume that Glooscap and his entire entourage wintered at this spot. Sinclair may have wintered there part of the time, but one of the most impressive things to the Mi'kmaq about Glooscap was his tireless explorations of the country. Mi'kmaq legends tell how, even before the first winter set in, Glooscap crossed the Nova Scotia peninsula to the Atlantic before returning to the Bay of Fundy.

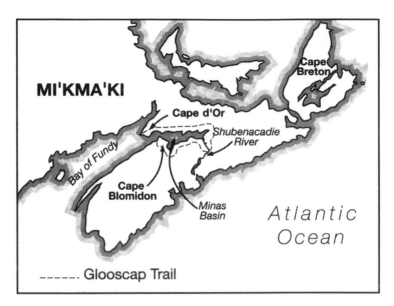

The Glooscap Trail

A general map of Nova Scotia highlighting areas attributed to the Mi'kmaq legend of Glooscap. Note how the Glooscap Trail is centered on the Shubenacadie River.

Cape Blomidon, on the south shore of the Bay of Fundy, is another traditional winter home of Glooscap. It was here that Glooscap supposedly lived among the Mi'kmaq. Surpassing even Cape d'Or, Cape Blomidon offers the most famous view of both the Annapolis Valley and Minas Basin.

Scots Bay, located below Cape Blomidon, is a rock hunter's paradise, with one of Canada's most prestigious deposits of amethyst. Interestingly, Glooscap was said to possess a magic belt with an amethyst jewel as its centerpiece. In *Glooscap Legends,* compiled by Stanley T. Spicer, amethyst is known as Glooscap's jewel.[8]

Through other Glooscap legends there occur several resounding themes centered around Glooscap's ability as a magician and his control over animals and nature. The legends tell that even the land was not immune, and structures of land and sea were attributed to his handiwork.

Beyond the casual observance, though, it's obvious that Glooscap/Sinclair would have carefully chosen both Cape d'Or and Blomidon for one very specific reason—their strategic locations. Both sites are positioned in such a manner as to offer unobstructed views of both the entire Bay of Fundy and Minas Basin. With the Cape d'Or promontory having an elevation of 500 feet above sea level and Cape Blomidon rising to 760 feet above sea level, on a clear day not only can the mouth of the Bay of Fundy at Grand Manan Island be observed, but also the Northumberland Strait across the low-lying Chignecto Isthmus.

Rivers running into the Minas Basin, Cobequid Bay, and Chignecto Bay often experience a tidal bore, a wave of water that moves upstream against the current, making it seem as if the river is running backward. Tidal bores occur regularly in the Macaan River and River Hebert near Amherst, the Chigonois and Salmon rivers near Truro, the Meander River that empties into Minas Basin near Windsor, and the Shubenacadie River.

The Shubenacadie is one of Nova Scotia's longest rivers and appears to split mainland Nova Scotia in two. It has become the locale for exciting white-water rafting as modern-day rafters ride the crest of the tidal-bore wave upstream. It can be said that Glooscap was certainly a fine military strategist to realize the seemingly impregnable defense that the tides meant to locating a settlement only accessible to those who possessed the knowledge to "ride the tide."

Michael Bradley has located Glooscap/Sinclair's settlement atop the highest hill at New Ross, Nova Scotia. When Bradley first viewed the site, one characteristic of the ruins that interested him a great deal were the large boulders that had been incorporated into the walls. In comparison, some Saxon and Norman churches in Britain also have large and irregular boulders embedded in the walls up to about the thirteenth century, but not often afterward. This detail, along with the general rubblework type of construction, suggested to Bradley that the ruin could be Norse or North Scots, dating from the thirteenth century or earlier. Bradley notes that the ruin could even date from the end of the fourteenth century if the builders were concerned only with making a rough "keep" or hill-fort.[9]

When I visited New Ross in 1992 for the first time, I had to admit that there appeared to be some inexplicable relationship between the castle ruins and Oak Island to the south.[10] It was hard to explain, but I just knew that New Ross had been chosen for its strategic location in relation to Oak Island. What clearly set me on this tangent was the realization that a Masonic lodge had recently been established directly across the street and to the east of the ruins. Surprisingly, I later confirmed with Michael Bradley that the Masonic lodge had not existed prior to the publishing of his book in 1988. And what was it about the fact that the castle ruins were located exactly eighteen miles from Oak Island? As I have previously noted, the clues remain; one only has to see them.

Arthur Conan Doyle endowed his fictional character, Sherlock Holmes, with the ability to see connections where no apparent connections lie and comments upon them specifically in *The Adventure of the Norwood Builder*. As it is starting to appear, Prince Henry Sinclair was also a builder in the North Woods—Norumbega, as it was known at one time. Curiously enough, the Masonic lodge located in New Ross is named the Norwood Lodge.

NORUMBEGA

Father Sebastian Rasle, the French priest who did missionary work among the Wabanaki Indians of Maine during the eighteenth century, thought he had found the source of the word *norumbega* in the Wabanaki name Aranmbegh.[11] Rasle translated this as "at the water's head," but more recent scholars have favored "at the clay inlet."[12] Others claim to have traced it to the Mi'kmaq Nolumbeka, which is said to mean "a succession of falls and still waters." Still another suggestion was Nalambigik, "pool of still water," while yet another relates it back to a modification of Norman Villa.[13] But it appears clear that Norman Villa and Norumbega were two different place-names. The usual theory is that the latter was the name of a river, while many have associated the Norman Villa with one of the legendary Seven Lost Cities.

The legend of the Seven Lost Cities began in eighth-century Spain. There the legend tells of seven Portuguese bishops who managed to escape by ship when the North African Moors descended upon the Visigoth, in the year A.D. 711.[14] With a considerable number of their flock, they reached an island somewhere out in the Atlantic, where they established seven cities. However, one of the greater mysteries relating to the exploration of the New World is by far the La Cosa map, dated 1500. This is the first map to indisputably show America. The map shows discoveries apparently made by the English, as it is decorated with no fewer than five English flags shown along the northern coastline.

Indeed, there is general agreement among most historians that La Cosa must have received some detailed information of the reputed discoveries made by John Cabot. The really interesting question is whether this derived merely from Cabot's voyage of 1497; or whether there is in the map unique data from altogether more mysterious voyages of an earlier era, such as Prince Henry Sinclair's.[15] And, if La Cosa's map is indeed of the 1497 Cabot voyage, then it incidentally provides the strongest possible evidence that Cabot's landfall had not been Newfoundland, but had been further to the south along the eastern seaboard.[16]

This brings us to the practice of "latitude sailing," when the European mariner sailed north or south to the latitude of his destination, and then sailed east or west as the case may be until he reached it. In Cabot's instance, it appears that he chose 45° north latitude to follow, for it is told that he first made for the French port of Bordeaux and then sailed west. Bordeaux is at latitude 45° 35' north.

In this light, Cabot's first landfall may possibly have been as far south as Maine, in which case Maine would have been his "mainland," and Nova Scotia his Isle of the Seven Cities. But the more favored view is that he arrived somewhere east of Nova Scotia's most southerly point, then worked his way northeastward along the coast and then back to Bristol. Coincidentally, together with Nova Scotia's Bay of Fundy, Bristol has one of the highest tidal ranges in the world, with its spring tides reaching a range of forty feet. A further coincidence has La Rochelle, being the port from which the Templar fleet disappeared on October 13th, 1307, located at 46° 15' north.

It is known that, during medieval times, the magnetic deviation of any compass could range from one to three degrees on average. This could mean that anyone sailing two thousand nautical miles across the Atlantic using latitude sailing, thinking he was sailing due west, was actually sailing somewhat southwest and could end up anywhere to 1° south of his destination.

Could this be the cartographic clue that allowed some Templars to sail directly to Nova Scotia on that fateful Friday morning of October 13th, 1307? Could it also be the clue as to why Norumbega and the Seven Cities have all been located in several different places along the New England-Maine-Nova Scotia coastline?

In turn, this brings us back to *The Zeno Narrative* and the question

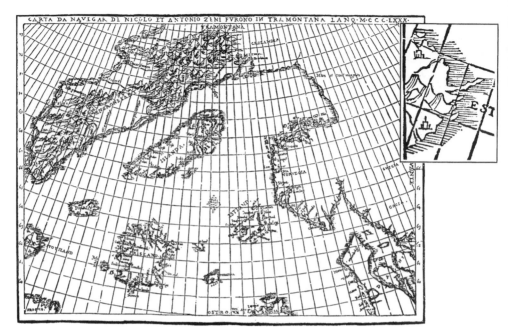

The Zeno Map

The Zeno map with an insert showing two castles representing settlements. Note how the two castles are shown separated by a difference of one degree in latitude.

of its authenticity. One remarkable fact about the Zeno map is that it illustrates none of the lost islands or cities that were so common on maps of this era—no Norumbega or the Seven Cities. What it does show is two settlements in Estotiland, represented by little castles that are separated by a river. One of these settlements is shown on the map at just below 63 degrees at the far right; the other is shown further down to the left just below 62 degrees—a difference of one degree. And since Estotiland can only be Nova Scotia because of the geographic features that fit *The Zeno Narrative* and apply only to Nova Scotia, then it can only be concluded that this large river must be an attempt to show the Shubenacadie River.

Pohl speculated that Sinclair sailed away from Nova Scotia in the spring of 1399 toward New England, where he explored the coast before beginning his homeward journey across the ocean. But no one knows whether this New England visit was a short stopover before returning to Orkney, or whether the detour to the south is of greater significance to Sinclair's New World travels.

Regardless of his intentions, a significant event appears to have occurred. It seems that the trip proved fatal to one of Sinclair's trusted knights, for the effigy of a fourteenth-century knight found on a rock ledge located outside Westford, Massachusetts, carries a broken sword, the symbol of death.

Following its discovery, Frank Glynn, then president of the Connecticut Archeological Society, and later, Frederick Pohl, visited Westford and made detailed drawings of the entire effigy figure. Both were able to make out the coat-of-arms on the knight's shield: a crescent, a five-pointed star, and a buckle above a masted ship. Although they were unaware of the significance at the time, the coat-of-arms proved to be that of the Gunn clan bearing the symbol of the galley of Orkney.[17]

I, in turn, have reproduced both Glynn's and Pohl's constructions, and determined that the figures do show a medieval knight. Ingeniously,

The Westford Knight

Graphic depictions of the Westford Knight by both Pohl and Glynn. Although somewhat different in artistic expression, both drawings show the relative detail of the knight's shield and sword. Note that both drawings depict a square formed over the right eye, possibly suggesting the notion of the alchemical "squaring of the circle."

the figure of the knight incorporates some marks made by nature along with those made by man. Where colored streaks and patches and parallel glacial scratches in the hard gneiss could serve his purpose, the effigy maker accepted them.[18]

While many investigators fail to agree on a definitive likeness of the knight, they all agree that several of the Mi'kmaq Indians who had guided Prince Henry Sinclair to the south were witnesses to the death of this important person. The following passages from *Legends of the Micmacs* suggest that this knight's name was indeed Gunn, or "Kuhkw," as pronounced in Mi'kmaq:[19]

He came from the east; went away toward the west. There he is still tented; and two important personages are near him, who are called Kuhkw and Coolpujot . . .

Kuhkw means Earthquake; this mighty personage can pass along under the surface of the ground . . . One of these seven visitors was wonderfully enamoured of a fine country; and expressed a desire to remain there; and to live long; whereupon, at Glooscap's direction, Earthquake took him and stood him up and he became a cedar-tree . . . seeds producing all the cedar-groves that exist in New Brunswick, Nova Scotia, and elsewhere . . .

The other men started and reached home in a short time . . .

The next day they prepared a festival, and all four are feasted and sumptuously entertained. They are then taken to the top of a hill which is very high and difficult of access. The ground is rocky, broken, and totally unfit for cultivation. On the very apex of this hill, where the sun would shine from morning until night, they halt; and Glooscap takes the man who had desired to live for a long time, clasps him round the loins, lifts him from the ground, and then puts him down again, passing his clasped hands upon the man's head, and giving him a twist or two as he moves his hands upwards, transforms him into an old gnarled cedar-tree, with limbs growing out rough and ugly all the way from the bottom. "There," he says to the cedar-tree, "I cannot say exactly how long you will live—the Great Spirit alone can tell that. But I think you will not be likely to be disturbed for a good while, as no one can have any object in cutting you down; . . . I think you will stand there for a good long while . . ."

What intrigues me about this whole episode is the fact that the noted investigators failed to question the obvious: is the design of the knight one big clue?[20] It's wonderful to realize that the knight was of the Gunn clan, but what of all the other strange markings that accompanied this figure? What of the fact that this knight, from his honorable mention in the Mi'kmaq legends, was obviously Sinclair's "right-hand man" when it came to underground exploration and mining? Also, just what effect did this event have on Sinclair's "Celtic" settlement, and just who did "Earthquake" bury under a cedar tree, and where?

MAPS

There is no question that *The Zeno Narrative* and the Zeno map were believed and used extensively by fellow Europeans for at least the following one hundred and fifty years. Giovanni Batista Ramusio was known to have used the Zeno map in his "Travels of 1574," while John Davis also referred to it in his explorations.[21] Purchas even referred to it in his treatise entitled *Purchas His Pilgrimes*. Even more surprising, a reconstructed polar projection of the Zeno map gives an amazing accuracy to the relative longitudes and latitudes of selected places, such as mainland Nova Scotia.[22] But how could this be? The art of navigation in the fourteenth century was still very elementary, although by the beginning of the century Venetian sailors had started to use a crude compass and the hourglass, as well as sailing directions based on estimated distances.

The great barrier was that, as previously noted, no one could determine longitude, the position in degrees east or west of a given point, with any accuracy. All mariners knew was that the determination of longitude involved the accurate measurement of time. As a result, master navigators of this time simply accepted the fact that no one had any way of accurately measuring longitude.[23]

But if Prince Henry Sinclair knew the accurate latitude and longitude of just one location in Nova Scotia, he could then have accurately mapped the entire mainland through the application of one simple geometric theory—the Pythagorean theorem. Knowing that the square constructed with a side equal to the longest side of a right triangle has an area equal to the sum of the areas of the squares whose sides are the other two sides of the triangle, extending a known area is as simple as adding another identical triangle using the known distance of any side of your first triangle. In its simplest form, the relationship of the lengths of the three sides of the triangle can be shown in the ratio of 3:4:5.

For Prince Henry Sinclair, the easiest starting point may have been Oak Island. It would have given him a true shot at Polaris, by which he could have established true north and accurately recorded his latitude. (Let us call this point A.) In support of this we have learned that there existed on Oak Island the distinctive stone triangle that established true north to an accuracy of one-quarter of a degree.

This stone triangle also established, or recorded, a magnetic deflection of approximately $6^{1}/_{2}$ to $7^{1}/_{2}$ degrees. Could Prince Henry Sinclair have used a magnetic needle as a backup system to verify his angles of sighting in relation to true north? Nonetheless, if one were to walk in a direction of true north from point A, using the North Star and a magnetic compass to verify his direction wherever he stopped (let's call this point B), he could fix his latitude at this new point and therefore calculate the distance in degrees—knowing that one degree is equal to sixty nautical miles. This distance could also be confirmed using a rope or a chain of a verified length and physically measuring the distance traveled, as modern surveyors do.

The fixing of distance on a straight line does not have to pertain only to points in a true north direction. As long as a person can continually sight along a specific bearing, even if point B cannot be seen from point A, an accurate distance can be attained by following either a compass bearing or sighting on physical elements that can be seen. For example, the lead man could take a bearing of 30° west of north (or 330°) using a handheld 30–60–90 degree triangle, sight a distinctive object on that bearing such as a tree or a rock outcrop, and proceed to that object. From this point all that would be needed would be another object to sight upon, and so on. An even better guide would be to do as the Indians have done for centuries and as Prince Henry Sinclair and his knights did on their arrival to Nova Scotia: use a smoke plume to sight one's line upon.

In medieval times, crude compasses that had the needle suspended by a thread from a peg in the center of a directional dial were known to be used by the Templars, among others. Navigators could then determine not only north, but their vessel's course in relation to north. Yet, unlike a circle that is divided into 360 degrees, the dial on a medieval compass's rim was divided into just 32 points.

This came about for both traditional and practical reasons and lingered in nautical custom until about a century ago. The tradition of 32 points represented not directions but "winds" that would blow a ship to a certain destination.[24] When conventional compasses were introduced, the 32 points were retained but changed into directions. Two points separated $11^1/_4$ degrees, and each point had a directional designation that navigators had to memorize. Reciting these designations clockwise around the compass was called "boxing the compass." Starting at north, the next point would be "north by east," "north northeast," then "northeast by north," then "northeast" and so on around the compass to "north by west."[25]

Therefore, if the man on the ground was dealing with a known declination of $7^1/_2$ degrees, then he could have followed a bearing of $30 - 7^1/_2 = 22^1/_2$ divided by $11^1/_4 = 2$ points west of north (more accurately termed "north northwest"). In fact, on this exact bearing from point A, or the stone triangle, on Oak Island, lie the ruins at New Ross. More specifically, point C falls on the so-called hermetic rock that Bradley illustrates in his survey of the ruins. Not as surprisingly, the accurate distance measured between these two points is exactly 18.0 miles, or 5760 rods or 1440 chains, using the set of ancient measures that would have been used at the time of Prince Henry's explorations. All three of these measurements are multiples of the number 9 (shades of the original nine knights), a fact unrealized by me when I first determined these relationships.

The measured distance between point A and point B is exactly 14.4 miles (4608 rods or 1152 chains) while the distance between point B and point C is 10.8 miles (3456 rods or 864 chains): a simple 3:4:5 right triangle! Having established the distances and bearings between the three points, Henry Sinclair and his trusted men, with the help of the Mi'kmaq, could have triangulated throughout North America, given enough time. Of a more curious nature is the fact that both points B and C are found on hilltops at exact elevations of five hundred feet above sea level.

Of further interest is the physical layout of point B, positioned between two small peaks known locally as the Pinnacles. The Pinnacles

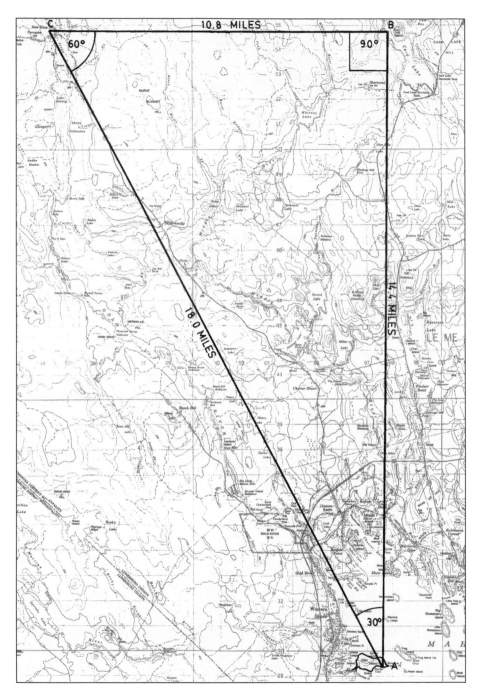

Simple triangulation showing relationship between Oak Island (A),
the Pinnacles (B), and New Ross (C)

*Once established, this simple relationship would allow an accurate mapping of
all of Nova Scotia.*

provide the perfect grove to sight the North Star from Oak Island, as if one were lying on one's back and sighting something between their raised knees. Prince Henry Sinclair indeed had his starting point.

The argument can be made that Sinclair didn't need a fixed latitude and longitude to map Nova Scotia. In essence, one could treat point A as the center of a sheet of paper and go from there. This is true. Once one has established a proper scale, all the distances are relative. But anyone who has ever created any type of map will realize that it is far easier to relate one distance to another if a central axis to the diagram is determined. Thus, by following a rough determining of Nova Scotia's shape, one would be inclined to run an axis not north to south but through the middle of the mainland—from its northeastern to southwestern points—from Hebron to Judique, for example. Again, if you were looking to base your map on geometric principles, would it not make sense or catch your imagination that this axis would be positioned exactly 30° north of east?

Whether Prince Henry had the ability to establish or accurately know a specific longitudinal location is a mystery in itself. Yet there is the clue of the illustration of the Templar knight on the Vopell map that Henry Sinclair is known to have explored, along with a reference of some ongoing "laboring" activities and of farms. Assuming New Ross was the mysterious Norman Villa, can this provide an explanation for a second castle? Can the second castle to the north represent the lost settlement of Norumbega?

Norumbega is supposed to have been a city "fifteen miles up a river," and appears as such on Cornelis Van Wytfliet's map of 1597, entitled "Norumbega and Virginia." The city is shown at 45° north and 315° east, for at this time longitude was measured easterly from the Azores Islands. Coincidentally, the latitude and longitude readings add up to 360 degrees. Was this a clue that Norumbega was considered to rest at the end of the earth, or "beyond the north wind," following a complete circuit, or the closing of a square?

Many other maps are just as suggestive, if not more so. The Gastaldi map of 1548 places Tierra de Nurumberg at the 315° longitude while L'Arcadia is positioned at 45° latitude. In turn, Zaltieri's map of 1566, although it does not give latitudes or longitudes, is interesting in that it has attracted a considerable amount of attention from modern institutions, such as Harvard, because of its remarkable representation of the entire continent of North America.

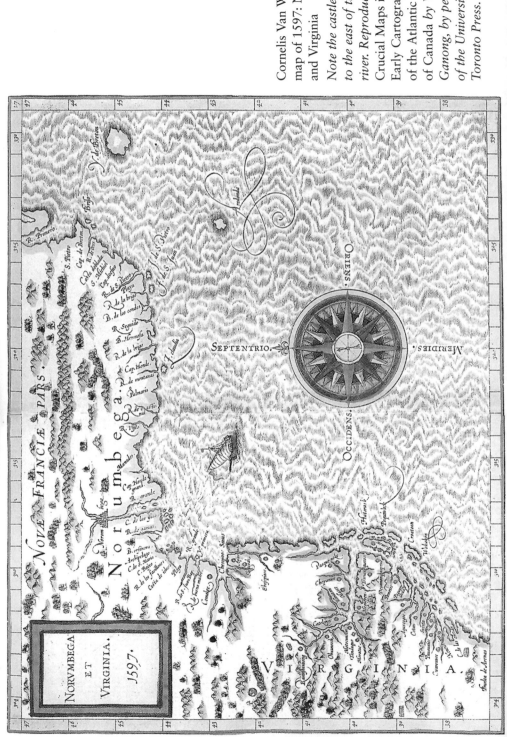

Cornelis Van Wytfliet's map of 1597: Norumbega and Virginia

Note the castle shown to the east of the large river. Reproduced from Crucial Maps in the Early Cartography of the Atlantic Coast of Canada by W. F. Ganong, by permission of the University of Toronto Press.

The Gastaldi map of 1548

Note the placing of Tierra de Nurumberg at 315 degrees longitude while L'Arcadia is found at 45 degrees latitude, adding up to 360 degrees in total. Is this a suggestion that the land of Norumbega and Arcadia are one in the same? Reproduced from Crucial Maps and the Early Cartography of the Atlantic Coast of Canada by W. F. Ganong, by permission of the University of Toronto Press.

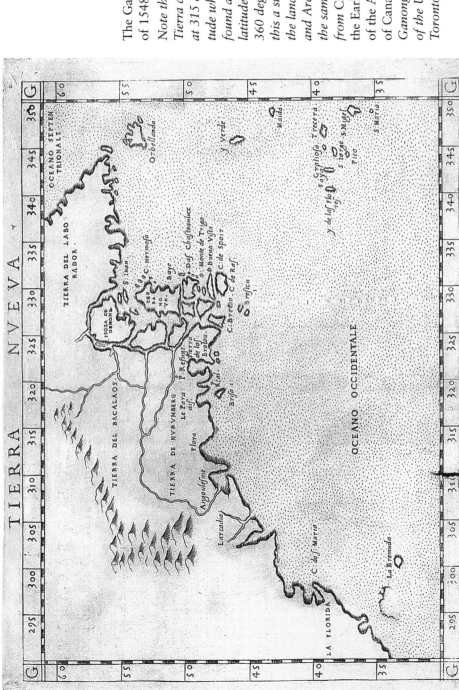

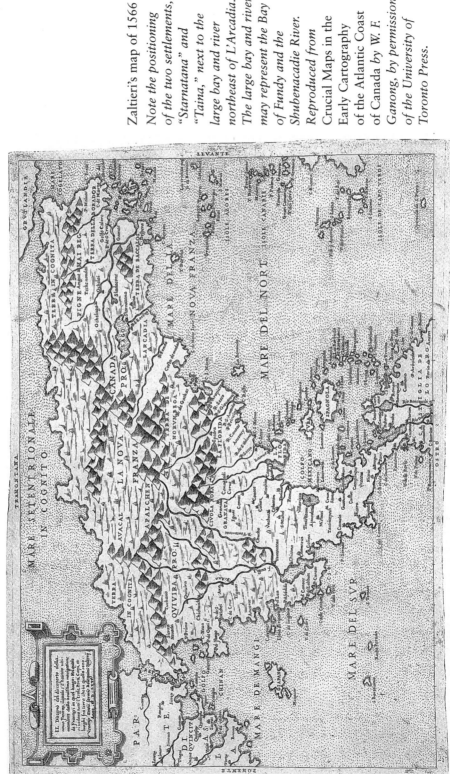

Zaltieri's map of 1566
Note the positioning
of the two settlements,
"Starnatana" and
"Taina," next to the
large bay and river
northeast of L'Arcadia.
The large bay and river
may represent the Bay
of Fundy and the
Shubenacadie River.
Reproduced from
Crucial Maps in the
Early Cartography
of the Atlantic Coast
of Canada by W. F.
Ganong, by permission
of the University of
Toronto Press.

A particularly important feature of this map lies in the positioning of a very large *lago* (bay) to the north of L'Arcadia, with two settlements positioned to the east of the "R. S. Lorenzo," which empties the bay into the Atlantic. These two settlements are noted in Latin as Starnatana (Star of Christ, or Star of David) and Taina (refuge). Geographically speaking, if the large bay is considered to be the Bay of Fundy, with the R. S. Lorenzo being the Shubenacadie River, then this indeed would position a European settlement of a size to be acknowledged in 1566 approximately fifteen miles up a river.

The Pseudo-Agnese map of 1556–1560 also shows a very curious feature that may relate to Prince Henry Sinclair's travels. Similar to Ramusio's map of 1556, it shows a stippled track running parallel to the coast; in the middle of the track is a square. While this has been drawn in a manner that could represent shoals and shallows—namely, the Grand Banks—it could also be taken as representing the Gulf Stream or North Atlantic drift. But why a perfectly square island? Could this be a hint of more ancient knowledge of land to the west?

The Paris Meridian is the original European marker of longitudinal measurement, established around 1670. It was replaced in 1884 by the British Greenwich Meridian, despite repeated opposition from the French. In contrast, Norumbega was repeatedly located 45° west of the Atlantic Meridian by Flemish and Venetian cartographers. Could there be meridians falling on strategic islands throughout the world that established longitudinal locations in medieval and even ancient times? If so, this could further explain the seemingly inexplicable accuracy of the portolans.

It could also go a long way toward explaining the floating square found to the south of mainland Nova Scotia. Was the square a telling code identifying a longitudinal meridian at this location, or did it suggest that the navigator must fix his position at this point? It's interesting that the clue would be represented by a square. The decoded *Rennes Parchments* speak of "a completion of the square." On one level, were the maps reflecting the ancient Egyptian practice of establishing the first corner to completing the square, and did that corner relate to a known meridian?

One last question before this chapter ends. Does the square in some manner explain why, according to Pohl, Sinclair virtually did a

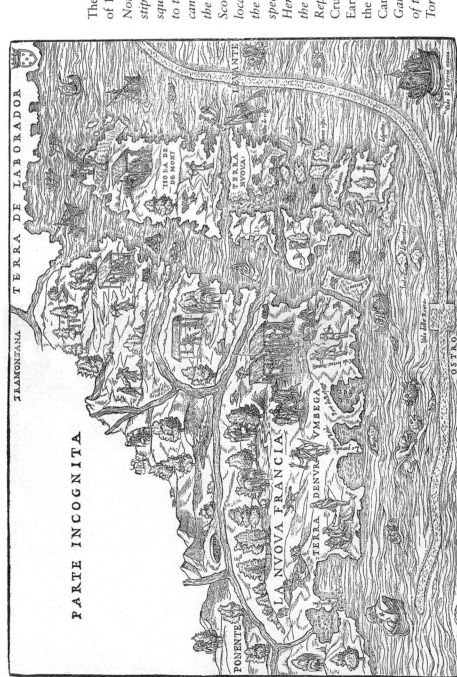

The Pseudo-Agnese map
of 1556–1560

*Note the very curious
stippled track and
square running parallel
to the coastline of what
can be presumed to be
the coastline of Nova
Scotia. Compare the
location of the square to
the location where Pohl
speculated that Prince
Henry did a U-turn off
the very same coastline.*
Reproduced from
Crucial Maps in the
Early Cartography of
the Atlantic Coast of
Canada by W. F.
Ganong, by permission
of the University of
Toronto Press.

180-degree turn in the mid-Atlantic and proceed easterly to where he first landed? Had he established his position by sighting a physical signpost, or had he determined his position through some method of navigational reconnoitering?

It's becoming obvious that Prince Henry Sinclair possessed some form of prior knowledge as to where he was heading. It's also obvious that a portion of this came from the hidden knowledge of the Templars. And it certainly appears that throughout the centuries there was a definite requirement to establish beyond a doubt that the mysterious lost colony, or land of Norumbega, could rightfully be theirs to claim.[26]

At least one other thing is certain. From the time he was born Prince Henry Sinclair received an amazing education, which enabled him to become the guardian of what many considered to be the true Holy Grail.

4

Mary, Mary
Quite Contrary

———◦———

Why was the notion of a direct holy lineage so important to the Knights Templar? The answer to this question might explain how the symbolism of the Holy Grail plays such an important role in solving this story's puzzle. However, one must bear in mind that the notion of a direct holy lineage, perpetuated by the Merovingians through to the sixth century and even later, may not be true. There remains the fact, though, that many people in the thirteenth and fourteenth century believed it to be true, as do certain modern organizations and individuals. Whatever the historical actuality behind the legend of the Holy Bloodline, one thing is known—the Merovingian dynasty was surrounded by an aura of magic, sorcery, and the supernatural.[1]

Traditionally, Merovingian monarchs were considered to be occult adepts, initiates in arcane sciences, and practitioners of esoteric arts.[2] According to one account, the tassels at the fringes of their robes were even deemed to possess miraculous curative powers. (Remember the curious funeral ritual of the French priest Berenger Saunière). The Merovingians were regarded not only as kings but as priest-kings, not unlike the ancient Egyptian pharaohs.[3]

There is very little evidence, though, as to the true origins of the Merovingians.[4] They claimed descent from Noah, whom they regarded as the source of all biblical wisdom, and also claimed direct descent from ancient Troy (remember the reference through the axis to Troy).[5]

According to the research of the authors of *Holy Blood, Holy Grail,* the ancestors of the Merovingians were supposedly connected with Arcadia's royal house as well.[6]

Whether the Merovingians derived ultimately from Troy or from Arcadia, or from Noah, does not necessarily present a problem of origin. According to Homer and early Greek histories, a substantial number of Arcadians were present at the siege of Troy, which was founded by settlers from Arcadia. The very name Arcadia derives from *arkades,* which means "people of the bear."[7] The bear was a sacred animal in both ancient Arcadia and Troy.[8]

Like the legend of the origins of the Merovingians, the pagan veneration of the bear also extends back beyond the time of the Greeks. The bear's holiness was universal in the Northern Hemisphere and, as a vegetation spirit, the male bear was sacrificed once a year to secure the renewal of life in the spring. Even as far back as the Upper Paleolithic period, drawings of bears with bleeding mouth, nose, ears, and dart marks were associated with the annual sacrifice of this animal.

The other aspect of the bear's holiness, specifically relating to the female, is her association with motherhood and her ability to provide sanctuary. Old European folk memories confirm that the bear was considered an ancestress similar to the deer and the elk-doe, and later linguistic evidence supports the association with the ability to carry and bear children.

In a similar fashion, many other customs and beliefs were also absorbed into the regime of the early Merovingians—including archetypal patterns that had as their basis such far-ranging sources as the Greek and Roman classics, Egyptian lore, Celtic myth, and the Old and New Testaments.[9] Indeed, we tend nowadays to take most of them for granted. They would include events such as birth, puberty, sexual initiation, death, and the cycle of the seasons, as well as more abstract concepts like the desire for escape to a soothing place of comfort.

Generally, archetypal patterns first found expression by means of symbols—Mother Earth is the best example. For instance, in the Upper Paleolithic period the Earth Mother was the single source of all life, who took her energy from the springs and wells and from the sun, moon, and moist earth.

Archetypal patterns are also frequently symbolized by anthropomorphic figures (many of which can be found in the tarot cards). The Earth Mother, the Hero, the Wanderer, the persecuted maiden, the femme fatale, the Lovers are all examples found within the tarot. The dying and reviving god, the wise old woman, the Hermit in the forest or the desert, the sacred Fool touched by God are other examples. One of the strongest archetypal patterns appears to have connected the Greek mythology of Queen Artemis and Arcadia with all that is rich, fertile, and nourishing.[10]

Significantly, the goddess Artemis the huntress, daughter of Zeus and Leto and twin sister to the sun-god Apollo, was a goddess of bears.[11] Greek myth suggests that the constellation Ursa Major—the Great Bear, with its seven principal stars—was an aspect of the goddess that had been transformed into the heavens.

Septentrion, which means "the gifts of the Holy Spirit of Wisdom," is another name for the constellation that guides the seafarer and never vanishes from the sky. The reference here is both to the polestar as the guide of mariners and to the magnetic attraction of the north. It is sometimes also called the "star of Arcady" because Callisto (another name for Artemis) had a son who was named Arkas, and they lived in Arcadia.[12]

At other times Artemis was known as Mellissae (meaning "bees"). The symbolic association of the goddess as Queen Bee may very well be the source of this imagery. (Over three hundred golden bees were found within the tomb of Clovis, the Merovingian king who ruled around the same time as King Arthur, around A.D. 500.) At other times Artemis was represented by the evergreen tree, the cedar.

One Greek myth tells of the hunter Orion who dared to violate a maiden of Artemis and because of this was severely punished by the perfectly aimed arrows of the mighty huntress.[13] Thus, the bow and arrow also represented Artemis.

Artemis is especially interesting in that accounts of Amazons were often linked with the goddess, thus relating to the myth of the Isle of Maidens. According to descriptions by both Pindar and Allimachus, Amazons founded the temple at the city of Ephesus (in the province of Lydia), Greece. Consequently, the temple was spoken of by the Greeks as a shrine of Artemis, and later by the Romans as a shrine of Diana. And although classical Greek accounts state that Leto gave birth to

Artemis on the island of Delos, Ephesians claimed that Artemis was born in a cavern at the foot of a mountain near Ephesus.[14]

Similarly, in many other temples and shrines throughout Greece, the image of the earth goddess, Demeter, was revered on the same level as Artemis. The month of Boedromion (September/October), when the crops of Demeter were harvested all through the land, was known as the time of the sacred mysteries. This was the time of the Thesmophoria—the nine days of the Greater Mysteries of Eleusis. Traditionally this was the time to remember the mythological abduction of Demeter's daughter Persephone by the master of hell, Pluto.[15]

To continue this connection even further, the best known shrine of Gaia, another variation of the Earth Mother/Goddess, lies beneath the later temple at Delphi.[16] The image of Gaia was closely associated with the sacred serpent. At the site of Olympia, Gaia was known as the oldest deity of that divine mountain. Even before Zeus was born, Gaia had been symbolized by the deep cleft that faced the southeast.[17] Here the priestesses of Gaia were said to celebrate the ancient rites of the goddess.

Some myths say that Gaia's Delphi priestesses were as "young as the leaves of springtime and innocent of the great knowledge they conveyed."[18] But others speak of long white hair and faces creased with lines of wisdom that only many years of life can bring. Crowned with a laurel wreath, sitting upon the ancient tripod, each in turn was said to throw barley, hemp, and laurel into the fire on which the sacred cauldron burned. Or the young priestesses were known to pay tribute to where the natural vapors poured from a fissure in the deep rock of a subterranean chamber, which was at that time considered to be the earth's holy of holies.[19] Here is the earliest association of the Goddess with the tripod and the inner sanctuary.

Other myths say that Dionysus was buried deep beneath the stone in the heart of Gaia's Delphi cavern. Yet it is also said that the cavern was the grave of the sacrificed python, Gaia's virgin-born serpent child, who was once known as Delphyna.

Homer, in turn, sang that young Apollo, finding the site of Python to his liking, decided to take it for his own.[20] But upon seeing Gaia's priestess Delphyna blocking his path to the holy chasm, Apollo used his torches and his arrows and dropped the pythoness Delphyna in an untimely fiery death, thus declaring the ancient shrine as his own. From that time on, Apollo assumes the attributes of the Goddess—the tripod and the inner sanctuary.

Euripedes tells another version, writing that a serpent, a child born alone of Gaia, guarded the cave of Gaia's oracle. Apollo then struck the serpent dead, and Gaia, in her wrath at this wanton act, sent nightmares to his men, so that they would know what penance they would someday pay. Other myths tell of Apollo's attempt to heal his guilt, for they proclaim that after he murdered Delhyna he went to Tempe Valley to purify himself by working as a shepherd.

Through interpretation of these myths, bears and snakes were seen as the guardians of the springs and sanctuaries of life and as symbols of life energy, cyclic renewal, and immortality. They are still considered as such in European folklore. By following these interpretations, it becomes evident that over the centuries a universal story line or archetypal pattern developed, a pattern where the Earth Goddess came to be represented by the evil serpent, while the virgin form of the Goddess assumed all of the bear's majestic attributes.

It was at Ephesus, the famous temple of Artemis, that the last goddess, Diana of the Ephesians (the Queen of Wisdom), survived well into the fifth century. But the citizens were transferring their allegiance from the virgin huntress to the virgin mother, and it was in A.D. 471, at the Ecclesiastic Council of Ephesus, that the seal of change was set. This final transfer of the goddess's attributes is known as the Marian Devotion. Yet, ever since this time there has been confusion as to which Mary is the subject of devotion, since there was certainly more than one Mary in the life of Jesus.

Not surprisingly, some of the stories within the Arthurian legends also appear to be echoes of pagan myth. Both Morgana and Guinevere of the Arthurian legends are figures taken directly from pagan antiquity, with a little bit of the Christian Mary thrown in for good measure. The change in Morgana's character from good to evil, as in Guinevere's, was due mainly to a shift in Church attitude. Celtic Christians had no deep animosity toward the pre-Christian religions. It is this notion, therefore, of the intertwining of continuous "life and death," "good and evil," and "pagan and Christian" cycles that leads us back to the earlier time of the "divine" goddess. (Remember the analogy of the wheels of a clock, except this time we're going back in time.)

The British authors of *Holy Blood, Holy Grail* were the first to call attention to the possible notion that Poussin's "shepherdess" was a link from the Christian Mary to the image of the pre-Christian Earth Goddess, an idea of immense importance. What the British authors did not realize is that, although the shepherdess is an explicitly Arcadian figure, embodying both medieval romantic and ancient philosophical tributes, she is in fact concealing something else. That something happens to be the fact that she is pregnant. This is quite evident in Poussin's painting *Les Bergers d'Arcadie—The Shepherds of Arcadia*. In the Rennes-le-Château parchment, the "no temptation" following this command obviously relates, on one level, to the fact that a pregnant lady does not present a temptation to the shepherds, since she is already with child.

As a result, instead of four figures there are five, the fifth being the "hidden" fifth element. Where, in esoteric circles, the number four traditionally represents endurance, firmness of purpose, accomplishment, and will, the number five represents adventure, restlessness, nervousness, and a quick temper, some of the very attributes that men attach to women when they are pregnant or emotional. The number 5 is the

Les Bergers d'Arcadie (The Shepherds of Arcadia),
Nicolas Poussin, circa 1640–42
Note closely the flowing garments of the "shepherdess." Does it not appear that the female figure is pregnant? Reproduced courtesy of the Louvre Museum.

number of the controller of the powers of nature. From this we can assume that the shepherdess is representative of Mother Earth, the life-giver and controller of the four seasons, and can be seen as a refuge/sanctuary/temple, with her womb as the inner sanctuary. On another level, the hidden fifth element represents Indian summer, that particular season in autumn where for only a short while the breezes of summer once again carry joy and warmth.

As this inner story line has now been completed, the mythical "good" side of the goddess/shepherdess as mother and nurturer has been exposed; but even paintings have been known to conceal the darker side. Knowing this, the evidence to date appears to confirm that Poussin's painting of the tomb is somehow linked to a deeper secret. This dark secret relates to the ancient mysteries, the mystery of Rennes-le-Château, the disappearance of the Templar fleet in 1307, Prince Henry Sinclair's explorations of the New World, and even to the development of the ceremonies and symbolism of the three basic degrees of Freemasonry. It is a secret that appears to support the notion that if Prince Henry were looking to establish a new Temple of Solomon in a New Jerusalem, then the application of sacred geometry and moral allegory, including archetypal patterns, would be required to sanctify the temple. It therefore appears logical that the symbols and rituals applied by Sinclair and his knights across the landscape of Nova Scotia may well relate to the three basic degrees of Freemasonry.

THE THREE DEGREES

Since it is impossible to provide a complete description of the three basic degrees of Masonry within this book, the reader should, for now, assume that the relationships described are based upon accurate accounts of the specific rituals. For those who are interested in a description of the entire ritual of the ceremonies I suggest John J. Robinson's *Born in Blood*.

Today, the initiation of an Entered Apprentice Mason, who is prepared by being half-stripped, blindfolded, relieved of all metal, and having a "cable-tow" placed around his neck, generally takes place in a permanent lodge room. The modern-day lodge room is equipped with an altar, chairs, and various symbolic props, such as rough and smooth ashlar stones. In the earliest meetings, which Masonic legend tells us were held "on high hills and in deep valleys," no so-called lodge furniture would have been available.[21]

Oak Island, Nova Scotia, is likewise situated within a deep valley along the shoreline of Mahone Bay and is surrounded on three sides by high hills of a uniform height of five hundred feet above sea level. The predominant limestone outcrop located to the east of Oak Island (if one "leapfrogs" the nearby Frog Island, remembering that the frog was one representative symbol of the Merovingian dynasty) is known as Aspotogan Mountain. Because of its whiteness, Aspotogan Mountain can be seen from great distances. It has been used for centuries by sailors as the first landmark to be sighted from the sea along the South Shore of Nova Scotia. (Sinclair changed his course once he had sighted something along the South Shore of Nova Scotia). Of a more curious nature is the fact that a small village called The Lodge is situated east of Aspotogan Mountain in the valley of St. Margaret's Bay.

The lodge symbol that would always have been made available to those secret meetings of the early Masons was the circle on the floor. This circle could easily have been traced on the ground in the center of a forest clearing or in the dirt floor of a barn, or in the sawdust scattered across a pub's floor. The circle obviously relates to the moon/sun or the golden ring, but on another level could identify the lodge as a "station."

During the American Civil War, blacks were ferried to Canada from the southern United States along the underground railroad from village to village, or station to station. As we have already learned, the French priest Saunière reinterpreted the Stations of the Cross within the remodelled village church of Rennes-le-Château. In Station XIV, which portrays Jesus's body being carried into or out of the tomb, there is a background of nocturnal sky dominated by a full moon. Was Saunière trying to intimate that Jesus was, as is suggested in Masonic ritual, seeking "light" when he was crucified and entombed in what we have come to interpret as Arcadia? (We should remember that Jesus had also once been an apprentice carpenter.)

Following Masonic ritual, if one wanted to develop a survey or geometric figure across the landscape starting at a single point (say, point A on Oak Island), then the necessary tools of the apprentice to complete the survey would be a compass and square and a "cable-tow." No one, including Masons, has been able to identify precisely what a cable-tow is. But in surveying, if one is following a compass bearing through a dense forest and measuring the distance by a chain—a sixty-six foot piece of flat metal wire—the easiest way to do this is to hook the chain to your belt at the small of your back so that your hands are free to hold the compass and to clear the path of limbs and branches. Accordingly, we can surmise that the Mason's apprenticeship is akin to that of a surveyor who starts his apprenticeship as a chainman.

In the first stage of initiation into Masonry, there is a reference to the apprentice being stripped half-naked. Could this not relate to the costumes worn by the shepherds of ancient Greece, as depicted within *The Shepherds of Arcadia*? Or could it relate on a different level to the poor apprentice chainman, who is required to trudge through some of the worst bog and scrub found in Nova Scotia along the South Shore? Any chainman will attest that it is very easy to lose both socks and boots and become completely disheveled when tramping through spruce and cedar bog.

The removal of all metal objects of any nature from the apprentice is as equally mysterious, unless one considers that the apprentice was using a compass to take his bearings and that any metal on his person could possibly alter the effectiveness of his compass readings. Blindfolding is just as easily explained if one considers that as the apprentice concentrates on his compass bearing he is, in fact, walking blindly through the woods.

Within the ritual of the Entered Apprentice, the newly confirmed Mason moves from the ground floor of Solomon's Temple, for the first station is only one of many that one has to pass through to reach his destination. This "journey of light" is likened to an ascent of a stairway that is accomplished step by step, or degree by degree, similar to the Stations of the Cross.

The newly initiated Mason is supplied with a white lambskin apron and is told that the white apron is an emblem of innocence. Surely this must be a direct reference to the purity of the Greek/Roman goddess Artemis/Diana. Hence, the apprentice is not only seeking wisdom, purity, and light through his completion of the Masonic stations, but he is also looking to build a new Temple of Solomon/Artemis/Diana/Demeter. And like the shepherd, the apprentice will be able to pay homage to the entombed, receiving guidance from the priests or deacons on what direction to pray to God for their deliverance.

At the close of the ceremony the apprentice receives his working tools, including the common gavel or maul, so that he may shape himself into a stone suitable for the Temple of God. Thus, by following this path of reason for a moment, it would appear that the "cornerstone" of the temple should be carved out of an appropriate material, such as limestone or gypsum, both of which are white and reflective like glass, and carved to represent a symbol of the goddess. Surely, Sinclair would have chosen a symbol that was also sacred to the Mi'kmaq, the bear, so that pagan, Hellenic, and Christian worship could be treated as one.

As to the second degree, the Fellow Craft, it is primarily a series of variations on the Entered Apprentice degree. After being guided through the ceremony by the Master Masons and passing around the lodge room from station to station, the candidate once again finds himself before the altar, still blindfolded, where he takes the oath of the second degree.

The bear in the wilderness

The author standing before a large limestone outcrop that depicts a bear drinking at a pool of water, reflecting notions of an earlier time when the bear was considered to be a guardian of the inner sanctuary. Photo by William F. Mann.

In this second part of his initiation, the newly made Fellow Craft Mason is directed to a spiral staircase, which symbolically leads to the middle chamber of the Temple of Solomon—only reached by passing between two columns. He is told that these columns represent the great bronze columns that flanked the outer porch of the Temple of Solomon. The initiate is then told that the original columns were hollow and protected the secret documents of Masonry from flood and fire, in a similar manner to the practices of the ancients.

The initiate next learns that Freemasonry incorporates both operative (working) and speculative (allegorical) Masonry, and is told that Freemasons built the biblical Temple of Solomon, in addition to many other notable stone structures. It is then explained that the Fellow Craft degree is founded on the science of geometry, which is the central theme of the entire Masonic Order. He is told that it is with this science that man comprehends the universe, the movements of the planets, and the cycle of the seasons. Especially important to the Mason is the use of geometry in the Masonic science of architecture; significantly, the initiate is told that geometry is so important to Masonry that the two terms were once synonymous. Finally, in the second degree, it is reaffirmed that speculative Masonry encompasses life and death, architecture, the arts and sciences, including astronomy, geography, and navigation.

Again, during the Fellow Craft initiation ceremony the initiate is blindfolded. Although there are obviously other levels of meaning, this action recalls the trickery and deception of the Master, or the Magician as depicted in the tarot. From this the initiate is to understand that even Masons of the second degree must be prepared for false clues and ruses. (An example of this is that even the most senior Masons over the years have remained convinced that Oak Island continues to be the final resting place of the "treasure.") The moral to the story so far may be that man should not be blinded by worldly goods, and that only through dedication to God and his Spirit will the Mason ascend to the higher levels.

At this point of the ritual, reference is made to the valley of "Jehosophat" and the "highest pinnacle of the Temple" in what appears to be an analogy of "on high hills and in deep valleys."[22] Remarkably, "Aspotogan" is an anagram to "Jehosophat" if one substitutes *J* (Jehovah) for *G* (geometry), combines the two *h*'s to make an *n*, and considers the *e* an *a* as in the Greek alphabet.

Equally surprising is the fact that from Oak Island the North Star is sighted between the twin mountain peaks known as the Pinnacles. It is becoming remarkably clear that the laying down of a sacred geometric figure across mainland Nova Scotia was either developed or fashioned to sublimely relate to the basic three degrees of Freemasonry. Or is it the other way around?

If this is in fact the case, the question remains, for what purpose? If Prince Henry Sinclair wanted to identify the area of a refuge/settlement, then signposts such as the planting of oak trees on strategic islands along the coastline of Nova Scotia would probably have been sufficient. Yet the clues left within the rites and ceremonies of Freemasonry appear to represent a quest, a quest that only the truly fortunate could complete. It is almost as though Sinclair was providing a challenge. Or was he suggesting that even among the initiated, only the pure of heart and morally strong will remain untempted by the supposed riches of Oak Island?

One has to remember that the pot of gold lies at the end of the rainbow, not the beginning. What lies at the beginning (Oak Island) is literally flood and allegorical fire (hell) for those who continue to seek true gold where it isn't. Do you remember the earlier reference to the rather warped or black sense of humor of the Knights Templar? Oak Island may have served their purpose.

There is a wonderful Greek myth that relates quite well to the enigma of Oak Island. It is the story of Tantalus, father of Pelops and Niobe. Either because Tantalus served his son's flesh to the gods, or because he stole their nectar or disclosed their secrets, he was condemned to eternal punishment in Hades. Here he sat forever in a pool of water that receded when he tried to drink from it and under fruit branches he could not reach. Alternatively his punishment was to have a huge boulder suspended over his head so that he could not enjoy the feast set before him. Is the small village of Tantallon, Nova Scotia, located at Head of St. Margaret's Bay, another sublime reminder that whoever discloses the secrets of Freemasonry will be tantalized by the unattainable for the rest of their lives? Are we to be reminded of the Templar belief that the soul lies in the head and not in the heart?

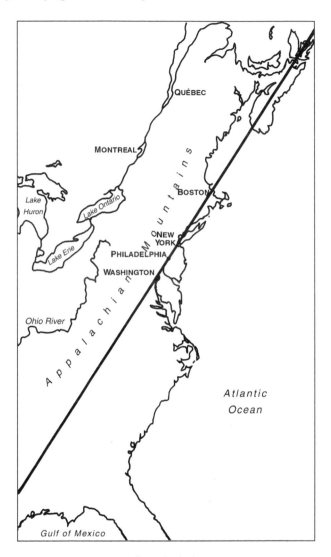

QUÉBEC

MONTREAL

Lake
Huron

Lake Ontario

BOSTON

Lake Erie

NEW
YORK

PHILADELPHIA

WASHINGTON

Ohio River

Appalachian Mountains

Atlantic
Ocean

Gulf of Mexico

Satan's Axis

A line depicting the so-called Satan's Axis running along along the eastern seaboard of the United States. Aside from the esoteric implications, the line obviously depicts the mineral rich Appalachian and Allegheny Mountain ranges, where large coal and manganese deposits are found.

If the inner secrets of Masonry do not lie in hell, where do they lie? Of course, they lie in heaven. But heaven needs hell. Thus, through Craft Masonry the initiate learns that the original columns of the temple were hollow and each supported a globe, one representing a map of the world and the other a map of the heavens. In many ways the *mapa mundi* produced in the fourteenth to sixteenth centuries reflects this notion, with one circle illustrating what was known of the eastern world at that time and the western circle representing the New World—L'Arcadia. Could *mapa mundi* refer to a world created by the Cathar god of evil—Rex Mundi, "King of the World?"

If so, then it goes a long way toward explaining why the lands of the New World purportedly fell along what was considered in the sixteenth century to be Satan's Axis, that line beyond what was known of the world at the time. Satan's Axis not only runs lengthwise through Nova Scotia but also extends through Boston, New York, Philadelphia, and along the Allegheny Mountains—all renowned areas of early occult and witchcraft practice.

Beyond coincidence is the fact that the largest manganese and coal deposits within Nova Scotia lie along this so-called Satan's Axis. And there is the evidence presented by Barry Fell in *America B.C.* that the majority of pre-Columbian relics and remnants found in North America also relate to this axis. In *America B.C.*, Fell convincingly presents the argument that a number of pre-Columbian artifacts relate to the ancients' quest for precious metals such as copper, tin, gold, and iron.

Of all these metals, manganese is an ore that possesses remarkable properties yet is readily accessible to primitive mining. It is used in the production of light blue steel, a steel that is lighter yet stronger than the normal "black" steel and is nonmagnetic. For these and other reasons, light blue steel was used in the production of bombers during World War II.

We have already learned that the Knights Templar forged their own steel weapons and possessed the finest weapons in all the world. If the Knights Templar did indeed possess the secret knowledge of a remarkable ore and its location, they would naturally have formulated any number of devilish ruses to prevent its discovery.

Manganese deposits occur in a variety of types, including the ores associated with carboniferous sediments, particularly those found in limestone, and the ores that filled fissures in precarboniferous rocks and surface bog deposits. Deposits of the second type have been found at New Ross. There, development work has shown that the deposits are extremely shallow. In the Windsor limestone beds, manganese oxides occur as masses of float near any contact with overlying red sandstone.

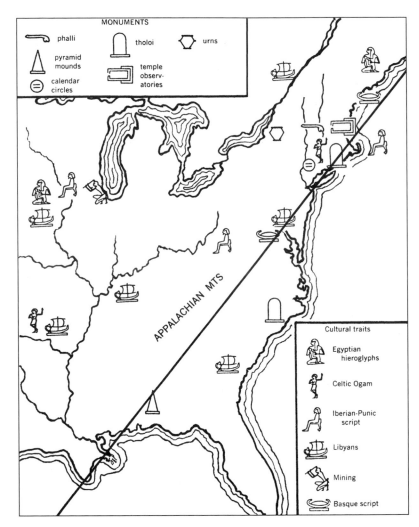

Pre-Christian New World Explorations

Based on a diagram first presented by Barry Fell in his America B.C., *the so-called Satan's Axis is shown relating to pre-Christian relics found along the eastern seaboard of North America.*

Logically, wherever surface sandstone is evident, manganese oxide is found relatively close to the surface in relatively pure concentrations.

Associated with the manganese oxides, limestone, gypsum, sandstones, and shales of the carboniferous rocks is coal, an obvious requirement for any forging operation. Even the most primitive of metal workers must have felt he was blessed by the abundance of raw materials available along the entire eastern seaboard. However, even at readily accessible depths the caves and crevices were located below the surface of the earth and therefore, figuratively, belonged to Satan. Could this explain the supernatural powers of King Arthur's sword, Excalibur? Could this new understanding not also forge another link in the chain of events that influenced the Templars' beliefs and actions?

The formation of the carboniferous rocks could also explain the many references to the original columns of the temple being hollow. To any geography student who's taken a course in physiography, it is elementary that Karst topography, where caves are readily present, is synonymous with carboniferous layering. Carboniferous sediments are present not only in Nova Scotia but in Great Britain and southern France as well. Not only have these natural areas presented opportunities to hide precious treasures throughout the ages, but, as we have learned, Berenger Saunière discovered secret documents within one of the hollow Visigoth columns that supported the altar stone within the Rennes-le-Château chapel. This also takes us back to the earlier Visigoth practice of burying their kings in a hollowed-out log below a diverted river course, then redirecting the course back to its original position above the sacred tomb.

Returning to the path of the Mason for the moment, the rites of initiation for the third degree, the Master Mason, are much more complex and dramatic than those for the Entered Apprentice and the Fellow Craft. They are much more complex and dramatic because they reveal the most enduring and most important mystery of all Masonic ritual—the legend of the murdered Master, Hiram Abiff, and "that which was lost."

The initiation of the Master Mason is the most interesting of the three degrees because it contains the unexplained allegory that gave Freemasonry its central identification with the construction of the Temple of Solomon in a manner unlike the biblical account. Indeed, the rituals and ceremonies of the basic three degrees appear to owe more to Greek myth than to the Old and New Testaments. The notion of a brother Mason flying to a brother's distress harks back to the magician Hermes' (Mercury) ability to travel the skies and protect the traveler.

When the Master Mason receives the ribbon and jewel of a Senior Deacon, it not only confirms that the Master Mason is knowledgeable in the inner workings of the temple but also that the Master is the keeper of the Jewel of the Royal Arch. Yet, the Master also is told that he must complete further journeys, assisted by a conductor (again, the railway station theme), before the inner secret is revealed to him. He goes on to learn that Hiram Abiff was murdered before he could complete the Inner Sanctuary, the sanctum sanctorum, and reveal its inner secrets. Curiously, this sounds exactly like what Prince Henry Sinclair wanted to accomplish by traveling to the New World and establishing a new Temple of Solomon.

Within the story of Hiram Abiff, Hiram is assaulted by the three apprentices at the south, west, and east gates of the temple. No mention is made of the north gate. Soon after, Abiff is temporarily buried in a "rubble" grave (Oak Island?), then dug up and reburied in "a grave dug on the brow of a hill." Are we to surmise that the second grave is located on the brow of a hill at the north gate? Significantly, although Abiff refused to divulge the inner secrets of the temple, several clues are given as to the true nature of the jewel. The candidate is accosted by a twenty-four-inch gauge, a square, and a setting maul, and by images of the three candidates. Again, are we reminded that a jewel with $24 \times 3 = 72$ right angles set within a circle and a square is the significance behind the jewel worn by the Master Mason? In many Masonic writings, God is identified as the Grand Architect. Does the jewel, or geometric application of the jewel, allow the Master Mason to directly meet God or a form of God?

The Jewel of the Royal Arch is the six-pointed Star of David that was adopted as a symbol of Jesus Christ. It now appears that "that which was lost" relates to the Jewel of the Royal Arch and the Star of David, the same configuration that I was compelled to apply to Nova Scotia following my recognition that it may be a key to the mystery of Sinclair's travels. Could part of "that which was lost" be a mummified body with nothing but a ribbon and jewel about its neck? Or could "that which was lost" be a reference to the earlier worship of the Goddess that appears to have been absorbed into Christianity?

Something of great historical value must be buried within the inner sanctuary, which in Poussin's most famous painting is represented by the tomb that is guarded by the Arcadian shepherds. A clue as to what might be hidden is provided by the enigmatic Rennes parchments that were apparently found within the hollow center of a pillar. Even if the parchments did not originate from a time before the Great Flood, someone went to a great deal of trouble to provide us with the necessary clues as to how the parchments should be interpreted. And what was it that Saunière was trying to convey when he moved the same pillar into the graveyard and positioned it beside the tomb of Marie de Blanchefort, whose gravestone epitaph suggests that "here lies [both] whore and virgin"? Are we to surmise that "that which was lost" can still be found?

5

Peace 681

━━▷◆◁━━

Through the years the Grand Masters of the Priory of Sion, Poussin, Saunière, and the authors of the *Dossiers secrets* all felt the need to speak of the incredible secret of Rennes-le-Château. But because they also felt a mysterious constraint, they spoke in endless riddles.[1] Perhaps they felt that the tantalizing hints and clues would eventually identify the truly initiated and deserving. Perhaps they realized the dangers of revealing the secret. Regardless of their motives, at least this much is known—the "underground knowledge" has led many on a false trail, including those who still believe that the Holy Grail lies in southern France or in Scotland.

The initial starting point to Henry Lincoln's discovery in southern France of what he terms the Holy Place is the supposed discovery of the two parchments inside the hollow pillar of the church altar at Rennes-le-Château.[2] What first piqued Lincoln's curiosity about the parchments was that the lines are arranged in a cryptic fashion, which suggested several hidden messages in code.

The second of the two parchments (see page 80) also has a strange symbol in the bottom right-hand corner.[3] According to Lincoln, this symbol could be interpreted as a direction indicator, especially as there is an *N* at the top, which could denote north.[4] More curious are the labels *NO* and *IS*, which appear at the left and right of the same device along with an upside-down *A* located directly opposite the letter *N*. Lincoln demonstrated that if the document is inverted in order to turn the letter *A* upright, the *NO-IS* converts itself simply to *SION* which could be interpreted to mean Jerusalem, or the Priory of Sion.[5]

ᵐᵛ̌ ÉTFᴬCTVᴍESTᴄVᴍIN
SᴀᴛᴛᴬTOSᴇᴄVNdₒPᴋIᴍO ᴀ
ᴛIᴋEPᴇᴋSᴄᴄETEЈᴀIЈ̧IᴘVLIᴬVTEᴍILLTᴋISᴄOE
ᴘEᴋVNTVELLEᴋESᴘIᴄᴀSETFᴋIᴄᴀNTESᴍᴀNTᴛVS + ᴍᴀNᴅV
ᴄᴀᴛᴀNTqVIᴅᴀᴍᴀVTEᴍᴅEFᴀᴋISᴀEISᴀT
ᴄEᴛᴀNTEIEᴄᴄEqVIᴀFᴀᴄIVNTᴅTSᴄIᴘVLITVISᴀᴛ
ᴛᴀTIS + qVOᴅNONLIᴄETᴋESᴘONᴅENЈᴀVTEᴍINЈ
ЈᴇᴛxTTᴀᴅEQЈNVᴍqVᴀᴍᴛOᴄ
LEᴄIЈTIЈqVOᴅFEᴄITᴀᴀVTᴅqVᴀ̃NᴅO
EЈVᴋVTIᴘЈEETqVIᴄVᴍEOEᴋᴀI + INTᴋOIᴛITINᴅᴄ̃ᴍVᴍ
ᴅEIEᴌᴘᴀNEЈᴘᴋOᴘOЈITIONIЈ   ᴋEᴅIЈ
ᴍᴀNᴅVᴄᴀVITETᴅEᴅITETqVI   ᴛIEЈ
ᴄVᴍEᴋᴀNTVxᵘᴏ qVIᴛVЈN O
NᴜIᴄEᴅᴀᵗᴍᴀNᴅVᴄᴀᴋESINON   ЈOLIЈ ЈᴀᴄEᴋᴅOTIᴛVЈ

(Pℬ)

Rennes Parchments, Parchment I

Allegedly discovered in a hollow Visigoth column in the church of Rennes-le Château by Berenger Saunière. From Gérard de Sède, Le trésor maudit (The Accursed Treasure).

Contrary to Lincoln's conclusion, I concluded that the inverted *A* represents the Aspotogan Mountain found in Nova Scotia. This symbol could therefore convey the notion that "SION" (the New Jerusalem) is "NOT" to be found at point A (representing the "ass-end," using Templar humor) but "IS" to the "NO," or north. The other device found on Parchment II, which could represent the squaring of the circle and the four compass points, confirms this.

In Parchment II, Lincoln discovered another hidden message which, when decoded, spells REX MUNDI.[6] This obviously refers to the Cathar belief that all physical matter was the work of a God of Evil, Rex Mundi, who opposed a supreme God of Good. Generally, Rex Mundi is considered to be Satan, although he was not quite the devil or the Antichrist of conventional Christianity. (For the Cathars, Christ was considered to be an equal to Satan.)

Lincoln identified yet another hidden message that could also function as a key to interpreting the Rennes-le-Château code. Through a further examination of Parchment II, Lincoln has revealed the first and last letters of the Greek alphabet, *alpha* and *omega*.[7] What this suggests, obviously, is a basic Christian tenet: Christ is the alpha and the omega, the beginning and the end. On another level, one of the alleged Grand Masters of the Priory of Sion, René d'Anjou, related *alpha* to

JESVSEVRGOANTCESEXdTPESPASCShAEVENJTTbEThQANTAMVKAT
JVEKAOTIAZA▪VVJMORTVVVJQVEMMSVSCTYTAVITIYESVSFEdCERVNT
.LAVIEM▪TTCAENAPMTbTETOMARTHAhMINISTRRAbATCbAJARVSO
VEROVNXVSEKATTE×dTSCOVMLENTdTLVSCVJMMARTALERGOACbCEP
TTLKTbRAMYNNGENTTJNARdTPFTJTICTQPRETTOVJTETVNEXTTPE
dPESTERVAETEXTEJRSTTCAYPTIRTSNSVTJPEPdESERTPTETdOMbESTM
PLFTTAEJTEEXVNGETNTTOdAEREdTXALTERGOVRNVMEXdGTSCTPVhL
TJETVTXTVddXVCARJORTTJQVIYEKATCVhMTRAdTTTVRVJQTVAREhO(CVN
.bEN VIVMNONXVENÿTTGRECENPdTSdEN3aRÿJETddaTVMESGTE
GENTÉS? dTXTNVFEMhOÉCNONQVSTAdEEG2ENTSPERRTINEbEAT
AdCVTMSEdQVhQFVKELKTÉTLOVCVIOShCahENSECAQVaCMVTTTEba
NMTVKPOTRabETEdTXTTEJKGOTEShVJSTNEPTLLAMVNTTXdIEPMS
EPVLGTVKAEMSEaESERVNETILLQVdPaVPJEKESENhTMSEMPGEKha
bEMTTSNObLTTSCVMFMEaVTETMNONSESMPERhaVbETISCJOGNO
VILLEKOTZVRbaMVQLTaEXTMVdaCTSTQVTaTLOLTCESTXETYENE
aKVNTNONNPROTEPRTESVmETaNT▪MMSEdVTLVZaRVMPVTdER
Éh~TQVEMKSVSCTaOVTTaMOKRTVTSCPOGTTaVKERVNTahVTEMP
RVTNCTPEJSSaCERCdOTVMVMTETLaZCaRVMTNaTERFTCTTRENTY
LVTaMYLVTTPROPQTEKTLhXVMabTbGNTCXVGT~2ETSNETCKCd
dEbANTITNTESVM

NO ☉ ₽ IS

JÉSV. MEdÉL2 .VVLNÉRVM ✠ SPES.VNa. PŒNITENTIVM.
PER.MaGdaLaNa. LaCKYMaS ✠ PECCaTa.NOJTRa. dILVaS.

Rennes Parchments, Parchment II
Note the strange symbol in the bottom right-hand corner. From Gérard de Sède, Le trésor maudit *(The Accursed Treasure).*

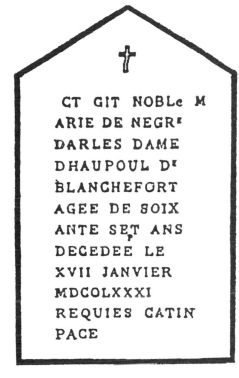
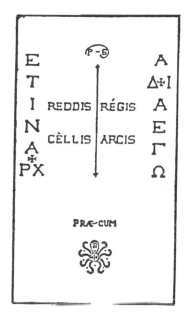

The headstone and horizontal slab found at the grave of
Marie de Blanchefort at Rennes-le-Château

Note how the phrase Et in Arcadia Ego *has been arranged to represent the two pillars of the temple. From Eugéne Stubelin, Pierres G de Languedoc.*

the "underground stream" and its source.[8] Somehow, we are now fixed with the notion of Christ and Satan (heaven and hell?) being located at the beginning and the end of an underground stream of hidden knowledge.

Once again, this notion conveniently provides us with a pathway back to the enigmatic Marquise d'Hautpoul de Blanchefort. It is her tombstone that the French priest, Saunière, defaced but that still lies in the cemetery of Rennes-le-Château.

Similar to the Rennes Parchments, the inscription on the headstone was deciphered by Henry Lincoln to yield further cryptic messages. The inscription on the stone has turned out to be a perfect anagram of the message that was distilled from the parchments that were found by Saunière.

The decipherment of this stone has also demonstrated several different layers of messages, although, of the several interpretations possible, only one seemed to make any sort of sense to Lincoln:

**AT ROYAL REDDIS [Reddis of the King], IN THE STORE-ROOMS
OF THE FORTRESS.**[9]

The third component of Marie de Blanchefort's gravestone appears to present a much more significant message to Henry Lincoln. To Lincoln, the two columns of writing found on the stone conceal the phrase *Et in Arcadia Ego*. The same words are written on the tomb depicted in Poussin's *The Shepherds of Arcadia*. Amazingly, following this decipherment Henry Lincoln learned that the tomb depicted within the painting could be found four miles to the east of Rennes-le-Château, not far from a former Templar stronghold called Arques.[10]

To understand further the relationship of Marie de Blanchefort's gravestone to the Arques tomb, we must go back in time to the early formation of the Knights Templar and one of Marie's direct ancestors. A vital connection between Rennes-le-Château and the Templars is Bertrand de Blanchefort, who was a Cathar and, more importantly, Grand Master of the Templars from approximately 1156 until 1169.

Bertrand de Blanchefort was probably the most significant of all Templar Grand Masters. It was he who transformed the Order into the well organized and highly disciplined military-political force that it became. Previously, the internal hierarchy and administrative structure of the Knights Templar had been disjointed and poorly organized. It was under Bertrand that the Order consolidated its position of influence in Europe, and, more specifically, in France. According to Baigent, Leigh, and Lincoln, it was also under the direction of Bertrand de Blanchefort, that something of great importance was concealed in the vicinity of Rennes-le-Château.[11] However, the only person who appears to have known with any certainty what that treasure was (and still may be) was Marie de Blanchefort. It also appears that when she knew herself to be dying, she conveyed the secret to her priest and confidant, Abbé Bigou, the reputed author of the Rennes Parchments.

In time, the suppression of the Templar Order was brought about by the French king Philip IV because of his desire to possess this very

Saint Sophia's Chapel
This little-known chapel in Glendaruel, Argyll, Scotland became the point of annual pilgrimages by the Mann family. It is dedicated to Saint Sophia, who was venerated by the Templars as the embodiment of wisdom. Photo by William F. Mann.

same treasure. But he needed an excuse to attack the Templars, so he started to circulate through his agents strange stories concerning the secret rites of the Templars. Consequently, rumors persisted that the Templars possessed a magical head of bronze named Baphomet. It was claimed that Baphomet was a demon-god who possessed various elements of both human and animal nature. Hence, Baphomet became associated with the mythical Beast and assigned the number 666.

It can be assumed that ninety-nine percent of the accusations laid against the Templars concerning their alleged heresy were nothing more than the product of Philip's desires. However, it is more probable that the Templars' only true "crime" was to venerate Sophia, the goddess of divine wisdom. That is, their only crime was to revere knowledge and understanding itself.[12]

The *Dossiers secrets* hint at the Templar desire to control both church and state by including three lists of names. These suggest that the Templars at one time were directly responsible for the administration of the holy state and appointment of the heads of the Church. The third list is the most amazing. It lists the successive Grand Masters of the Priory of Sion, otherwise referred to as the Navigator or the Helmsman.[13]

The third list is as follows:[14]

Jean de Gisors	1188–1220
Marie de Saint-Clair	1220–1266
Guillaume de Gisors	1266–1307
Edouard de Bar	1307–1336
Jeanne de Bar	1336–1351
Jean de Saint-Clair	1351–1366
Blanche d'Evreux	1366–1398
Nicolas Flamel	1398–1418
René d'Anjou	1418–1480
Iolande de Bar	1480–1483
Sandro Filipepi (Botticelli)	1483–1510
Leonardo de Vinci	1510–1519
Connetable de Bourbon	1519–1527
Ferdinand de Gonzague	1527–1575
Louis de Nevers	1575–1595
Robert Fludd	1595–1637

J. Valentin Andrea	1637–1654
Robert Boyle	1654–1691
Isaac Newton	1691–1727
Charles Radclyffe	1727–1746
Charles de Lorraine	1746–1780
Maximilian de Lorraine	1780–1801
Charles Nodier	1801–1844
Victor Hugo	1844–1885
Claude Débussy	1885–1918
Jean Cocteau	1918–

Four names (a square?) are immediately noticeable in relation to the story of Prince Henry Sinclair (the hidden fifth element?): Jean de Saint-Clair, Blanche d'Evreux, Nicolas Flamel, and René d'Anjou.

The first of these, Jean de Saint-Clair, was born around 1329. Not much is known of him except that he was descended from the French houses of Chaumont, Gisors, and Saint-Clair-Sur-Epte, the same network of interlinked families from which the Sinclairs of Rosslyn descended.[15]

On the other hand, a great deal is known about Blanche d'Evreux. She was born in 1332 (notice that the year equals the number 666 × 2) and is best known for marrying Philip VI, King of France, in 1349. It is through her that the Merovingian dynasty once again became aligned with the state of France. Numerous stories have also suggested that Blanche d'Evreux, who was in fact Blanche de Navarre, daughter of the king of Navarre and the countess of Gisors, was immersed in alchemical studies and experimentation. It was also said that she was a personal patron of Nicolas Flamel, the alleged Grand Master between 1398 and 1418.[16]

According to his own account, around 1361 a twenty-one page manuscript entitled *The Sacred Book of Abraham the Jew* came into Flamel's possession. For many years he could not fully understand the text. The story goes that eventually he met an old Jew who assisted him in performing a transmutation that produced the philosopher's stone. This apparently was achieved on January 17, a date persistent in the mystery of Rennes-le-Château.[17] As a result of his success, Flamel became fabulously rich and influential.

Somewhat surprisingly, Flamel remained a modest man who did not revel in power and lavished much of his wealth on charitable works. By 1413 he had apparently founded and endowed fourteen hospitals, seven churches, and three chapels in Paris and a comparable number in Boulogne.[18]

Coincidentally, this was immediately following the time that Prince Henry Sinclair was apparently making a series of transatlantic voyages to gold-rich Nova Scotia. Could there have been a better way to conceal the true source of immense deposits of gold than to supposedly have created it in a laboratory?

It is René d'Anjou, however, who has provided a wealth of material that possibly relates to Prince Henry Sinclair's activities in the New World. Born in 1408 (shortly after the death of Prince Henry), René d'Anjou not only was a major contributor to the formation of the Renaissance academies, but also was one of the first proponents behind one of the Priory of Sion's favorite subjects—*Arcadia*.[19]

In René's work, the Arcadian theme of an underground stream, frequently symbolized by a fountain or a tombstone, is rich in symbolic and allegorical meaning.[20] In addition, it appears to relate to the underground esoteric tradition of Pythagorean, gnostic, kabbalistic and hermetic thought. But it might also portray some very specific factual information, a secret of some sort, such as an unacknowledged and thus "subterranean" bloodline or, in reality, a subterranean labyrinth of gold mines that lie in a New World.[21]

In the Renaissance academies the symbolism of the underground stream was widely applied on a number of levels. During the height of the Renaissance, the theme of Arcadia reached two of the Renaissance's most illustrious poets and painters, Botticelli and Leonardo da Vinci, both alleged Grand Masters of the Priory of Sion.[22]

Most of the Renaissance painters were also fascinated by the relationship between sacred geometry's Golden Mean ratio, appearing as a rectangle with sides equal to 1 and .618 ($^8/_{13}$), and the pentagram and were equally intrigued by its infinite reproducibility. To the Renaissance painters, the Golden Mean was clear mathematical confirmation of their esoteric belief that the microcosm and the macrocosm were related.

Upon reflection, if we relate the Templar history to the ongoing battle between church and state and the Templar's appreciation of always being three steps ahead of their enemies, the numbers 6, 1, and 8 take on a deeper meaning.

The Templars were known to apply chess positions to their secret ciphers. If one relates 1 and 8 to the rook or castle positions, as the state, and relates 6, whether counted from left to right, to the bishop's (or the church's) position, could the number 681, as identified in the Rennes cipher, not be a reference to the knight's desired peace between church and state?

The chess piece known as the knight also has the ability to jump over any of its own pieces, in a manner relating to the autonomy that the Templars enjoyed between church and state. On another level, the Templars benefited from a network of strongholds and castles that allowed them to make their curious moves, to "leap-frog" their adversaries. Just as importantly, this network allowed them to move information and other valuables from station to station.

Another example of this desired peace is between man and woman. 6 + 8 equals 14—the esoteric number assigned to woman. Within the tarot sequence, the number 14 is also assigned to an angelic female, Temperance. In comparison, 6 + 8 + 1 equals 15—the number given to man; the tarot sequence assigns the number 15 to the Devil. Could this be another example of Templar humor based on their belief that woman deserved higher veneration than afforded by the Church?

This type of relationship can almost be taken too far. What may be more believable is that Henry Lincoln discovered, in the Rennes area, a pentagram that can be determined within a natural circle of mountains. And that the pentagram encompasses a number of medieval churches that cover earlier holy (pagan?) sites.

The churches of Rennes-le-Château—Cassaignes, Bugarch, Serres, Saint Just-et-le-Bezu, and Coustaussa—all stand on pagan and Celtic sites. The Rennes-le-Château church apparently stands as well on Visigothic or Merovingian Christian foundations, thus supporting the Templar belief that early Christian doctrine had been built upon the foundations of earlier pagan and ancient practices.

As we have learned, one such ancient practice, the alchemical squaring of the circle, was performed to figuratively form the two sexes into one. The alchemist was to make a circle out of a man and a woman, derive from it a square, from the square a triangle, and from the triangle a larger circle, which then forms the philosopher's stone. Could this be what is meant by Peace 681—eternal peace between man and woman, between church and state? And could this be what Nicolas Poussin was trying to emulate in the phrase *Et in Arcadia Ego* (Even in Arcadia am I to be found) found on the tomb in his paintings on the *Shepherds in Arcadia* theme.

A PAINTER'S TRANSFORMATION

Art critics generally regard Nicolas Poussin as the greatest neo-classical French painter of the seventeenth century. He was born near Les Andelys in Normandy. From here he moved to Paris in 1610, and worked there until 1624, at which time he moved to Rome. Very little is known of him before his thirtieth birthday, although it is said that his skill was recognized at a very early age. Tradition suggests that he spent most of his time in Paris studying the paintings of the Renaissance masters. His first significant commission was to illustrate Ovid's *Metamorphoses*—a series largely based on the concept of transformation—for the Italian poet Marino.

It was in Rome in 1624 that Poussin met two patrons who were to become lifelong activists on his behalf: Marcello Sacchetti and Cardinal Barberini. During this period, Poussin appears to have evolved (like any other serious classical painter) into a seeker of "truth and light." In 1629, he completed *Et in Arcadia Ego,* his first version of *The Shepherds of Arcadia.*[23]

From then until about 1633, Poussin appears to have been fixated upon themes from classical mythology and ancient legend, producing such biblical scenes as *The Worship of the Golden Calf.* However, the mystery thickened considerably when, in 1640, he traveled to Paris on the express orders of Cardinal Richelieu, King Louis XIII's "right-hand man," and painted *The Shepherds of Arcadia.* At the same time, Poussin formed a valuable friendship with Freart de Chantelou and received a commission from de Chantelou for a series of paintings depicting the Seven Sacraments. Once again, Poussin completed not one but two series of paintings.

This repetition of theme and duplication of subject may have come about from Poussin's deeply religious and moral transformation. During the 1640s and 1650s, Poussin started to choose rather amorphous mythological heroes who showed no human emotion, and his style took on a further rigid and austere tone. His landscapes became geometrical and more classical. There evolved an objectivity and coldness to his paintings, as though he were trying to reveal the conflict that

Et in Arcadia Ego, Nicolas Poussin, 1629
Devonshire Collection, Chatsworth. Reproduced by permission of the Duke of Devonshire and the Chatsworth Settlement Trustees.

a dying man finds within himself. Perhaps Poussin's health was deteriorating and he was desperately searching for the true spirit of Christ and the meaning of life. Or he may have known a great deal more of Rennes-le-Château, its mysteries and secrets, than he wished to share with his public audience.

Poussin did not try to simply paint the surface of his canvas. Under the stark, external, classical stillness there is evidence of a more mysterious, vibrant inner life. One suggestion was that, through his many paintings of dancing and sacred groves, Poussin was trying to relate Christian mysteries to pagan myth.

Yet it is also possible to see hidden Christian symbolism in his works, specifically within *The Shepherds of Arcadia*. The woman and the two kneeling men at the tomb may be meant to represent Mary Magdalene, Saint John, and Saint Peter at the empty tomb on the first Easter morning. The standing figure with his arm outstretched may symbolize the risen Christ. He wears a crown of leaves which could be a hint at the crown of thorns. The use of water in baptism is symbolized by the female's feet immersed in water. Could this possibly suggest that the female figure, the shepherdess, is indeed Mary Magdalene, because it was she who anointed Christ's feet during the sacraments?

In the earlier depiction, the shepherd standing nearest the tomb traces the inscription with his right hand, while a rather removed fourth figure sits off at a distance to their right. This appears to signify that the seated figure with his back to the viewer symbolizes the risen Christ. Behind the tomb there looms a dark, black cliff, which possibly represents one of the pillars of the temple.

On another level, the black cliff could symbolize the fertility of the Goddess and Arcadia. Significantly, the tomb bows out like an arc. It is here that Poussin may have been hinting that Christ's spirit followed the arc of the rainbow to a land in the west, from "the beginning to the end."

The most significant difference between the two pictures is the shape and position of the tombs. The 1629 version shows the tomb as more of a scroll, while in the 1640–42 version the tomb has taken on a specific geometric form. Could this be a suggestion that the temple and tomb evolved from a natural mountain setting to a more formalized architectural construction and appearance?

The *Shepherds of Arcadia* theme attracted other well-known

Self-portrait, Nicolas Poussin, 1649
Reproduced courtesy of the Staatliche Museum, Berlin.

painters as well. Guercino painted his version in 1618; it shows two shepherds looking at a skull on which a bee rests. A late sixteenth-century engraving by the German Albrecht Dürer carries the same inscription, although it portrays the king of the New Sion dethroned after starting a new Golden Age.[24]

The idea that Poussin was among those who knew of a powerful secret is hinted at if one compares two self-portraits that were executed by him, the first in 1649 and the second dated 1650. In the latter,

Self-portrait, Nicolas Poussin, 1650

Note in the later self-portrait Poussin is prominently wearing a Masonic ring and is depicted with a number of right angles, created by the corners of the picture frames in the background. Reproduced courtesy of the Louvre.

Poussin is displaying a ring clearly of a Masonic nature. When combined with the various square corners of the art frames in the background, Poussin seems to have been suggesting in a very sublime manner his initiation into a secret society that was "on the square." What can be concluded from all of this? The answer appears to be that Pythagorean thought and its associated geometry is one of many underlying keys to the location of the Arcadian tomb.

If this is the case, then Poussin's 1640–42 painting should be re-examined using the oldest of the Mason's suggested knowledge—sacred geometry. At this point, is it surprising that a right-angled triangle can be aligned to the eyes of the four figures? Probably not! Just as telling is the fact that an equilateral triangle found by a mirror image of the right-angled triangle reflects the geometry found by Henry Lincoln within the first of the Rennes Parchments.

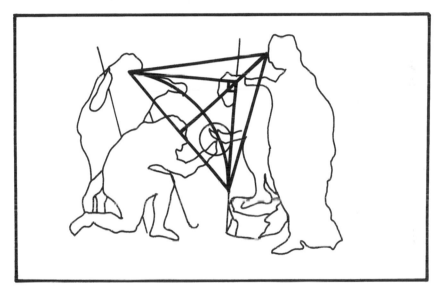

Note how a geometric construction of equal proportions is determined through the relationship of the four figures relative to the rough stone located at their feet. It is also interesting that we find an angle of 45 degrees and its reflection, 54 degrees, within the two constructions.

In *The Shepherds of Arcadia,* the kneeling figure and the figure somewhat concealed by the shepherdess are both pointing to the location of the actual tomb. One interesting aspect to this is that the kneeling figure, the only one with a beard, has his eye parallel with the tomb's location as well as in line with the female's navel. Is there a hidden meaning to this, since this figure's eye also represents the base, the right angle of the first triangle? Are we to gather that if one finds the true location, the meaning of the tomb, then a direct link to God can be established?

Was Poussin relating the painting to a specific location, or did he have an inkling that the simplest geometry had to be applied to a specific location—one that he learned of during his two years in Paris through his relationships with Fouquet and de Chantelou? In retrospect, it makes sense that Poussin's *Et in Arcadia Ego* of 1629 was nondescript in terms of location. But its theme had attracted the interest of someone who could help Poussin locate the allegory to a specific point considered to be the navel or the center of the earth.

Nicolas Poussin was an artist capable of producing remarkable levels of painting that transcended the classical geometry that most Renaissance masters imposed on their compositions. Henry Lincoln discovered just this fact when he asked Professor Christopher Cornford of the Royal College of Art to analyze Poussin's *The Shepherds of Arcadia*.[25]

According to Professor Cornford, during the Renaissance there were two basic types of layout available to the artist.[26] The first system was based on the account of the creation given in Plato's *Timaeus*. The second type of system derived from the older Masonic tradition. This system seems to have survived to this day but is often surrounded by an air of secrecy.[27] From all historical accounts, it would seem that Poussin would have constructed his paintings in conformity with the Timaean system; indeed, Professor Cornford found evidence of this.[28] As he continued his analysis, Cornford found evidence of an underlying Masonic-geometric system. Unexpectedly, Cornford was surprised at the degree to which it was possible to conform with both methods simultaneously and harmoniously. [29]

What Lincoln and Cornford fail to realize is that their analysis does not consider that not only pentagonal geometry was involved during Poussin's initial development of the painting, but that other principles of sacred geometry, such as the Golden Mean, were also applied to the overall layout of the canvas. Therefore, by applying the Golden Mean ratio to height, being 1.0, and using the corresponding width or length of 1.618, we learn that Poussin centered his second painting not only on the forehead of the shepherdess (as Lincoln demonstrated) but also on the third eye of her guardian. What this suggests is that Poussin quite remarkably not only used two intertwining geometric systems to lay out his composition, but he also developed two relative scales to his painting: an outer circle, which Lincoln and Cornford demonstrated, and an inner circle, which will now be demonstrated.

By eliminating a portion of the painting that includes only the sky and trees, Poussin may be suggesting that it is not the heavens that matter but only the earth and physical matter, in accordance with earlier Cathar thought. On the other hand, he could be suggesting that it is the connection between the earth and the skies, between heaven and earth, to which the clues found within the painting lead.

Upon further examination of the relationship of the five figures (remember the unborn child within the womb) to one another, it becomes apparent that the figures are also linked by historical events and other allegorical relationships. This suggests that if the unknown land is symbolically the Greek Arcadia, then the figures are the gods of Mount Olympus, which may just be depicted in the background. Therefore, the figures can be linked by the five Olympic rings, whose diameters and radiuses are determined by the shepherds' staffs, feet, head, hands, or eyes.

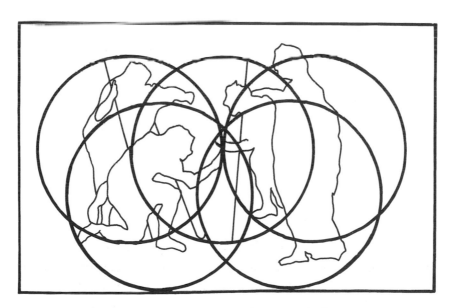

Poussin's figures relating to the rings of Olympus

Note how the arc of the various rings appears to sever the right hands of those figures who appear to be "in on the secret" as to where the tomb is located. Could this be a suggestion as to the penalty awaiting those who reveal the secret?

Nowadays, the five Olympic rings represent the five continents as they were known during the first Olympics. The suggestion here may be that the hidden "child," the hidden fifth element of the painting, may lie on the continent which, during Poussin's time, had only recently been "discovered" by the French—the New World—North America.

Just as important to the overall scheme of things is the fact that the four figures are all pointing to the center of the painting, where the five rings come together. On another level, the rings provide an aura to the central point where the letters *ARC* lie upon the tomb. Does Poussin present this as another hidden message? Can the spirit of the long lost gods be found on an arc (ark?), at the point of a cocked bow where the archer's hand meets the arrow's head?

By applying the earlier pentagonal geometry to the painting's new dimensions, the center of the new pentagon and its related circle falls between the eyes of the figure who is now seen as the both the archer and the steward. He is the only other figure aside from God himself (the

Application of the Masonic square and compass to Poussin's
The Shepherds of Arcadia
Note how the inner jewel again falls on the "third eye" of the guardian.

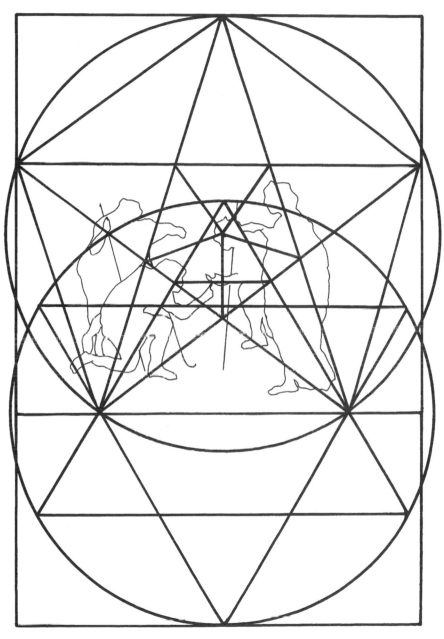

The esoteric balancing of male and female elements found within
Poussin's painting, *The Shepherds of Arcadia* (1640–42)

Olympian Zeus?) who knows exactly where the tomb lies. By constructing an inner triangle based on the archer's third eye, or the eye of the initiate of the inner circle, there is conveyed the message that only the guardian of the shepherdess knows the true location of the tomb.

On yet another level, the tools of the Mason (the compass and the set-square) can be positioned in a manner suggesting that by adept application of these two tools, the inner jewel or wisdom of the all-seeing third eye may be found. This also suggests that only by reflecting the hidden knowledge and understanding of Masonry can the holy treasure be found.

This dominant theme can be found yet again through the juxtaposition of the masculine six-pointed Star of David and the feminine five-pointed pentagram. The result is the intertwining of the two circles bringing together man and woman, Earth and Spirit, and pagan and Christian belief into the symbolism represented by the *vesica pisces*.

Was this what was conveyed by Prince Henry's application, both esoterically and physically, of the alchemical or geometrical "squaring of the circle" across mainland Nova Scotia? Maybe another piece of the puzzle lies in a further examination of the coded messages found in the Rennes Parchments and their relationship to both the medieval Knights Templar and their modern-day counterparts, and the Christian beliefs of these two brotherhoods.

6

The Temptation of
Saint Anthony

——◆——

A great deal of biblical material, including references to such events as the construction of Solomon's temple, can be found within the Royal Arch degrees of Freemasonry and the higher Order of the Knights Templar. There is also a considerable emphasis on several Christian saints. This includes Saint Anthony, the patron saint of the medieval Templars, and his dedication to the spirit and teachings of Christ. Even the deciphered Rennes Parchments speak of Saint Anthony and his many temptations.

Saint Anthony the Hermit was born at a village south of Memphis in Upper Egypt in A.D. 271. As tradition has it, following the death of his parents the rich young man heard those famous words of Christ: "Go, sell what thou hast, and give it to the poor, and thou shalt have treasure in Heaven."[1]

Soon afterward, Anthony became a model of humility and charity. He sold his estate and gave the profits to the poor. His only food was bread with a little salt, and he drank nothing but water. He never ate before sunset, eating sometimes only once in three or four days, and when he rested he would always lie on a rush mat or the bare ground.

The story goes that before his death Saint Anthony visited his monks, for he was then the head of a desert monastery, and told them that he would not die among them. His orders were that he should be buried in the earth beside his mountain cell by two of his disciples,

Saint Anthony Tormented by the Demons, Martin Schongauer, c. 1480–90
Reproduced courtesy of The Metropolitan Museum of Art, New York.

Macarius and Amathas. Hastening back to his solitude on Mount
Kolzin near the Red Sea, he soon died, whereupon his disciples followed his orders and buried his body secretly in that place.

The life of Saint Anthony could easily have inspired the Knights Templar in their quest for the Holy Grail. Surely the Knights would have related to Anthony's discarding of all earthly treasures and comforts in his quest for wisdom and closeness to God. Other stories tell of Saint Anthony's ongoing struggle with the many temptations of the flesh, to which the Templars must have also related. These temptations and evil visions are often depicted in art.

Another famous painting depicts the story of how Anthony buried Paul with the help of two lions.[2] Could Prince Henry and his knights have related to this notion as well, that like Anthony and the two lions, their purpose was to bury and protect the relics of Christianity? Did the Templars possess the remains of the disciple Peter or another symbol of the Christian church? Or did they see themselves as the device by which the formal church, represented by Saint Paul's teachings, would be buried, whereby, a new form of the church, one that more closely followed the teachings of the original pillars of the temple, would be resurrected.

Saint Anthony is also the saint to whom one prays in order to recover a lost or stolen article.[3] The small prayer to Saint Anthony is as follows: "Saint Anthony, help me find that which was lost."

This seemingly relates back to the Third Degree Master Mason ceremony that provides the basis to search for "that which was lost." As such, it seems reasonable to speculate that Prince Henry Sinclair left clues within the Nova Scotia landscape relating to Saint Anthony the Hermit and his pilgrimage into the desert wilderness. Based on the traditional story of Saint Anthony's life, did Prince Henry position something "right under Anthony's nose" that was to provide a constant temptation? And if Saint Anthony was as true and pure as the story goes, what "treasure" could have tempted him beyond mere gold and silver?

What if the treasure was what many early saints struggled to find through their journeys into the wilderness, namely wisdom? The Bible tells us that God once offered King Solomon any one wish he desired, and he chose well, for his choice was wisdom. From then on Solomon possessed the ability to choose between good and evil and thereby was able to accumulate a great treasure.

When Jacques de Molay, the last officially recognized Grand Master of the Knights Templar, was awaiting his death in France, legend has it that he conveyed a message to his nephew, Count Guichaud de Beaujeu. The message apparently was that the main part of the Templar treasure lay within one of the two pillars that stood at the entrance to the tomb of the Grand Masters.[4] Even though many key-signs have been found throughout Europe among Templar holdings, no one has possessed the wisdom to decipher the great secret as to the location of the Templar treasure.

The castle of Arginy in southern France contains the Tower of the Eight Beatitudes (or Tower of Alchemy, as it has come to be known). It is here that a number of the key-signs have been found. Written in Latin on the main archway of the Tower of Alchemy is the following riddle:

Thou shalt fashion this mysterious dwelling
Thou shalt give it three hundredfold
of main measure—length—longitude.
Fiftyfold latitude—width
Three in solidity—thickness
And according to the same measure thou shalt
make the extent
Orbicular
accessible in its upper part to Light.
Its widening in the opposite part
Thou shalt make these parts low, double
and triple.[5]

Over the years many ciphers, symbols, and secret signs have been used for the concealment and possible later disclosure of their treasures by the initiated, but even the initiated had to know in what part of the world to look. In this manner, since Nova Scotia is apparently where Prince Henry Sinclair carried the Templar treasure, let us try to relate the riddle to the first diagram that I developed from my great-uncle's disclosure.

Mainland Nova Scotia is exactly three hundred miles in length and fifty miles in its widest north-south (latitudinal) width. By applying the third ring of the trinity, the Star of David (orbicular in shape) can be fitted into the diagram. Through the positioning of this star, the upper or most northern and easterly portion of the inner circle lies within the fertile and heavenly Annapolis Valley, while the opposite or most southerly portion rests along the desolate and rocky South Shore, more specifically on Oak Island.

Another clue relating the Templar riddle to Nova Scotia rests within the use of the feminine number 3. A basic rule of thumb is that all of the geometric diagrams have to be constructed through numerology based on a factor or multiple of 9. Three doubled, or 3×3, equals 9. Three tripled, or $3 \times 3 \times 3$, is 27; 27×3 equals 81, which can be interpreted as 9×9. This, in part, can yet again be interpreted as the "squaring of the circle." Logic tells us that it requires the application of the squaring of the circle (the Star of David/Seal of Solomon) to the center of mainland Nova Scotia to continue the quest.

Let us first examine another legend of the Templar treasure. This story surrounds a manuscript that points to the castle of Val-de-Croix, or the Valley of the Cross. Unfortunately for French treasure hunters, there is no castle or place called Val-de-Croix in France. What remains is the second enigmatic riddle:

> *Under the ancient castle of Val-de-Croix lies*
> *The Treasure of the order of Templars. Go and*
> *seek it. The Saint and Truth will show you the way.*[6]

If the two riddles are intertwined, it becomes apparent that the hiding place is most likely where

> *The orbicular extent is accessible in its upper part to light,*
> *where "The Saint and Truth will show you the way."*

The Saint appears to be Anthony, but it could also be Peter, Paul, John the Baptist, John the Evangelist, Andrew, Joseph of Arimathea, Catherine, and/or Bernard, all of whom influenced Templar belief.

INTO THE WILDERNESS

Saint Peter, otherwise known as Simon or Simon Peter, was leader of the Apostles. He was a native of Bethsaida, located near the Sea of Galilee,

and a brother of Andrew. It was Andrew who introduced Peter to
Christ. Both Andrew and Peter were fishermen by profession and Peter
may have been the leader of a "cooperative" that included the sons of
Zebedee. In any list of the apostles, Peter is always listed first. He was
also one of the three apostles who witnessed the Transfiguration.

The meaning of Peter's name (*Cephas,* meaning "rock") was
explained by Christ when, in answer to Peter's famous confession of
faith, Christ told him that he would be the rock on which his church
would be built. He was also told that he personally would be given "the
keys of the kingdom of heaven."[7] From the earliest times, therefore,
Peter was invoked as a universal saint and considered to be the heavenly doorkeeper of the church and the papacy. Accordingly, his principal attribute is a set of keys, which coincides with the passing down of
the wisdom of the mysteries from the master to the student.

Saint Paul, on the other hand, is known as the Apostle of the
Gentiles. According to tradition, he was martyred at Rome during the
persecution of Nero and beheaded at Tre Fontane.[8] Paul was not only
a tireless missionary but also a powerful thinker, steeped in the Mystery
of Christ. Consequently, his epistles led to the development of Christian
theology. His key ideas included that of redemption through faith in
Christ and the concept that Christ is not only the Messiah, but also the
eternal Son of God, preexisting before the Incarnation and exalted after
the Resurrection to God's right hand. Ultimately, it was through Paul's
teachings that Christ assumed a more spiritual role within the church
of this time.

Peter and Paul are now recognized as the pillars of the Christian
church. Yet, in many circles outside official church doctrine, the teachings of Paul are still considered hollow and false. This is based in part
on Paul's teachings that the church is the "Body of Christ" and that
Christ was not only the Messiah, but also the everlasting, eternal spirit.

On another level, the teachings of Peter and Paul can be likened to
the messages supposedly found within one of the hollow pillars of the
church altar at Rennes-le-Château.[9] In a similar manner, these messages
were composed from the gospels and, like the teachings of Peter and
Paul, can be interpreted many different ways.

Likewise, all that is known about Saint John the Baptist also comes
from the gospels. We are told that he was the son of Zachariah, a tem-

ple priest, and that his wife Elizabeth was a cousin of the Blessed Virgin Mary. He was supposedly born after the foretelling of his birth and the choice of his name by an angel. Nothing more is heard of him until the age of thirty (a rather common theme?), when he began his mission of preaching and baptizing in the river Jordan. His way of life and style of preaching closely resembled those of some Old Testament prophets. Like most, his message was one of repentance and preparation for the coming of the Messiah and his Kingdom. Of course, his greatest deed was when he baptized Christ and recognized him as the Messiah.

John the Baptist has always been held in high esteem within various monastic orders due, in part, to the story of his solitary and austere life in the desert, similar to that of Anthony. However, his stated purpose on earth was to prepare for the coming of Christ within the hearts of the people. Significantly, various attempts to link John the Baptist with either the Mandeans or the Essenes have been made throughout the centuries.

The other John, Saint John the Evangelist or John the Apostle, was a son of Zebedee who with his brother James and Peter belonged to the small group of apostles of Christ. This small group was privileged to witness special events, such as the raising of Jairus's daughter and the Agony in the Garden.

The tradition that identified John as the author of the fourth gospel goes back to the second century. It has been said that John wrote about the events he witnessed in a contemplative way, emphasizing the theological reality and presupposing his readers' knowledge of Christ's life. Above all, he clearly stressed the divinity of Christ, who is "both Light and Life," and the importance of charity *(agape)*. Charity was seen to be the bond between Father and Son and between Christ and his disciples, as well as among the disciples themselves.[10]

Saint Andrew, the apostle and martyr, was the brother of Simon and Peter. A fisherman by trade, his home was at Capernaum where he was a disciple of John the Baptist before becoming an apostle of Christ. In art, Andrew is normally depicted with the saltire cross (X), commonly called Saint Andrew's Cross, which represents Scotland on the Union Jack.[11] His other symbol is a fishing net because of his connection with the story of Christ's feeding of the five thousand.

Each of the four gospels relates in one way or another the story of

Saint Joseph of Arimathea, the secret follower of Christ and uncle of Mary Magdalene, who on the day of the Crucifixion came forward to provide a sepulchre for the body of the Lord. But perhaps the strangest and most interesting of his traditions is the story that connects him with Britain and the foundation at Glastonbury of the first Christian church in these islands.

The legend that occurs in some of the Grail romances of Saint Joseph possessing the Holy Grail was never accepted by the monks of Glastonbury Abbey during medieval times. Instead, they believed that he brought with him to Britain two silver cruets that preserved the blood and sweat of Christ. The monks believed that these were buried with Joseph of Arimathea somewhere on or near the Glastonbury Tor. Tradition has it that these cruets lie with the saint in his grave and foretells that when the grave is found, "open shall these things be and declared to living men."[12] The meaning of this is unclear; and the burial place of Saint Joseph has never been discovered.[13]

Saint Catherine is yet another saint who was honored as the patron of learning, loved by ordinary people and by a variety of artisans of whose trades she was the protector. Many churches are still dedicated in her name. She was also the special patron of young unmarried girls, carpenters, saddlers, and ropeworkers. As well, she was the patron saint of wheelwrights, carters, millers and others whose work was in some way connected with wheels.

The story of her brief life and her death by torture (on the infamous Catherine wheel) has been related in certain early Greek and Latin texts. According to the best known version of her legend, she was the talented and beautiful daughter of a noble family living in Alexandria at the end of the third and beginning of the fourth centuries. Although she was only eighteen years old when she died, she was already renowned in the city for her deep love of learning. By birth and upbringing she was a pagan. Tradition tells us that, after seeing the Virgin Mary and the Jesus child in a vision, she became interested in Christianity through her studies and eventually was converted to it.[14]

After her death, Saint Catherine's body is said to have been carried by angels (more likely, monks) to the top of Mount Sinai and buried. Later, at the site of her burial, a great monastery containing her shrine and dedicated in her name was built.

Many of the churches dedicated to her were built on hilltops, often near the sea or dominating land highways. In these, beacons frequently burned for the guidance of travelers and more particularly of sailors. It has been suggested that this connection with warning lights sprang from the tradition of her birth at Alexandria, where the most famous lighthouse of the ancient world stood.

Saint Catherine was also associated with fire in other ways. The wheel, the emblem of her martyrdom, is an ancient fire symbol, an image of the life-giving sun. Since it was by this wheel that she was most commonly identified, it was almost inevitable that she should be regarded as a fire saint and, since fire is associated with fertility in pagan thought, to some extent as a saint of fertility also.

The wheel was also often associated with water, the opposite symbol to fire, and many ancient springs, pools, and holy wells were dedicated to Saint Catherine. Saint Catherine's Holy Well, or the "Balm Well" as it was known to the Saint Clair family, was located four miles north of Rosslyn. (Remember that the tomb that Lincoln discovered at Arques was four miles from Rennes-le-Château.)

The Balm Well was held to be an inexhaustible fountain of healing, for it possessed a black oil believed to be constantly renewed by Saint Catherine. Traditionally, the black oil was a remedy for many ills, including many types of skin disease and inflammations. When Prince Henry Sinclair was born, his father immediately anointed him with oil from this well with the belief that it would protect him from the plague.[15] It was also to Saint Catherine's Well that Prince Henry would go for inner strength during his younger years.

Therefore, it would not be surprising when, years later on the other side of the ocean, Henry's men reported they had found a brook flowing with black balsam (at modern-day Stellarton, Nova Scotia), and that he would feel it to be a sign of continuing good fortune from Saint Catherine. He would likely have interpreted it as proof of her guidance and that a major stage of his quest had been reached. On a more scientific level, Prince Henry Sinclair would surely have recognized that the evidence of the oily balsam meant that rich deposits of coal lay just beneath the surface—coal that was necessary for any type of metal refining.

The last saint to be examined is the most enigmatic due to his direct relationship with the Templars. Although a member of the Cistercian order that purported to practice seclusion from the world, Bernard of Clairvaux (the house of Saint Clair?) became one of the most charismatic and influential personalities in the cause of reform during the twelfth century.

Bernard, like the Knights Templar, thrived on conflict. He not only attacked both Peter Abèlard and Gilbert de la Porrèe, two of the most important scholars of his time, but he also severely criticized Cluny as well as the traditional Black Monks, the Benedictines. The result was that he made some powerful enemies. Possibly the greatest failure of his life was the Second Crusade. This he had preached with immense energy and determination. Unfortunately, it also ended in disaster.

Bernard's character can best be studied in his writings and recorded sermons. These include his *Letters,* which reveal the passion of his sermons on the Canticle. One of the most attractive, as well as one of the most simply written, is his treatise on the love of God, which has become a spiritual classic in fostering devotion to the human nature of Christ.

Yet probably the most significant contribution of Bernard to the Templar mystery occurred in 1131. It was during this year that Bernard received the Abbey of Orval, vacated some years before by the monks from Calabria, the same mysterious monks who had been led by an individual called Ursus—"the Bear."[16]

THE COMPLETION OF THE SQUARE

How does all of this background information concerning the life and times of the various saints relate back to the Rennes ciphers? Part of the answer lies with the three men and the woman depicted in Poussin's *The Shepherds of Arcadia.* On one level, these four figures may be considered to be four saints who influenced the Christian beliefs of the Knights Templar—John, Peter, Andrew, and Catherine. On another level, they may represent the earlier pagan veneration of the four seasons. On another level still, they may relate to specific Greek gods; and, on yet another level, they may relate to the four Grand Masters who were responsible for the transfer of the mysterious Templar treasure to Arcadia.

This is a significant point: the "completion of the square" found within the Rennes ciphers can occur on several different levels. What is just as interesting is that the figures seem to be in a position where they respond to one another and support one another's beliefs. In a similar manner, we have seen how the background elements found within the life stories of the various saints support the now familiar notion of the early Christian reconciliation with the pagan and ancient beliefs.

What if we were to go one step further and try to relate the figures to the Merovingian history that many different groups seem so determined to preserve? It appears logical to assume that if Poussin had the ability to position his figures on several geometric planes, then maybe on another level the figures can relate to a time when the last great king of the Merovingian line ruled. Could a clue lie within the fact that Dagobert II died just before A.D. 681?

It is known that Dagobert II claimed direct descendancy from the House of David. Thus, if one were to assume that the figure within Poussin's painting who was earlier identified as Christ also represents Dagobert II, then the kneeling figure represents kings David or Solomon. In his positioning of these two figures in relation to one another, Poussin may in fact be suggesting that through Dagobert II, the wisdom and mysteries of Christ and King Solomon live on.

When these two figures are then related back to the right angle of the triangle discovered within the painting, it could be concluded that the kneeling figure, God/Solomon/David, provides the true (90-degree) corner to the Trinity, while a combination of God the Father, God the Son provides the Trinity's base.

If the remaining two figures are examined in relation to what has already been surmised, we see that the eye of the female figure is positioned at the 30-degree angle of the triangle, or Trinity. From this it can be concluded that there is a direct relationship between the three figures that form the angles of the triangle. The kneeling figure is meant to represent God the Father and the royal House of David. The rather ephemeral figure is Christ or Dagobert II, and the female represents Mary, either the mother or the wife of Christ, or Dagobert II's mother or his first wife, the Celtic princess Mathilde. All the while the all-seeing or inner eye of the triangle falls on the fourth figure.

All of this appears to support the notion that the royal Merovingian line was a direct descendant of the House of David through a union between Christ and Mary Magdalene. If this were true, it would mean that the completion of the Trinity would suggest that the Holy Spirit indeed represented Mother Earth and all women, or more specifically, a particular woman.

Let us not forget that the painting is suggesting that the base of a larger equilateral triangle can be formed, leading from the Christ figure to the rock at the base of the tomb. Could this rock represent Peter? Could this representation of a triangle with three equal sides not also suggest that the female figure was meant to be an "equal" of Christ and God the Father?

Side-stepping this question for the moment, let's examine the enigmatic fourth figure in detail. The "inner" figure appears to be suggesting to the shepherdess that he knows exactly where the holy tomb lies. The fourth figure is also resting his left foot on a rather large rock. Could he be suggesting that the tomb of the king of New Jerusalem is located at a spot where a new cornerstone awaits shaping?

Many Christians make the sign of the cross with their right hand when they enter a church or any other holy place. Again, could the spirit of Christ and the Holy Spirit, or holy lady who appears to be leaning on the fourth figure for support and guidance, be found through the geometric layout of the temple? It shouldn't be forgotten that the lady is carrying a fifth figure within her womb, an inner sanctuary in the truest sense.

If we once again relate back to the clues found within the three basic degrees of Freemasonry, this leads to the conclusion that "that which was lost" can be found within the inner sanctuary, or holy of holies, of a new temple of Jerusalem. This suggests that the fourth figure is not only the protector or steward of the holy treasure and the royal family but also the one who, through his knowledge of the hidden arts and sciences, was responsible for the construction of the temple and the hiding of the treasure.[17]

In other words, the fourth figure is the architect Hiram Abiff, as well as Joseph of Arimathea and the Supreme Grand Masters of the Knights Templar, all guardians of the Holy Grail at one time or another. The fourth figure is both the architect and the warrior/monk who, through his use of the hidden knowledge, has completed the square, the foursome. The rock that he guards is the rough cornerstone of the new temple of Jerusalem that requires shaping.

At this point it is important to try to relate the four figures to Greek mythology, knowing that the basis of Freemasonry can also be found in ancient mythological allegory. It has already been concluded that the kneeling figure represents the supreme Greek god, Zeus, while the ephemeral figure behind him is the dual Apollo/Artemis, whose mother was Leto/Demeter. This leaves the guardian figure as the magician/trickster Hermes, the protector of all travelers, similar to the position that Joseph of Arimathea fulfilled in relation to the fleeing holy family. Here can be found new insight into the saying "lean on me."

Can the guardian figure also be seen as representing those who follow the voice of hidden wisdom—truth that is beyond reason? With the figure's position within the triangle relating to the all-seeing third eye, Poussin's message appears to be that those who possess the knowledge and understanding—the true initiate—acknowledge God the Father, God the Son, and the Holy Spirit as equals.[18]

Unfortunately, if an attempt were made to interpret Poussin's most famous painting on every possible level, then the larger mystery would never be solved. If the reader so wishes, he or she can take the time to determine how the four figures relate to everything from the earth's forces to the four seasons, but it is suggested that one continue with the story and then return to the puzzle as further clues unfold. Remember that one figure can possibly be represented by two aspects because of the Cathar tenet of duality.

Within Solomon's Seal, there are also several elements, with each carrying a particular significance. The triangles on one level symbolize heaven and earth meeting at a single point, heaven on earth. On another level, the intersection of the two triangles represents the balanced union of man and woman. On a third level, the Seal of Solomon represents man in a state of balance with nature. Therefore, it makes sense that the Seal of Solomon would be used to represent that spot on earth where man is one with heaven and earth (woman)—the Garden of Eden.

The Jewel of the Royal Arch, which depicts the Seal of Solomon/Star of David within a circle, is a Masonic jewel given to a Companion of the Holy Royal Arch. The Royal Arch is a level of knowledge that must be achieved by a 3rd-degree Master Mason if he wishes to proceed to the Knight Templar level. According to the *Royal Masonic Cyclopedia,* the key to the Jewel of the Royal Arch is known as the Triple Tau.[19] The Hermetic Tau (represented by the letter T) was an ancient hieroglyphic representation of God; consequently, the Triple Tau in its simplest form represents the Trinity. Saint Anthony was known to wear the Tau on his clothing.

What this means is that the key to finding the Jewel of the Royal Arch within the Nova Scotia landscape must be through the use of the Trinity and the Saint. As part of the Templar riddle says:

The Saint and Truth will show you the way.

Could not the Trinity in its simplest geometric form, an equilateral triangle, be considered to be Truth? Within an equilateral triangle, in geometrical value, there are eight right angles. The same number of right angles can be found within the Triple Tau ($8 \times 8 = 64$, the same number of squares on a chessboard).

The Masonic Companion's Jewel of the Royal Arch is a double triangle depicting the Seal of Solomon/Star of David within a circle of gold. At the bottom is a scroll bearing the words *Nil nisi clavid deest*—"nothing is wanting but the Key." Beneath this is the Triple Tau, which not only signifies God but the temple of Jerusalem, *Templum Hierosolyma*. It also means *Clavis ad Thesaurum*—"A key to a treasure"; and *Theca ubi res pretiosa deponitur*—"A place where a precious thing is concealed"; or *Res ipsa pretiosa*—"The precious thing itself." In the simplest of terms, the key leads to a temple of Jerusalem where a "treasure" lies. Or the wisdom and truth gained through the discovery of the Temple is, in itself, the treasure.[20]

All that is left is to apply the Jewel of the Royal Arch to mainland Nova Scotia and the critical starting point on Oak Island. In doing so, amazing relationships come to light. The balance of opposites between the South Shore and the Annapolis Valley have already been touched upon, but other coincidences, if we still dare use the word, appear like magic. Is this the wisdom that the Jewel radiates?

One sure conclusion is that, through the squaring of the circle, Prince Henry Sinclair was employing the simplest of geometric forms (a right-angled triangle) to survey the countryside. Arranging his survey stations on the uniform hilltops, his men could have proceeded station to station with relative ease, once they traversed the lower, swampy lands found along the South Shore.

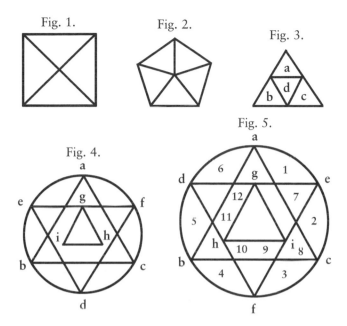

The Jewel of the Royal Arch

By its intersections, the Jewel of the Royal Arch forms a given number of right angles (72) which can be taken in five combinations. Note that in the simplest form, the square, an inner fifth element—the apex or center of the figure X— is found.

Another aspect relating to the application of the Jewel of the Royal Arch is the fact that a Maltese Cross could be constructed within the same circle defined by the star. Was this Sinclair's way of reconciling the notion that there should be peace between the Knights Templar and the Knights of St. John of Malta? This also suggests that Sinclair must have possessed something in physical terms that was venerated as a direct symbol of God, something that even Saint Anthony would have been tempted to possess or protect.

It also suggests the more complicated notion that this Star of David is the mate to the five-sided pentagonal figure that makes up Lincoln's "Holy Place" in southern France. If this is the case, it can be concluded that the figure of the Star of David established by Prince Henry across Nova Scotia points to an area where the treasure of the Templars and, possibly, the treasure of the temple of Jerusalem and Solomon, was ultimately transported and hidden. Whoever determined this massive figure,

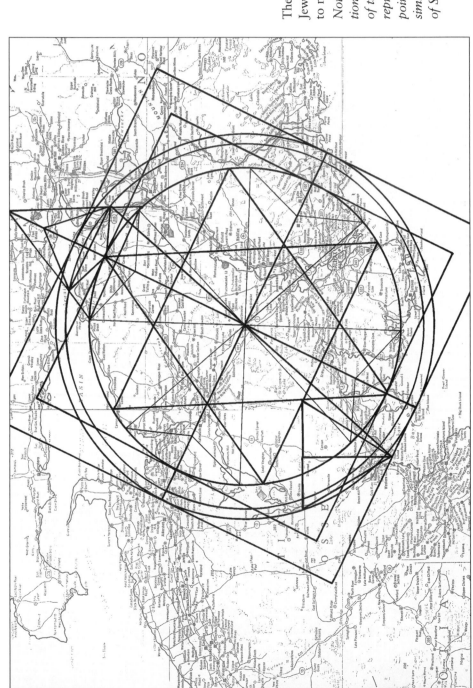

The application of the Jewel of the Royal Arch to mainland Nova Scotia

Note how the triangulation in the upper reaches of the circle can be seen to represent a drawn arrow pointing to the north sky, similar to the zodiac sign of Sagittarius, the Archer.

with a dimension of sixty-three miles by sixty-three miles across the landscape of Nova Scotia, certainly did not go to all of the trouble just to locate and map a settlement.

Nicolas Poussin must have had at least an inkling that the holy treasure had been transported to Nova Scotia/Arcadia following that fateful night when the Templar fleet disappeared from La Rochelle in 1307. But the question still remains as to whether the treasure, or maybe just a portion of it, was transported directly to Arcadia or was first taken to Scotland. Understanding the reasoning of the Knights Templar as we now do, it appears that the Templars would have divided the treasure to make sure "their eggs were not all in one basket."

Could portions of the treasure have gone with the Knights who made for Portugal, Scotland, and the Baltics, while the true Holy Grail was shipped for safekeeping directly to Arcadia (again, completing the square)? This makes perfect sense and does not lessen Prince Henry's role within this grand conspiracy. Sinclair's role could have been to retrieve the missing portion of the treasure from its temporary hiding place within Oak Island and to conceal it in a more strategic location. And what better location than at the head of the Bay of Fundy, guarded by the highest tides in the world?

If this was the case, anybody possessing the old keys to the location of the treasure needed an updated survey, just as in modern times anybody wishing to sell any property is required to provide an up-to-date survey. How better to compose this survey than through the very beliefs and teachings that supported the Templar dedication and devotion?

The strongest evidence of the Cathar teachings is the understanding of opposites and the balance of nature. By applying Sinclair's Jewel of the Royal Arch (accepting that Oak Island was the beginning and located on the outer circle) along an axis that runs through Mt. Uniacke, the opposite end falls at a little community within the inner circle called Green Oaks. And while on Oak Island there remains the mystery of the planted red oaks, at Green Oaks there exists an equally mysterious grove of English White Oaks. Red (birth) and white (death)—the colors of the Knights Templar and the colors of the clothing of two of the figures in the Poussin painting (again, the beginning and the end).

Green is the color of the clothing of the male figure found kneeling in Poussin's painting. Traditionally, it is the color of the Green Man, the prevalent Celtic vegetation god, whose image pervades all of the more conventional Christian decoration found within Rosslyn Chapel.

Significantly, by Bruce's time Celtic tradition, the Grail mystique, and Templar values had fused into a single, but often confusing, belief. For example, the ancient Celtic belief that the head contained the soul figures most prominently in the myth of Bran the Blessed, whose head, according to tradition, was buried as a protection and fertility talisman outside London. This function surfaced later through the Grail romances into the so-called Green Man cult.

In *The Sword and The Grail,* Andrew Sinclair confirms that the Sinclairs not only sanctioned but also welcomed and protected these practices (as is evident by the carvings of Rosslyn Chapel).[21] Therefore, if Prince Henry Sinclair and those who came before him had established a settlement at Green Oaks in the Celtic tradition, it makes sense that he would have paid tribute to the fertility and sanctity of the refuge. Furthermore, it makes sense that the majestic white oak would have been planted to provide future shipbuilding materials and to act as a signpost to later generations of initiates.

The concept of planting a tree as a tribute to the gods cannot only be traced back to the story of Hiram's grave being marked with an acacia tree, but to the ancient knowledge that the coffin of Osiris was embedded in the trunk of a tamarisk tree. It also harkens back to the Glooscap legend of the man buried within the cedar tree. And in Canaan, as elsewhere in the ancient world, the worship of the goddess Astarte, similar to Artemis and Demeter, involved trees and pillars erected in sacred groves and on hills as symbols of her divinity.

These common threads guide us back to the stories of the saints who were venerated by the Knights Templar. The stories of the saints reflect the pre-Christian belief that sanctity and a closeness to God could be found upon the highest hills, in the deepest wells or valleys, in the wilderness or forests, and through hardship and diversity—all of which in turn reflect basic Masonic teachings. Therefore, Prince Henry Sinclair would have believed that a talisman depicting the Seal of Solomon was necessary to ward off the evil spirits encountered on a holy quest and to identify exactly where heaven on earth could be found.

Similarly, in order for a modern-day Mason to proceed to the degree of a Knights Templar, he is required to pass through the Royal

Arch ritual. A portion of this ritual tells, symbolically, how the Jews were freed from captivity in Babylon in the sixth century B.C., and how they returned to Jerusalem to rebuild King Solomon's temple. This, in turn, fittingly describes Prince Henry's desire to build a new Temple of Solomon in a New Jerusalem.

It now only remains to identify the proper keys and to unlock the doors in the proper order.

7

The Keys

————◆————

Following the emergence of the mystery cults and the adoption of Christianity as the official religion of the Roman Empire, a spiritual movement arose in the Middle East. It attempted to combine the best elements of paganism and the new Christian beliefs.[1] This spiritual movement was known as gnosticism and its followers were known as Gnostics. Among other beliefs, the Gnostics claimed to have preserved the real teachings and mystery rites of Jesus that had been suppressed by the Church.

The Gnostics derived their spiritual inspiration from a variety of sources. Gnosticism most closely followed the writings of the Persian spiritual teacher Zoroaster, who was a priest of the Indo-Iranian religion, which worshipped the elemental forces of water and fire.

According to religious tradition, at the age of thirty Zoroaster had a vision during which one of the Iranian gods appeared to him and said that he was the Supreme Being. Following the vision's direction, Zoroaster broke away from the established religion and taught his own philosophy based on the universe as a cosmic battleground between the opposing forces of light and darkness. Accordingly, the enlightened follower had to choose eternally between one and the other of these principles.[2]

In its later stages, Zoroastrianism became associated with the mystery cult of the bull god Mithras that originated in Persia. Mithras was a scholar god of light who was born in a cave surrounded by animals and shepherds at the winter solstice in December. Here again, we are fixed with the notion that earlier beliefs became melted and forged into what became the "pillars" of the temple.

Another of Poussin's paintings, entitled *The Ordination,* or *Christ Handing the Keys to Saint Peter,* certainly supports this notion.[3] Painted quickly between June and August 1647, it captures the inner radiance of Christ just prior to his death. In the painting there is a remarkable juxtaposition between the figures in the foreground and the architectural elements of the background, including a bridge, towers, and the Temple of Solomon.

According to some art historians, the pillar engraved with an *E* was a last minute addition. Could this mean that Poussin only received a clue as to what the hidden fifth element actually was just in time to incorporate it within his picture? It's curious that *E* was also the top letter shown in one of the two columns of the inscription found on Marie de Blanchefort's gravestone. This suggests that the two columns of the grave slab inscription are meant to represent the pillars of the temple. The column can therefore be read as *Et in Arc*—the first half of the message, *Et in Arcadia Ego.*

What can be inferred from this? Was Poussin confirming the ortho dox belief that Saint Peter received the keys to the temple and its hidden

Christ Handing the Keys to Saint Peter, Nicolas Poussin, 1647
Reproduced courtesy of the National Gallery of Scotland, Edinburgh.

wisdom? Or alternatively, was he hinting that Mary Magdalene was actually the one who received the secrets of the original rites? On yet another level, is it just possible that Poussin was suggesting that proof of the life and teachings of Christ still lie within the hollow base of the pillar of the unfinished Temple of New Jerusalem?

It even appears that Poussin provided in his painting the necessary elements to locate the temple and to bridge the knowledge between old and new, between good and evil. It would be useful to examine these elements in relation to the intertwining mystery of Prince Henry's application of the Seal of Solomon across Nova Scotia and the secret societies of the seventeenth, eighteenth, and nineteenth centuries that promoted a return to the esoteric ways and ancient religions.

THE LITTLE KEYS OF SOLOMON

Esoteric tradition suggests that those who possess the secret writings known as *The Little Keys of Solomon* possess the understanding and knowledge of where the temple may be found. *The Little Keys of Solomon* are known to relate, on one level at least, to the esoteric principles that could be found within the ancient mysteries.[4] According to ancient writings, the keys include the proper application of androgyny, dualism, numerology, astrology, and etymology (the play on words).

Kabbalists, Masons, and occultists agree that the twin pillars in front of the Temple of Solomon represent the masculine and feminine energies, which are the basis of creation.[5] A further suggestion is that their position on either side of the entrance to the temple may represent the female labia. In ancient religious belief the temples of the Goddess, whether as Astarte, Ishtar or Isis, and even Solomon's temple, were known to have been designed and dedicated as symbols of her body.[6]

Reflected within its architecture, the most sacred part of the Temple of Solomon was considered the inner sanctum, or holy of holies, which symbolized the womb of the Goddess. It was here that sacred treasures, including the Ark of the Covenant, which was considered to be a direct conduit to God, were stored. Judaic tradition tells that only the high priests were allowed to enter the inner sanctum where the treasures and the Ark were kept. What this meant, in direct contrast to the beliefs of the Cathars and the Templars, was that only the high priest could communicate directly with God.[7]

The nineteenth-century occultist Alphonse Constant, a former Roman Catholic priest who took the Jewish pseudonym Eliphas Levi, wrote extensively about Baphomet as a conduit to God. According to Levi, the head of Baphomet is seen to combine the characteristics of a dog, a bull, and a goat, which are meant to represent the three sources of the pagan Mystery tradition. These three sources were the Egyptian

Baphomet, as conceived by the nineteenth-century occultist Eliphas Levi
From *The Key of the Mysteries.*

jackal god Anubis, who was the guide of the dead to the underworld and is identified with the Greek Hermes, the Indian sacred bull who may be the origin of Mithras, and the Judean scapegoat sacrificed in the wilderness to cleanse the sins of the tribe.[8]

Baphomet's androgynous nature is emphasized by one arm being muscular and masculine while the other is of a more feminine nature. One hand points upward and the other downward, curiously similar to the depiction of Christ in Poussin's *The Ordination*. The hands point to one black and one white crescent moon signifying the lunar phases that occur every twenty-eight days. According to occult tradition, these phases symbolize the duality of human nature and the male and female principles, whose union brought the universe into being.

In alchemy, the Dual Mother archetype is seen as the fusion of good and evil, positive and negative, the sun and the moon. Another alchemical symbol of the Dual Mother is the astrological sign of Cancer, the Crab. Lasting from June 22 to July 22 (the period of the summer solstice), the fourth sign of the zodiac is a water creature that avoids the sun and buries itself in the crevices of the sea floor. Cancer is also the only zodiacal constellation ruled by the moon, the so-called Lady of the Waters. And, because of the moon's effect on tides, the crab is a symbol of the primal water, and hence, motherhood. But it must be remembered that the crab also possesses the ability to kill its victims.

In many ways, the watertraps of Oak Island can be likened to the duality of the crab.[9] The natural sinkhole within the ocean floor may have provided safety and comfort for the Lady of the Waters but for anyone trying to penetrate her outside shell, the watertraps controlled by the tides have presented real terror and danger.

The opposite and mirror image of the zodiacal sign of Cancer is Capricorn. While Cancer (Oak Island) is the archetype of the womb, the moon, and reincarnation, Capricorn (Green Oaks) represents the struggle for ascension. The sign of Capricorn is a cardinal earth sign that covers the period from December 22 to January 20, the period of the winter solstice, the birth of Christ, and the Epiphany.

Compared to Cancer, which expresses the urge to fuse with nature, Capricorn, the Goat, embodies the urge to conquer nature. This same urge is demonstrated by the archetypal Magician of the tarot cards. The goat is an appropriate representation because of its slow, patient, and concentrated efforts that allows it to conquer hilltops and mountains.[10] Capricorn is also seen as the gate to the spiritual life that can only be opened through conservatism and concentration on a personal level.

This all relates back to the notion conveyed through Poussin's *The Ordination*. Does a belief in Christ and his teachings represent a key to ascension into heaven? Is one of the other keys a belief in the Cathar notion of dualism? The Knights Templar certainly believed both to be true.

By relating this notion of dualism to the physiography of Nova Scotia, another fantastic clue to the relationship between Oak Island and Green Oaks can be identified. The type of geological formation found at the east end of Oak Island is known as the Windsor Group. It was formed during the carboniferous period of the Paleozoic era roughly 300 million years ago. Within this type of formation are glacial deposits and layering of limestone, siltstone, gypsum, anhydride, salt, and sandstone. The amazing thing about this is that the surrounding area of Oak Island is made up entirely of a later formation known as the Meguma Group that contains slate, schist, and migmatite—three very hard deposits that prohibit natural caving and mining.

What is all the more remarkable is the fact that Green Oaks is located within an extensive band of the Windsor Group that runs the entire length of the Annapolis Valley. Therefore, any settler with the knowledge of where fertile land could be found would associate richness and fertility with the topography of the Windsor Group.

This type of topography is known as Karst topography and is characterized by natural sinkholes, caves, glacial layering or stratification, and fossiliferous sediments. In simpler terms, the settler would have been amazed at the abundance of raw materials such as gypsum, limestone, coal, red clay, and rich mineral deposits including copper, gold, manganese, and silver. Add to this its moderate climate and the Annapolis Valley must have appeared to be heaven to the first settlers, or at least the Elysian Fields of Pythagorean times. As a result (for the moment at least), the pathway leads back to the Greek philosopher's time and the science of numerology.

Of all the primary numbers, the Pythagoreans considered the number 9 as the most complete and highest achievement because it is the last and highest of the series from 1 to 9, and because a human child is normally born nine months after conception. As the number 9 also marks the transition from one series of numbers to a higher series, most initiation rituals therefore take the form of a mock death followed by a rebirth after a period that incorporates the number 9.

Nine also represents creativity and brilliance because it is made up of 3 × 3 and therefore has the force of three, or the trinity, tripled. On another level, this can be considered to be a three-dimensional force. Its completeness and self-sufficiency is reinforced by the fact that a circle has 360 degrees and 3 + 6 + 0 = 9, and by the fact that if multiplied by any other number, 9 always reproduces itself: 3 × 9 = 27 and 2 + 7 = 9, and so on. Accordingly, one can see how the original nine Knights of the Temple of Jerusalem felt that their numbers would always multiply and the Order could never be crushed. This also accounts for, in part, the egotism and obstinacy associated with the Templars.

Within the geometric diagrams that have been applied to the physical landscape of Nova Scotia, it has become obvious that the numerical basis for all of the workings is also the number 9. For example, the original triangle developed by Prince Henry between Oak Island and New Ross has exact dimensions of 18.0, 14.4, and 10.8 miles, all multiples of the number 9.

The Jewel of the Royal Arch or Seal of Solomon that has been applied to mainland Nova Scotia is composed of 9 × 8 = 72 right angles. The square that results from the squaring of the circle has dimensions of 63 × 63 miles, or 9 × 7 by 9 × 7. The exact distance between Oak Island, which lies on the outer circle, and the small community of Green Oaks which lies on the inner circle, is 63 (6 + 3 = 9) miles. The diameter of the inner circle is exactly 54 (5 + 4 = 9) miles with a radius of 27 (2 + 7 = 9) miles.

Number 9 is also the number assigned to the Hermit of the tarot's Major Arcana. To have discarded all material value in search of the pinnacles of mental and spiritual achievement and ascension into a higher realm is certainly characteristic of the passion and solitariness attributed to the number 9. Therefore, to find "the Saint and the Truth" one must search out and apply the number 9.

In the story *The Aeneid* by Virgil, Aeneas and the Sibyl seek out the Elysian Fields. There Aeneas meets the spirit of Anchises, his father, who reveals to him the workings of the universe and the purifications through which men could be admitted to Elysium. (In a similar vein,

Prince Henry must have gained through his father the knowledge and understanding that would allow him to maintain what he rightfully thought belonged to God and the heavens.)

On a higher numerical level, the numbers 666 and 72 are often repeated in relation to sacred geometry and can be shown to provide the basis for the construction of both the pentagram and hexagram. The number 72 is the base angle of a pentagram and is a reflection of 27, a product of 9. The reciprocal of 666 is 15, which is known to represent Osiris, the Lord of the Underworld, or the half-man/half-beast minotaur that guarded the labyrinth and the Golden Fleece. Therefore, it's easy to see why both the numbers 666 and 72 are considered numbers of the devil and Satan.[11]

Yet several societies have acknowledged the numbers 666 and 72 as expressions of order and the balance of nature. In the Kabbalah, the solar Father of Light is given a value of 666 while the lunar Mother of Forms is assigned 1080. Their relation of polarized light, or as positive to negative, may be expressed as 1.6 (1080/666)—the Golden Mean. Their sum is 1746. (Many readers will immediately recognize 1746 as the year of the Battle of Culloden and the beginning of the end for Bonnie Prince Charlie and the House of Stuart.)

In mythology, the Mother of Forms (1080) creates the Holy Grail to contain the Father's Seed of Light (666, or the Blazing Star, the Star of David). All the while the *elohim* (angelic Grail maidens), bring the Grail (now 1746, both Seed and Vessel) down to earth (to the 12-sided Grail Castle) for Adam (assigned the number 144), who is considered by many to be the original Grail knight and Grail bearer.

Adam is assigned the number 144 (again, 1 + 4 + 4 = 9) because 144 is the maximum number of individual elements to be found in the universe and Adam, as man, expresses the full potential for the 144 elements. What the Kabbalah emphasizes is that Earth, Adam, and Light create the harmony of our world. In other words, God is Light, Adam is man, and Earth is woman. Not to belabor the point, it nevertheless appears that only through the fusion of 666, the man-beast, and 1080, Mother Earth, can the light be found. Was this what Prince Henry Sinclair was attempting when he applied the Star of David (a symbol representing the union of man and woman) to the landscape of Nova Scotia?

The number 9 has also been identified as "the Strength of the Lion."

In the tarot card Fortitude, a powerful woman stands astride a lion/serpent, holding its jaws open in triumph and controlling its strength. The lion represents the king, and the sun and star represent evolution. Thus, 9 is the logo of the sun and the stars and can be considered to represent light and wisdom. It therefore requires no great imagination to realize that the Templars considered themselves to possess the strength of lions and to be in harmony with nature, all the while searching for light and wisdom. It also requires little thought to realize that the Templars believed that the earth, the ultimate mother/goddess, controlled their quest.

Basically, the fertile Annapolis Valley could supply Prince Henry and his men with all of their needs from natural provisions, game, and fish, to raw materials and minerals in overwhelming quantity. To this day, Annapolis Valley is a veritable Garden of Eden. With their bellies full and the sun shining, Prince Henry and his men must have danced and laughed with joy. Coming from a land of hardship, overcrowding, persecution, and the Black Plague, they must have felt mischievous and full of tricks. To a group who believed that they had completed their quest and found heaven on earth, the cornucopia of life—the Holy Grail—they certainly must have believed in the magic of the Holy Spirit.

But, being ordinary men, they must have also known that their refuge/sanctuary could not last and that the demands of their mother country, Scotland, still awaited them. In this way, it appears logical that they developed a set of rituals, a plan, that would allow only the initiated to rediscover the secrets and treasures that they possessed. Or maybe they just adopted or modified earlier Templar and other, more ancient initiation rituals to their own special situation.

One of their biggest advantages over their enemies was their command of many languages. Prince Henry himself was well versed in Gaelic, French, Latin, Norse, and what at that time could pass for English. So one of their greatest devices to prevent the discovery of their secrets was etymology, or the play on words.[12]

The question remains as to how Nova Scotia place-names appear to relate back to the history and stories of the eleventh- to fourteenth-century Knights Templar. The explanation might be that, following the expulsion of the Acadians in 1755 by the British, various place-names reverted to Anglicized variations of the Mi'kmaq place-names.

For example, throughout Nova Scotia there are place-names such as

Harmony, Gibraltar, Saint Andrew's, Kennetcook, Jeddore, Canaan, and many more that appear to recall what is known of the Templar history. But many people attribute the place-names to the background of the first settlers, whether they be Irish, French, Scots, or a combination of a number of these. This is just the point. The Templars of Nova Scotia were all of these. What is of further interest is that many of the place-names such as Brookfield, St. Mary, and St. Anne, to name a few, are repeated throughout Nova Scotia, as if the intent was to confuse.

Of even further significance is the fact that many of the place-names are referenced as stations or corners, although they do not fall along railway lines or are located at crossroads.[13] Alternatively, a high percentage of these place-names do fall within Prince Henry's Seal of Solomon and are positioned at critical survey station or corner points. Examples abound, but a few are Wyse Corner, Smith's Corner, East Mines Station, and Newport Station.[14]

This may sound a little far-fetched but there is at least one example that provides an important key to the location of Solomon's new temple.

To the east of Green Oaks lies a number of larger communities along the main route that links the capital of Nova Scotia, Halifax, to the northern part of the province. These communities are known as Bible Hill, Truro, Hilden, Brookfield, Stewiacke, and Shubenacadie and reasonably form an "arc" when joined together. If one relates these communities to the coded message found on Marie de Blanchefort's tombstone—*Et in Arc*—and employ a little of the Templar etymology on the place-names, we arrive at the phrase: Jerusalem's (Bible Hill's) true gold (Truro) lies hidden (Hilden) next to the brook and field (Brookfield) and belongs to the steward (Stewiacke) who is dedicated to guarding the tombs of Shuben and Acadie (Shubenacadie).

Similarly, author David Wood was the first to recognize that the Rennes pentagram fell on the Paris Meridian that was established by Louis XIV in A.D. 1666.[15] But the question remains as to how a figure attributed to the ancients, the Celts, and the Templars could possibly relate to a longitudinal line that was established in the mid-seventeenth century. Is it just possible that a group possessed the knowledge to establish longitudes on an accurate level prior to the development of the telescope and chronometer?

As has already been discussed, a hypothetical method existed long before Louis XIV that allowed for the establishment of an accurate longitude. But the problem was that the method was not reliable at sea. The only known method of establishing longitude before this time was by timing an eclipse, whether it was an eclipse of the sun or the moon.

However, there are two problems associated with this. The first was that one had to be able to predict when the eclipse was going to occur. The second was that two parties, one west of the other, had to simultaneously record the time of the eclipse in local time. This way, if the parties involved compared the relative observed hour of eclipse wherever they were, and multiplied by 15 to convert time into arc (1 hour of time = 15 degrees of longitude) between the base station and the other station, then the result was the longitude west of the base station.

To simplify matters, if the base station was located in the mainland of the Orkney Islands at Brognar, at a modern-day longitude of 3° 15' west, with the second station located at a modern-day longitude of 63° 15' west—and an eclipse of the sun or moon was locally recorded at 8:00 A.M. at Brognar and at 12 noon at Green Oaks, then the longitude west of the base station would be 60° west.

But in order to calculate the difference in longitude, one had to possess the ability to predict an eclipse and be in a position to accurately record the local time. In other words, the ancients needed to possess an accurate calendar and recorder. In fact, there may have been ground almanacs positioned throughout the world. These would be the mysterious megalithic rings and circles, the prehistoric monuments, and ancient ruins found throughout the world.

Stonehenge is certainly the most celebrated, but within the British Isles alone there are over nine hundred stone rings still existing. Their existence may just indicate the mysterious motivation of the Neolithic, Bronze Age, and some say Celtic, people who built them throughout northern and western Europe over many centuries, from 4000 B.C. to 1500 B.C.[16]

It was the English professor Alexander Thom who first surveyed many of the stone circles and rings and proposed that they were used to pinpoint exact days of various solstices and to predict both solar and lunar eclipses. For example, Thom determined that Temple Wood in

Argyll, Scotland was used to make precise observations of northern and southern moonsets at the major standstill.[17]

This very simple explanation concerning the thousands of mega-lithic sites positioned throughout the world certainly raises a fascinating idea.[18] It is the idea that a specific society or societies were able to establish their relative positions by both latitude and longitude and therefore, through the simplest geometry, to map their positions. Could this explain why the portolans were so accurate in their east–west measurements? Could it also explain why the portolans were based on an azimuthal equidistant projection?

Using the hidden geometry demonstrated by Poussin, including the application of the Golden Mean and right and equilateral triangles, and applying it to an azimuthal equidistant projection of a world map, demonstrates some very relative and equally remarkable relationships. Among other things, a north–south axis projected through Genoa, from the North Pole to the equator, allows two right-angled triangles to be

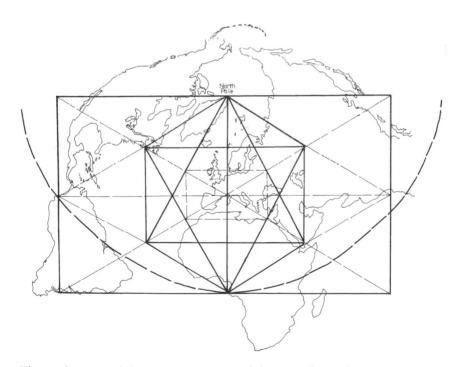

The application of the sacred geometry of the Star of David to an azimuthal equidistant projection of the world

established between the equator, Alba, and the North Pole in one instance, and the equator, Cape Verde, and the North Pole, in another.

Furthermore, equidistant geometric relationships appear between port-to-land stations such as Genoa, the Canary Islands, and, of all places, Green Oaks, Nova Scotia. As a result, Nova Scotia becomes the upper corner of a rectangle that encloses the known world during the Phoenician/Carthaginian era. (Remember that Christ is pointing with his hand to the farthest upper corner of Poussin's *The Ordination*.) What is also evident is that the majority of crucial stations fall along the routes of the various explorers of the Age of Discovery.[19]

What is totally remarkable is the fact that the Star of David/Seal of Solomon can be constructed by the various geometric relationships between the known ports of land. Just as Prince Henry Sinclair was able to construct his diagram across the Nova Scotian landscape through an application of simple geometric principles and mathematical keys, the ancient mariner was able to map the relative positions of the various ports that he visited within his realm of trading.[20] Just as fascinating, all of these symbols are connected with the secret societies of the Knights Templar, the Rosicrucians, and the modern-day Priory of Sion.

66–72

The Order of the Rosy Cross, the Rosicrucians, is alleged to have been founded by ex-members of the Knights Templar after their suppression by King Philip. The earliest writings about this order began to circulate in Europe at the start of the seventeenth century. These writings claimed that before the Crusades, members of the Rosicrucian Order secretly worked in the Holy Land for the common good of humanity. Certainly, it has been documented that both the Templars and the Rosicrucians used the symbol of the Rosy Cross at different times and were dedicated to roughly the same political and religious reform. Other writers allege that both groups, while outwardly Christian, seem to have been secretly engaged in occult and pagan practices under the cover of orthodoxy.

The medieval Rosicrucians were popularly credited with possessing a wide range of magical powers, including the ability to prolong youth, the knowledge of summoning spirits, making themselves invisible, creating precious stones from thin air, and transforming lead into gold.

The term Rosy Cross and the word Rosicrucian were said to derive from the Latin *ros,* meaning "dew," and *crux,* or "cross," which refers to the chemical sign for light.

According to this translation, the Rosy Cross is a symbol of the alchemical operation of transforming earthly matter into spirit, of turning lead into gold. On a simpler level, the Rosy Cross stands for the twin pillars of wisdom, knowledge, and understanding and the rose itself is identified with the sun. Could this be another link to the chain that holds the present to the past?

Historically, there are a number of important links between the Priory of Sion's alleged Grand Masters of the seventeenth and eighteenth centuries and European Freemasonry that proliferated during the same period. For example, the Sinclairs of Rosslyn, the Scottish branch of the Norman Saint-Clair/Gisors family, have long been associated with both Freemasonry and the Order of the Rosy Cross; and Rosslyn was located only a few miles from the former Scottish headquarters of the Knights Templar at TempleBallythorpe.

As well, in Staffordshire, England, there still exists a rather more mysterious piece of the overall puzzle.[21] Here remains Shugborough Hall. During the eighteenth century, it was the residence of William Anson, brother of George Anson, who ultimately became lord admiral of the British navy.

The story goes that following a rather noble and daring naval career that included sailing home in triumph with some two million pounds in Spanish treasure in 1744, George Anson died peacefully in 1762. Later, as tribute to Lord Anson, a poem was read aloud in the British Parliament, which included the most significant stanza:

> *Upon that storied marble cast thine eye.*
> *The scent commands a moralising sigh.*
> *E'en in Arcadia's bless'd Elyssian plains,*
> *Amidst the laughing nymphs and sportive swains,*
> *See festal joy subside, with melting grace,*
> *Any pity visit the half-smiling face;*
> *Where now the dance, the lute, the nuptial feast,*
> *The passion throbbing in the lover's breast,*
> *Life's emblem here, in youth and vernal bloom,*
> *But reason's finger pointing at the tomb!*[22]

Many writers appear to have connected this stanza to Poussin's *The Shepherds of Arcadia* and its inscription—*Et in Arcadia Ego*. Just as mysteriously, between 1755 and 1758, as a further tribute to Lord Admiral Anson, a headstone known as the Shepherd Monument was erected on the grounds of Shugborough. Immediately below the headstone's bas-relief, which is a reproduction—reversed, mirror-fashion—of Poussin's painting, there appears a secret coded message, which no one has ever satisfactorily decoded (until now):[23]

O.U.O.S.V.A.V.V.

D   M

In the seventeenth and eighteenth centuries there existed in Britain a secret society known as the Illuminated Ones.[24] Whether this society was an offshoot of Freemasonry is not known. However, the celebrants' colors were red and white, the same as those of the Knights Templar. In their rituals, it was said that the candidate was presented as a slave, and stated that he wanted to liberate society from tyranny.

In 1786, a raid upon the house of an influential Reform lawyer named Zwack revealed secret papers connected with the order, and it is through these that many of the inner workings of the organization became known. Men were to be influenced through their womenfolk and a large-scale plan for initiating women members was at an advanced stage of development. Also found among the papers was the following cipher:[25]

A	B	C	D	E	F	G	H	I ⌣ J	K	L	M
12	13	10	9	8	7	6	5	4	3	2	1

N	O	P	Q	R	S	T	U ⌣ V	W	X	Y	Z
13	14	15	16	17	18	19	20	21	22	23	24

If this cipher is applied to the inscription found on Lord Admiral Anson's tomb, one possible interpretation is:

	O.	U.	O.	S.		V.	A.	V.	V.	
D	14	20	14	18		20	12	20	20	M
E		66					72			N

REVERSE 72–66 NE

This appears to suggest that in order to find the mirror image or reflection of the Rennes-le-Château tomb found in Poussin's painting, one must apply a diagram with 72 right angles on an axis of 66 degrees pointing northeast. The reference to the northeast is interesting in itself. Deciphered by taking one letter beyond both D and M (beyond the three basic degrees of Masonry to, once again, complete the square), this suggests that Lord Anson belonged to a society that was a step above basic Freemasonry, as are the modern-day Knights Templar. In a somewhat simplistic fashion, it could be said that the Illuminated Ones were the "inner core" of the apple.

During his many ocean voyages, Lord Anson, one of the first to circumnavigate the world, could well have visited sites on coasts that once had belonged to Visigoths, Merovingians, and Templars. As well, in his many naval encounters he could have taken important French and Spanish prisoners who were willing to exchange secrets of ancient treasures for their lives. It is also recorded that he visited the important British port of Halifax, Nova Scotia on several occasions. All of this means that Lord Admiral George Anson would have had plenty of opportunity to visit both Oak Island and Green Oaks.[26]

Was it at Green Oaks that Lord Anson saw the true tomb of Arcadia on the Elysian plains? Had Anson been able to decipher a variety of the keys necessary to unlock the mystery of Poussin's painting? His tribute refers to "reason's finger pointing at the tomb," which appears to be a direct reference to the figure identified as the guardian found in *The Shepherds of Arcadia*. It certainly now appears that the Lord Admiral must have discovered something of far greater value than just the gold and silver that he "liberated" from the Spanish.

8

La Val d'Or

Another key just as important to finding the lost settlement of Prince Henry Sinclair appears to follow the thread of seemingly unrelated evidence found within the classic legends and myths. It is a thread that even appears to have been followed by great men such as George Anson—namely, the desire for gold. Associated with this eternal quest for the most elusive and sought-after metal ever is its famed legendary origin, la Val d'Or (the Valley of Gold), which has been sought for thousands of years. From the earliest times, the Valley of Gold was known by many names but the most prominent is Ophir, the place of King Solomon's mines.[1]

Some have said that Ophir lies in what was called the New World. It has been established that Hiram's and Solomon's vessels were at sea for forty-two days before reaching their destination.[2] Thus, North America not only appears as likely as any to be a good candidate for the location of King Solomon's mines and the land of Ophir, but also may be the Templars' and the Stuarts' private source of gold.

Barry Fell, in *America B.C.,* contends that over three thousand years ago a band of roving Celtic mariners crossed the North Atlantic to discover, and colonize, North America.[3] Fell supports his theory by the hundreds of inscriptions found among stone ruins during the course of an archaeological survey of New Hampshire, Vermont, and other eastern seaboard states of America.[4] Systematically, he traced the remnants of North American Celtic civilization throughout the New World, along with Egyptian hieroglyphs and Iberian-Punic script.[5]

A fascinating connection to this theory is that a majority of the ancient inscriptions are located along the previously noted Satan's Axis. Therefore, let us return to the time of the ancient mariner and examine his legends and myths for further clues.

One of the most compelling ancient myths is Ovid's story of the Minotaur, which suggests that the labyrinth or maze of clues that lead to the mines of Minos can be rediscovered by following the golden thread of Ariadne. The story of the Minotaur tells how Minos's wife Pasiphaë had fallen in love with a white bull with a black spot between his horns; from their union, she had given birth to a child, half-bull and half-man. To hide the horror, Minos employed Daedalus to build the labyrinth with its innumerable mazelike passages, and the Minotaur was consigned to its depths.[6]

The Minotaur was fed every nine years on the blood of seven Athenian youths and maidens. Twice this tribute was paid through human sacrifice, but the third time a youth named Theseus volunteered as one of the seven young men who were to be sent to Crete. Ariadne, daughter of Minos, gave him a ball of golden thread to unwind when he entered the labyrinth. Theseus slew the Minotaur and by winding the thread up again found his way back to the entrance of the labyrinth and escaped.[7] The labyrinth in which the monster was found may represent a cave, although it has also been compared to a tomb or temple and even a Minoan palace. Virgil told of a painted representation of a similar maze near the entrance to the underworld near the Golden Bough. But the labyrinth also recalls the mazes marked out as ritual dancing patterns in many countries. Such mazes have also been identified in the intricate passages and signs of Paleolithic sanctuaries.

As for the labyrinth's symbolism, both the winding path that the Hermit follows and Ariadne's golden thread relate to the understanding of life after death. The labyrinth also represents the steps of initiation that one takes in learning the mysteries of the dead that lead to the otherworld.

The clue to the symbolism can also be found within the classic fairy tales, like the fatal spindle of Sleeping Beauty and the ball of wool that the kitten unwinds before Alice goes through the Looking Glass. On another level, the acceptance of there being another, "inner," world is found within such classics as Beauty and the Beast and Jules Verne's *Journey to the Center of the Earth*.

Historically, Minos was the king of the Minoans who existed between the seventeenth and sixteenth centuries B.C. During this time, Ugarit was a flourishing kingdom on the Syro-Phoenician coast and the town of Ugarit included what was the world's first great international port. In the kingdom of Ugarit there existed a number of Minoan settlements. The famous Ugarit poems, mainly of the fourteenth-century B.C., belong to the northwestern branch of the Semitic languages and are written in Canaanite alphabetic cuneiform. The poems foreshadowed the Phoenician alphabet, which was to come to Greece in the eighth century B.C.[8] The Ugarit poems have strong links not only with the Old Testament but also with the Homeric cycle, as there are very many detailed echoes of these poems in the *Iliad* and the *Odyssey*.[9] For example, the *Odyssey* speaks fondly of dogs, which were popular at Ugarit but nowhere else in the Semitic world.

Does this link between Homeric and Ugarit poems indicate a literary association in the eighth century B.C. between Homer and the Phoenicians who had taken over Ugarit traditions? This was the time when the Greeks borrowed the Phoenician alphabet and the many artistic features, fantastic monsters, and the like, for which Phoenicia was known.[10] This may just explain how Greek myth and poem adopted stories of labyrinths and half-man/half-beast monsters from the Phoenicians, who in turn had taken some of their stories from the ancient mariners of Ugarit.[11]

There is a similar connection between the pagan Phoenicians and the Tribe of Benjamin, of which Hiram Abiff was a member. The Tribe of Benjamin evidently supported the followers of Belial, a form of the Mother Goddess often associated with images of a bull or calf.[12] There is even reason to believe that the Benjamites themselves revered the same deity. In fact, the worship of the Golden Calf in Exodus may have specifically been a Benjamite ritual.[13]

In Greek myth, one actually finds a record of the exodus of Benjamites from Palestine. There is the legend of King Belus's son Danaus, who sails to Greece with his daughters. Traditionally, it has been said that Danaus's daughters were the ones to have introduced to the Greeks the cult of the Mother Goddess, which became the established cult of the Arcadians.[14]

The great mythological cycles of the Greeks, including the worship of the Mother Goddess, are also closely connected with Minoan and Mycenaean sites. The legendary Minos, who became monarch and judge of the dead, is also the generic name for the kings of Crete during their Minoan sea-empire of the second millennium B.C. He is described as the son of Zeus and Europa, and his wife, Pasiphaë, is often regarded as a moon goddess, since her father is identified with the sun. Pasiphaë was also worshipped through Greek ritual that, though not associated with her name, may have a bearing on the Minotaur myth: yearly an Athenian woman was "married," in a building called the cattle stall, to the bull-god Dionysus.[15]

Greek literature also relates that Jason and the Argonauts eventually fulfilled their quest of obtaining the Golden Fleece but only through the help of three goddesses: Hera, Athene, and Aphrodite. Aphrodite bribed her son Eros to shoot an arrow into the heart of Medea, the daughter of King Aeëtes, the keeper of the Golden Fleece, kindling the flame of love.

We are told that before Aeëtes would part with the fleece, he imposed on Jason a terrible test. The test was to plough a field with wild, fire-belching oxen. Next, the ground was to be sown with the teeth of a monstrous serpent and the armed men who would spring up from them must be defeated and destroyed. Jason, with the help of Medea's magic ointment, ploughed and sowed the field. Warriors sprang up, but Jason had the wisdom to hurl a boulder, which started a fight among them and helped him to kill them all. Medea then led Jason to the sacred wood where, by her arts, his quest was fulfilled. Chanting a spell, she dipped a fresh sprig of juniper in her magic brew and sprinkled the eyes of the giant serpent that guarded the Golden Fleece. Finally, the serpent fell into a trance and Jason was able to snatch the fleece from the oak on which it hung.

The Argonauts then started home but on the way encountered the wailing winds that drove them off course. Hera, who wanted Medea to return home safely with Jason, bade Iris (the goddess of the rainbow) to calm the winds for the Argonauts, who by this time had escaped the Wandering Rocks and come to the Phaeacian island of Corcyra. There, while searching desperately for fresh water, the Argonauts came to the sacred garden of Atlas and to the Hesperides, whose golden apples had been stolen by Hercules. It was here that Jason found the spring that had been struck from a neighboring rock. Without one of their party, who had been killed by a snake, they embarked again and Triton emerged from the depths as their guide. They sped northward, stopping at the island of Aegina, and from there they sailed peacefully homewards.

This rather shortened account of Jason and the Argonauts is wonderful in itself, but when compared to Pohl's account of Prince Henry Sinclair's expedition to the New World, it's beyond fascinating—it's downright eerie.

Pohl states that Sinclair and his men sailed away on the tides after fulfilling their quest. However, according to Pohl, the prevailing winds blew them off course to the site of Westford where one of Sir Henry's knights died, possibly as the result of a snakebite.

Jason and the Argonauts were also blown off course to the Phaeacian (Phoenician?) island of Corcyra after passing through the Wandering Rocks. Is it just possible that the traditional image of the Wandering Rocks was associated by Prince Henry and his men with the phenomena of the rising and falling of the Bay of Fundy tides? It also appears beyond coincidence that both Prince Henry and Jason would lose one of their trusted crew to a snakebite. Surely, Prince Henry and his Templars would have taken heart knowing that they were following in the footsteps of Jason and the Argonauts and their quest for the Golden Fleece.

There is a further relationship between the legend of the Golden Fleece and the location of Prince Henry's settlement. It would be a natural inclination to identify the mythical island of Jason's quest as the Isle of Rams, since the ram assumed much of the symbolism that was evident within the pagan mysteries and rituals practiced in Celtic times. For instance, Hiram (high ram) was obviously the high priest who conducted the rituals, and the sacrifice of an older ram would have been a normal practice.

In Pindar's *Ode*, as in Apollonius's epic, Jason's quest for the Golden Fleece ended successfully. It was told that the fleece had belonged to the flying ram on which, with the help of Hermes, Phrixus and Helle escaped from their father, Athamas, and stepmother, Ino, at Orchomenus. According to most versions of the myth, Helle fell off and was drowned in the Hellespont River, but Phrixus reached the land of Colchis, where the ram was sacrificed to Zeus and its fleece given to the local king, Aeëtes. Based upon this, the fleece became a sort of magical treasure of which heroes go in search, and Aeëtes had to fight in its defense because the luck of his kingdom was bound up with the possession of the fleece.

Even in ancient times the story suffered many rationalizations. The Greek philosopher Strabo believed Jason was in fact looking for gold, using the explanation that the Colchians collected the dust from the river in fleecy skins. Even further, according to the Byzantine Suidas, the fleece was a parchment book explaining hidden knowledge on everything from obtaining gold by alchemy to preserving the soul after death.[16]

THE ART OF ALCHEMY

The art of alchemy is almost as old as human civilization and is documented as far back as the Greeks and Egyptians. The alchemists of the Middle Ages learned their art from the Arabs in Spain and southern Italy, who in turn had adopted it from the Greeks who adopted it from the Egyptians. Thus, alchemy extends its roots into Egyptian religion

The Magical Circle

The magical circle of the alchemist, or goldmaker, which allows the initiate to dispel the Golden Dragon.

and the Hellenistic figure of Hermes Trismegistus, who is the model for the Roman Mercury and medieval Mercurius.

The Golden Dragon is an alchemical term that relates to a time when a goldmaker's work was threatened by the "winged dragon." In reality, since many of the early European alchemists, or "goldmakers," performed their work in poorly ventilated caves or labyrinths, the winged dragon represents the fumes and closed conditions that would cause many miners and goldsmiths to hallucinate. Hermetic treatises claimed that only by performing the metallic transmutations within a magical circle could the Golden Dragon be defeated. Better still, if the miner had the simple forethought to create a labyrinth of airshafts, the dragon could leave whenever it so desired. It is scientific fact that within any primitive forging operation, if a raw iron is smelted to extract gold or other by-products such as manganese, there is a considerable amount of sulphur-mercury gas given off, which would cause even the most "enlightened" goldmaker to become light-headed.

But it was the Knights Templar who perfected the use of alchemy, not for the transmutation of metals, but to fit their allegorical code of life. After all, a quest was a quest. What honest knight could forego the opportunity to vanquish a few dragons, especially if it just meant having to inhale a few extra fumes in order to "see the light?" And what better way, then, to attract initiates into your ranks than to claim to have the power to change base lead into gold?[17]

This ruse appears to have been practiced by not only Prince Henry, but by many of the past Grand Masters of the Priory of Sion.[18] Nicolas Flamel was the first Grand Master to have claimed to perform a successful alchemical transformation. Sir Isaac Newton, another alleged Grand Master of the Priory of Sion, was also a practicing alchemist. Other alleged Grand Masters such as Leonardo da Vinci and Robert Boyle also dealt extensively with alchemy and alchemical experimentation. Between 1675 and 1677 Boyle published two alchemical treatises—*Incalescence of Quicksilver with Gold* and *A Historical Account of a Degradation of Gold*.[19] Leonardo is said to have encoded his successful transmutations within one of his many codexes.

However, all of this information concerning the past Grand Masters tells nothing more concerning the location of the gold mines that the Templars appear to have tapped during the fourteenth century.

The more sensible approach might be to apply a bit more of the Templars' ability to "forge" seemingly unrelated elements into a twisting tale of subtle intrigue.

As such, throughout the history of the Knights Templar, Prince Henry Sinclair, and the tales of King Arthur, there appears a recurring theme of the magical swords of the Knights of the Round Table. In many ways, the sword was considered a guardian and protector on the same level as the goddesses and saints, and became a separate object of veneration. For example, Fay Vivien, known as the Lady of the Lake, was guardian and protector of Lancelot during his childhood and was the same enchantress who gave King Arthur the magical sword, Excalibur.[20] Its blade was lighter and stronger than any weapon in the realm and its silver and gold scabbard protected the warrior who wore it.

Arthur's mysterious sword may well forge the tie between Arthur's Avalon and the Merovingian bloodline in France. There are numerous references to a sword of extraordinary power scattered throughout the Grail romances. In the *First Continuation of the Conte del Graal*, there is the account of Gawain's adventure at Montesclaire (Mont Saint Clair?) and his winning of the sword. Although his story bears no resemblance to the early history of the weapon that Perceval's sister related in the *Queste*, there are similarities throughout the romances as to the weapon's fragility and stroke, which destroys the fertility of any land.

In the later romances, authors have borrowed from the *Matter of Britain* by describing the hilt as made in part from a serpent and in part from a small fish. The symbolic meaning of this is inescapable. In *La Queste du Saint Graal*, when the ship containing the bed and the sword was ready to sail, Solomon's wife attached to the scabbard a girdle of hemp. When the king protested, she replied that she had nothing worthy to sustain so high a sword, but that in due time a younger maiden would provide a better girdle. This prophecy was fulfilled when Perceval's virgin sister produced from a casket a girdle made of silk, gold thread, and her own hair, attached it to the scabbard in place of the old girdle, and hung the weapon at Galahad's side. Thus, the hidden message reflected the earlier theory that the Virgin Mary of the Testaments superseded the Mother Goddess of the ancient beliefs.

Is the relative notion of a succession of chivalrous guardians protecting "Motherhood," regardless of the form that she takes, the golden thread that joins Greek and Roman allegory, mystic symbols, saints' legends, and Celtic themes to the Priory of Sion? The cover design of the modern-day Priory of Sions' publication titled *Circuit,* which shows a Star of David and a Merovingian sword superimposed over an inverted map of France, seems to indicate this.[21]

One of the most significant aspects of the design is that the sword is pointing upward in a manner reminiscent of the tarot card Justice.[22] If one were to superimpose the same sword on Prince Henry Sinclair's Star of David (remembering that the map and therefore the sword is inverted), the point of the sword falls on Oak Island, Nova Scotia.

Could this suggest that the Green Oaks area of Nova Scotia was the refuge of the guardians of the Grail and their secret source of forging operations? The Glenmore Mountain range, which includes the community of Green Oaks, is well known for its large gold-bearing deposits and high-quality ore. Might there just be more than a glen and a mountain waiting to be investigated by a modern-day goldminer? Even further significance can be drawn from all of this by recognizing that the golden hilt or original shaft of the sword would rest at the waterfall at Green Oaks.

THE FOOL'S PRECIPICE

For a very long time, investigators of the Oak Island mystery have contended that the inscription found on the coded stone within the Money Pit is a code of instructions on how to open and shut off the water traps. Others believe the inscription is part of a complex mathematical equation that is required in order to match wits with the unknown designer. Another concept is that the inscription is an important piece of a puzzle and may have an astrological interpretation. Yet another theory dates the burial of an ancient person of royal status.

It is unlikely that the originators of the Money Pit left a simple coded message giving the exact amount and depth of buried treasure. But it is certain that the stone and an inscription did exist, since it is mentioned in all of the early accounts of the Money Pit. Therefore, the beauty of this whole ruse is that the inscription was meant to be found and deciphered. It was composed, on one level, using a very simple code so the message would continue to inspire the foolish.

As a result, too many investigations of the Money Pit have ignored the obvious. In the most popular version of the story of the original discovery of the pit, there is mention of a ship's block that hung from the severed branch of the oak positioned directly adjacent to the enclosed pit. This indicates that someone wanted the pit to be found. Beyond the obvious, if someone had taken the time to peer through the "eye" of the block to the east, they would have noticed that Aspotogan Mountain looms in the background.[23]

Indeed, whoever wanted future treasure seekers to concentrate on the Money Pit certainly achieved their purpose. But for the true seeker of wisdom who could recall the traditional habit of Celtic gods closing one eye to gain the secret of magic, the eye of the block directed the initiate on the true quest.

Edgar Allan Poe wrote his famous treasure story *The Gold Bug* in the nineteenth century. At one point in the story the treasure seekers, by following the pirate Kidd's instructions, identify a critical point to the discovery of the treasure by dropping a little gold bug through the eye of a skull that hung from a very old tree.[24] It definitely appears that Poe was influenced by early accounts of Oak Island's Money Pit. But the point to be recognized is that, as in Poe's story, a spider's web or labyrinth had to be followed after the critical point was identified. Therefore, the labyrinth identified through a reconstruction of the Seal of Solomon confirms that Oak Island is only the starting point in the treasure hunt.

This leads to the idea that, although pirates were involved in perpetrating the idea that the Money Pit was the true resting place of the treasure, they were not the original developers of the Oak Island labyrinth of water tunnels and traps. However, there is a definite connection between the Templars, Freemasonry, and the pirates and corsairs who plundered Spanish gold during the seventeenth and eighteenth centuries.

One theory concerning Oak Island proposes that it was constructed as a communal treasure bank by a number of pirates or privateers. According to this theory, incline tunnels were driven from the bottom of the Money Pit to large, watertight vaults situated at various

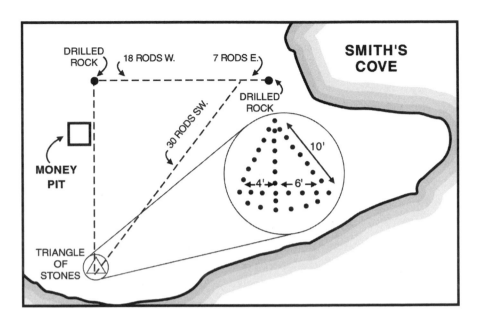

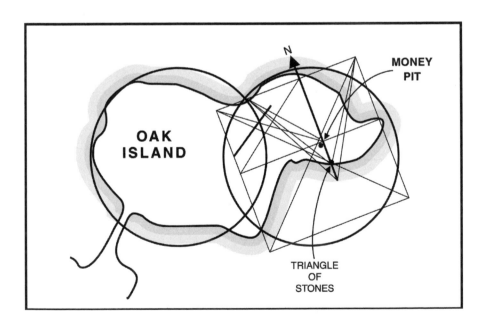

The stone triangle found on Oak Island

Note how the second drawing demonstrates the application of sacred geometry to Oak Island and the relative location of both the Money Pit and the stone triangle.

locations such as the center of Oak Island, the mainland, and even nearby Frog Island. The position of these vaults would then be pinpointed from measurements and bearings determined from the island's stone triangle.

The engineering aspect of this concept is certainly practical, especially in the soft limestone subsurface of the east part of the island. Yet, on the surface, it is difficult to believe that pirates could have organized such a massive endeavor. If they had constructed the underground labyrinth, rumors of the conspiracy would have eventually leaked out and surfaced in legend or recorded history.

Most people accept the fact that the pirates were individual rogues out for themselves; but this was not particularly the case. Many of the earlier pirates demonstrated immense loyalty to their country and cause. In fact, many of them were Freemasons. Therefore, it is reasonable to assume that if they were privy to the secret of Oak Island, they in turn would maintain the secret.

The more reasonable solution is that the pirates assumed possession of the Oak Island underground works and converted them for their own purpose—just as the Knights Templar before them had done not only with Oak Island, but with tarot cards, chess, alchemy, portolan maps, astrology, sacred geometry, and perhaps King Solomon's mines.

Indeed, the Knights Templar can be likened to the little flea that attaches itself to a dog or the hermit crab that takes over an abandoned shell. Or they can be likened to the magician who assumes another's identity to suit his own purpose.

The story behind Prince Henry is a fine example of this philosophy. As Glooscap, he commanded respect and admiration from the local Mi'kmaq, who in turn provided the local information and manpower that was required to complete his quest. The mythical proportions that the story of Glooscap and his deeds assumed over the centuries have served to disguise Prince Henry's true purpose and the location of his settlement.

In a similar fashion, since the beginning of time, individuals or specific groups have assumed another's principles and called them their own. An example of this is the proliferation of mystery and esoteric cults that have evolved from the earliest Greek and Egyptian mysteries.

Another example is the alleged assumption of the inner circle of the Knights Templar by the Priory of Sion, the Rosicrucians, or even the nineteenth-century Hermetic Order of the Golden Dawn.

One of the most notable links between the Knights Templar, the Priory of Sion, the Rosicrucians, and the Order of the Golden Dawn was the most famous of all Rosicrucian thinkers, Francis Bacon (1561–1626). It was Bacon who immersed himself in a mystical, hermetic philosophy, all the while acting as chancellor of England during the reign of King James.

Bacon was also a practicing alchemist and once wrote that alchemists were like the son of a man who told them he left gold buried in the vineyard. By their vigorous digging they found no gold, but by turning up the mold around the roots of the vines, they produced a plentiful vintage. Thus, said Bacon, the attempts to make gold brought to light many useful inventions and advanced society in innumerable ways.

Sir Francis Bacon was a Utopian who hoped to enlighten religion and increase education and the knowledge of science, and thereby create the New Jerusalem. Bacon proposed a blueprint for the new Golden Age through an allegorical novel called *The New Atlantis*.

The New Atlantis, Bacon's magnum opus, was published in 1627 shortly after the foundation of the English colonies in the Americas. It describes the creation of a scientific institute within the colonies along the lines of the Invisible College advocated in the Rosicrucian manifestos.[25] These ideas were later to provide the impetus for the Royal Society founded by the Order of the Rosy Cross during the reign of Charles II.

Bacon expressed his views on this subject several times, claiming that the new kingdom on earth (Virginia) was as it is in the kingdom of heaven. He was more explicit in a speech to Parliament when he made a reference to the establishment of Solomon's House in the American colonies. In his clear reference to King Solomon's temple in a New Jerusalem, Bacon was stating that the founding of the colonies in Virginia in 1606 was a spiritual as well as a political act.

Yet Bacon's largest and most enduring claim to fame is the theory which suggests that Bacon wrote Shakespeare and that his original manuscripts lay in a vault beneath Oak Island, deposited there by the earliest privateers who supported Bacon's hatred of the Spanish.

This theory comes from those who say that Shakespeare (1564–1616) couldn't have written the works for which he is credited; whereas Francis Bacon possessed all the qualities that Shakespeare is said to have lacked. Bacon might have felt that his original works deserved to be stored in the new Temple of Solomon until the world was prepared to recognize them as classic literature.[26]

To complete the "circuit" one more time, Ovid has given us the classic story of the beautiful Atalanta. She was the daughter of King Schoeneus of Boeotia and the story is centered around her courtship with Hippomenes. Apparently, Atalanta was quite vain and had many suitors. But she refused them all, devising a game where no one could have her unless he had first beaten her in a foot race. Hippomenes realized that he didn't normally stand a chance to beat Atalanta in a fair race. Therefore, he prayed to Venus and was rewarded with three golden apples, which she had plucked from a golden apple tree beside her Temple at Tamasus in Cyprus.

The story recounts that as the race started, Atalanta's love for Hippomenes grew stronger. Yet this did not dissuade Atalanta from drawing ahead, even though she ran as slowly as she could. Thankfully, Hippomenes, remembering the apples, threw one of them in front of Atalanta. As she stopped to pick it up, Hippomenes caught up to her. But it was not to last, as she soon started to outrun him once again. So he threw the second apple hoping for a better result, only to experience the same as before. Finally, they approached the finish line:

> And then, to keep her longer from the course,
> To the field's edge he threw, with all his force,
> The glittering gold. At first the girl seemed slow
> To follow after, but I made her go,
> And, as she took it, added to its weight,
> By loss of speed to make her yet more late.
> And, lest my long-drawn tale as slowly run,
> The girl was beaten, and her hand was won.[27]

Hippomenes had won the love of his life. But he later incurred the wrath of the mother goddess Cybele by making love to Atalanta within her temple walls. As a result, Cybele turned both Atalanta and

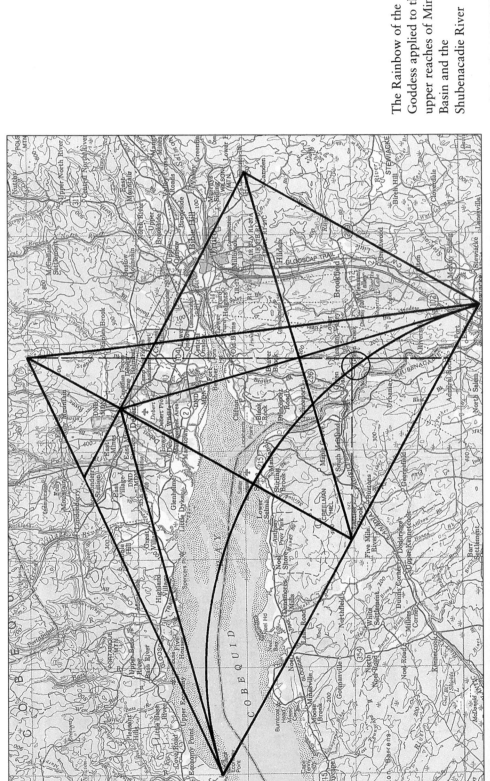

The Rainbow of the Goddess applied to the upper reaches of Minas Basin and the Shubenacadie River

Hippomenes into the lions that drew her chariot. In another version of the story, the lovers are transformed into the stone lions that guard the entrance to the temple, which is also the entrance to the underworld. It was here that both Venus and Cybele first assumed the status of the neglected and vengeful goddesses of many folk tales.

In the *Aeneid,* the descent of Aeneas to the underworld, while belonging to a widespread pattern, especially resembles the journey after death found in the myth of Malekula in the Melanesian New Hebrides. At Malekula, the journey starts in a cave near the seashore with a female companion, a maze or labyrinth at the outset of the quest, and a ferryman. In both cases a staff or wand is necessary as a talisman. In Virgil, it is the Golden Bough.[28]

Again, if we relate this myth to Sinclair's travels across Nova Scotia, it can be said that Prince Henry's own journey to the underworld starts at the natural cave at Oak Island near the seashore. Once he is ferried across Mahone Bay to the South Shore, he constructs a labyrinth (in this case a total-station survey) that leads him to the Gates of Sleep and the Temple of the Goddess.

Thus, it becomes obvious that the oaks planted on Oak Island were planted to provide a talisman of sorts. As to who Prince Henry's female companion was, we can only guess. If a direct descendant of the Holy Bloodline, she would have become the high priestess of the new temple. But where exactly did Prince Henry Sinclair's temple lie? Since Nicolas Poussin was probably the supreme seventeenth-century exponent of Ovid and Virgil, let us reexamine his elegiac painting of Arcadia's shepherds and shepherdess once more.

It was demonstrated earlier that the four figures found in *The Shepherds of Arcadia* (1640–42) can relate back to Merovingian historical figures such as David; Dagobert II; his wife, Mathilde; and the steward or guardian. It was also demonstrated how the geometric relationship between their eyes plays an important part in determining the construction of the Seal of Solomon/Star of David diagram across the Nova Scotian landscape.

What would happen if this logic were continued and the landscape surrounding Green Oaks, which is located adjacent to the Shubenacadie River at the headland of Minas Basin, was again examined? The result is that some very interesting relationships come to light

Rose Point from the valley of Green Creek
Can this be the northerly compass point of Prince Henry's Star of David? Photo by William F. Mann.

between the communities of Debert (Dagobert II?), Maitland (Mathilde?), Noel (David?), and Stewiacke (the steward?). By applying the same triangle to the location of the communities, the result demonstrates the same "eye-to-eye" logic that was earlier demonstrated.

If one assumes that Lower Debert is Debert's, or Dagobert's, eye; that South Maitland is Maitland's, or Mathilde's, eye; that Hayes Cave, the largest known natural limestone cave found in Nova Scotia, is the Noel Shore's, or David's, eye; and that Admiral Rock is Stewiacke's, or the steward's, eye; then the eye of an arc (the Rainbow of the Goddess?) formed across the base of the triangle falls directly on Green Oaks.

Although this may appear too much like hocus-pocus or too far-fetched to be true, consider for a moment the family relationships that Poussin's painting is suggesting. Only through the mother and wife was a direct link from the House of David to Dagobert II established.

Therefore, the relationship demonstrated within the Nova Scotian landscape between Debert and Noel through Maitland is a logical one. Another relationship shows that the tomb can be found in the valley on a line parallel to David's eye. Again, within the scheme of things, Green Creek is found on the same latitude as the point of land located directly across the river known locally as Rose Point, 45° 15' north.

There is one more fascinating clue that confirms that Green Creek is Prince Henry's Valley of Gold. It relates back to Virgil's use of the Golden Bough as a talisman. As noted previously, on the south slope of the ridge between the hilltop of Green Oaks and the valley of Green Creek, there is a large grove of magnificent white oaks. Remarkably, when viewed from the air or from the adjacent hilltop, especially during the fall, the grove takes on the outline of a giant golden bough or golden wing. Could the golden apple of Venus lie at the tip of this bough?

The practice of planting oak trees is definitely Celtic, and there may well have been an ancient Celtic origin of Prince Henry's sanctuary. If so, Sinclair may well have been reestablishing a secret settlement on earlier Celtic foundations, not only building upon its physical ruins, but by applying an ancient Celtic spirit to the occupants' everyday lives.

Aerial photo of the Green Creek and Green Oaks area
Note how the sweeping ridge of mature white oaks suggests a golden wing when viewed from the air.

9

The Fortress of Glass

The Celts were ultimately the ones who developed the idea of a paradise on earth by bringing together a number of the elements of the Elysium Plains, the Gardens of the Hesperides, and the Fortunate Isles. Included among these stories was the recurring theme of "The Fortress of Glass" that floated in the air, to which ascended the spirits of the bards. Hence, the essence of the "spirit" as a separate entity was born.

Taliesin, the sixth-century Welsh bard, referred to this same enchanted palace or tower and declared that the spirit of Arthur was not confined to its enclosure. Sometimes this palace was even represented as a glass mountain, and the early Teutons buried the claws of bears in the graves of their dead in the mountains to assist the spirits in climbing its crystal sides.

The Britons held several different opinions about the region of the departed but, broadly speaking, two principles prevailed. It was believed that either the soul passed into a sort of fairyland by way of a hill, or it migrated to an island. When compared to the earth and the sky, water was thought to be a more effective barrier against spirits (remember the elimination of the sky when the Golden Mean was applied to Poussin's *The Shepherds of Arcadia*). The second belief therefore came to achieve the greater popularity. Gradually, Islands of the Dead became geographically located, usually in the direction of the setting sun.

The Britons' enchanted isles, caverns of sleeping heroes, and so forth, impressed even classical authors. Plutarch mentions them, and

Procopius, around the same time as Taliesin, speaks of a country of "shades or shadows beyond the channel."[1] But at some stage of British culture the myths tended to concentrate and form into combinations. Thereby, a single Island of the Dead emerged more and more clearly as the accepted otherworld.

Although the pagan Britons certainly had notions about such a place, to the Christians Glastonbury Tor was undoubtedly Avalon, the Isle of Glass.[2] Avalon was translated as "apple orchard," but to some recent scholars the name Avalon is more related to the name Avalloc, or Avallach, a Celtic demigod who was supposed to have officiated over the otherworld. This is not to say, however, that the Island of the Dead could not support bountiful orchards of apples or the human guardians of the dead.

The actual date of Glastonbury's first Christian presence remains a mystery. However, it is known that the monastic legends have grown around the single fact that the church that Joseph of Arimethea was alleged to have built did exist. Historical records show that in 1184 fire destroyed a simple structure where the Chapel of the Lady stands today. Known still as the Old Church, apparently it was already on the site in the sixth century and was dedicated to the Virgin Mary, a fact that hints at pre-Christian Glastonbury having been a Goddess sanctuary.

The site at Glastonbury is well fitted to have been a pagan Celtic sanctuary. To this day, it provides enough fresh water to maintain the sacred pools and springs first described by classical writers. The prominent natural—and previously forested—hill of the Tor is a feature that would also support the ideal concept of a sacred grove sanctuary. As well, the existence of a great pagan sanctuary would explain the foundation of an early Christian monastic settlement at Glastonbury, perhaps even a hermitage.

The other possibility is that the site was the settlement and the stronghold of a local chieftain. Because of the steepness of the slopes leading up to the summit, and the excellent view of the approaches in all directions, the Tor was naturally defensible in a manner common to all Celtic earth forts. In a similar vein, from the collection of early Irish and Welsh tales known as *The Mabinogion,* it is not difficult to recognize that the Fortress of Glass (the Grail castle?) was originally an earth fort. Or perhaps it was simply a cave or stone dwelling that protected

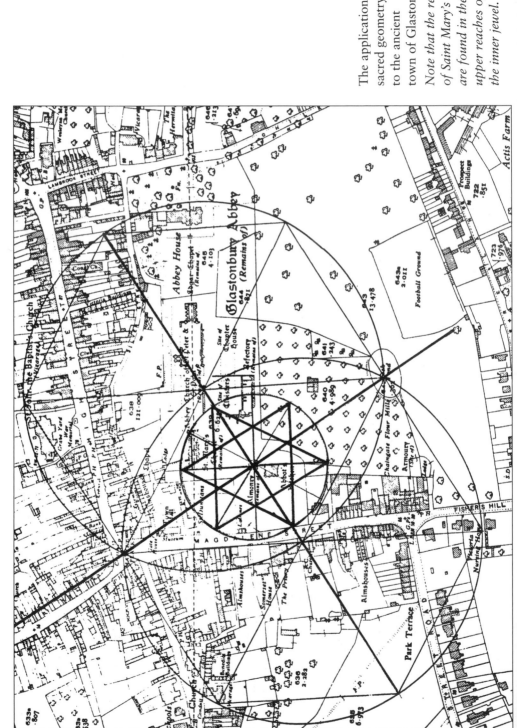

The application of
sacred geometry
to the ancient
town of Glastonbury

*Note that the remains
of Saint Mary's Church
are found in the
upper reaches of
the inner jewel.*

the inhabitants from the basic elements and provided burial chambers for the dead.

Over time, these simple dwellings became the thatch huts of peasants and hermits. By the time of the creation of the Celtic Elysium, they had become the grand courts and halls of kings and knights, where old age and disease were unknown and every desire was fulfilled.

In both the Irish and Welsh tales, it is just as easy to recognize the recurring theme of how stories of the Grail castle came to be embellished. For example, while the Grail castle was originally seen as remote and inaccessible to the common folk, the blissful dwellings of Gwyn were now accessible. In the story of Saint Collen visiting the castle of Gwyn, son of Nudd, king of the fairies, he finds his host seated on a magnificent golden throne. One description of the Grail castle tells of a royal hall where the visitors were supplied without pause, and though they remained there for eighty years, appeared no older than when they came. It was then believed that Gwyn's castle was situated on Glastonbury Tor, and that the royal hall was situated on the island of Grassholm (remember Glenholm Mountain in Nova Scotia), some where off the Welsh coast.

A more elaborate description of the Grail castle is found in the first sequel to *Le Conte du Graal* told by the first continuant of the poem (formerly called by scholars Pseudo-Wauchier). Here, Gawain's visit is nothing like the scene first told by Chrétien de Troyes. Instead, there is a visit to an otherworld castle, which resembles but embellishes two other Irish *echtrai* (adventures). The poet who introduced this Grail adventure into a continuation of Chrétien's work replaced the valley castle with a magnificent mansion at the end of a causeway far out at sea (remember that the priest Saunière built both a tower and a mansion).

In the Irish *Adventure of Art, the son of Conn,* it is the hero's turn to take on a greater status. The story is told that by his marriage to an evil woman, King Conn brought an evil enchantment on his kingdom, making the land sterile. Thus, to restore fertility to the land, Art set out in a small boat (a coracle) across stormy seas until he landed on a mysterious island. There, he found a hall, thatched with colored birds' wings, with bronze doorposts and doors of crystal; nearby, hazel trees were dropping their leaves and fruits into several wells.

Within the hall it was said that he saw the niece of the sea-god

Manannan and her invalid husband, Daire, who was being tended by his servants. Art was led to the fire by an invisible spirit. Then food-laden boards rose up before him (similar to a story concerning Rosslyn Castle) and a drinking horn appeared, though he could not see who fetched it, and he feasted until he could eat and drink no more.

In yet another Irish adventure, *The Adventure of Cormac in the Land of Promise,* there is a strong relationship between the otherworld palace of Conn and the palace that King Cormac discovers.[3] In the adventure, King Cormac, grandson of Conn, allowed his wife to be carried off by a great warrior, who is described as the lord of a land where there was no old age, decay, or sadness. Setting out to recover her, Cormac came upon a palace described in almost the same terms as the hall of Manannan's niece (a Merovingian princess?), with beams of bronze, roof thatch of birds' wings, and hazel trees overhanging a spring. The warrior and a beautiful woman welcomed him and invisible hands washed his feet. After being entertained lavishly with plentiful food, Cormac was informed by his host that he, Cormac, was Manannan mac Lir. The next morning he awoke unharmed and found himself on the lawn of Tara, together with his wife and a truth-testing cup.

One of the most enchanting of the Grail romances is *Perlesvaus,* the Welsh Elysium, which recounts the story of Perceval and how he came to possess the Grail castle. In this story, the castle was overlooking the sea, and inside its walls were the finest halls and the fairest mansions that one was ever to see. A river encircled the castle, which had three names: Edein; the Castle of Joy; and the Castle of Souls. The castle lay within a grove of trees and at the base of the highest tree there was a fountain that concealed a cave.[4]

Similarly, within the Judaic inner temple it was normal for the high priests to conceal the sanctuary from the choir by a curtain. A veil or curtain of this type can clearly be seen in Poussin's *Penance,* which is a depiction of Christ and the twelve disciples gathered around the temple's altar, celebrating his last Passover. This painting is included in the second set of sacrament themes that Poussin painted that also includes *The Ordination.* Christ is shown having his feet washed and anointed by Mary Magdalene, while many of the disciples appear out-raged and offended by this act.

The relationship of the veil to the waterfall can also be found through a close examination of the relevant tarot cards and, on another level, Prince Henry's ancestral home of Rosslyn, Scotland.[5] The name of the castle perfectly describes its position. The castle is perched atop a precipice or promontory, known as a *ross,* and just below the castle site is a pool or waterfall, known as a *lynn.* When combined to form the name Rosslyn, the site reflects the notion that the castle is both a sanctuary and a veil that guards and conceals the activities of its occupants.

What the castle of Rosslyn concealed was a natural rock formation and caves that lie beneath the eight stories of masonry and wood. These caves supported a number of fascinating features that were not known to those outside of the castle walls. Andrew Sinclair, in *The Sword and The Grail,* recounts that the library of the Templars was stored in the caves below old Rosslyn Castle.

It even seems possible that some or all of the lost Templar treasure may also have been temporarily hidden at Rosslyn Castle, for Sir Walter Scott later wrote:

> *From the inner edge of the outer door*
> *At thirty feet of old Scotch measure,*
> *The passage there, that's made secure,*
> *Leads to the holy Roslin treasure.*

This clue may also relate to another castle that Prince Henry built at his settlement in Nova Scotia to disguise and conceal the activities that may have occurred within the underground caves at Green Oaks.

In all probability, Prince Henry and his men engaged in ore-smelting and goldmaking activities. Or they secured the passage of the New World sanctuary where the Holy Grail was ultimately to lie, following its circuit or pilgrimage throughout the Old World. And by following the notion that Green Oaks lies on an ancient world circuit, the system of sanctuaries or castles that the Templars developed along the pilgrim routes across Europe and the Middle East can be seen to be the temporary resting places for the spirit of God.

One of the first strongholds of the Knights Templar was the medieval city of Carcassonne, France. In A.D. 506, Clovis laid siege to the city but withdrew, believing it was impossible to conquer the city, and only during the twelfth century did the Templars secure the city

Rosslyn Castle

Note how the bridge's arch suggests that those who wished to enter the inner sanctuary of the castle must first cross over the arc(h). Photo by William F. Mann.

through negotiation. The interesting aspect of the fortifications that remain to this day is the inner castle square with four towers, one at each corner, and a larger tower within these walls. This reflects exactly the same description of the Grail castle found in *Le Conte du Graal*.

There is another mystery centered on the French village of Coustaussa and its ruined Templar stronghold, whose name may be linked etymologically with the word *custodien*.[7] The theory is that there is the possibility that the street layout had been deliberately designed to reflect an ancient "boat of the dead," including the gigantic outline of a dead warrior, with the main *château* or tower positioned where the eye of the warrior would lie.[8]

Another stronghold, the Castle of Gisors in Normandy, where the alleged separation between the Knights Templar and the Priory of Sion took place, has a most distinctive octagonal keep. After the falling out, the Castle of Gisors continued as the headquarters for the Priory of Sion and continued as its main commandery from 1306.[9] It is said that the commandery was connected, via an underground passage, with the local cemetery and the subterranean chapel of Saint Catherine. In the sixteenth century, this chapel, or a crypt adjacent to it, is also said to have become a depository for the archives of the Priory of Sion.[10]

The fourth and most prominent stronghold of the Templars/Priory of Sion was Stenay, which was also known as Satanicum.[11] Stenay was the old capital of the Merovingian dynasty, near where Dagobert II was assassinated. Yet surprisingly, in 1591, an important Protestant leader (at least outwardly Protestant) acquired the entire town of Stenay.[12] His name was Henri de la Tour d'Auvergne, the possessor of Godfroi de Bouillon's old title.

It was during this same period of the Reformation that the rules against representational art were adopted by some of the more austere forms of Protestantism. This was particularly so in Scotland. Yet the Catholic Church had no such misgivings and seized upon the design principles of sacred geometry, utilizing them to augment its own purposes.[13] From the period of the Gothic cathedrals on, sacred geometry in architecture had gone hand in hand with representational art as an integral component of Christian churches and monasteries.

In the design of Gothic cathedrals, geometry and its application to a specific site became the single most important factor. Therefore, the position of the chief designer and mason was formally elevated to a level reflective of its importance. The construction of any such edifice, including Rosslyn Chapel, was conducted under the direction of the so-called Master of the Work. Each master devised his own geometry depending upon the local conditions.

Most early masters were essentially proficient craftsmen and draftsmen, whose skills were wholly practical. Some of them, however, were versed in something more. Their work, it is believed, reflected a metaphysical, spiritual or, in the language of Freemasonry, "speculative" character that attests to a high degree of skill and knowledge. From several early references, it appears certain that some masters had access to hermetic and Neoplatonic thought during the Renaissance, well before such thought came into vogue in western Europe. But prior to the Renaissance, such thought would have been extremely dangerous to its adherents, who were therefore compelled to secrecy. Consequently, an esoteric, or hidden, tradition of initiated masters would have risen within the guilds of "operative" stonemasons.

Within this esoteric tradition of initiated or speculative masters, it was believed that sacred geometry allowed one to build a reflection of the divine. For the initiated masters, a cathedral was much more than just a house of God. A cathedral was considered a musical instrument, tuned to a particular spiritual pitch, like the harp of an angel. The feeling was that if the instrument was tuned correctly, God himself would resonate through it, and his immanence would be felt by all who entered.

But how and where did God specify his design requirements? Sacred geometry provided the general principles, the underlying laws, but what locations on earth provided the essential contact points to utilize a larger form of conduit?

There is one Old Testament context in which, it was believed, God had very precisely and specifically instructed his worshippers on how to reach him. This context was the building of Solomon's temple and its dedication. And within the description of the building of Solomon's temple, God actually taught the practical application of sacred geometry through architecture. In this manner of association, the building of the temple assumed supreme importance for the stonemasons of the Middle Ages. It makes perfect sense, therefore, that God's chief pupil,

Hiram of Tyre, would be adopted as the model to which every true master builder and Freemason must aspire.

It has long been claimed that the Gothic cathedrals of France are secret textbooks of hidden wisdom. Using complicated linguistic arguments, Fulcanelli, the alleged author of *The Mystery of the Cathedrals,* declared that the hidden secrets are those of alchemy, awaiting a student capable of understanding them.[14]

Upon reflection, the general outline of a Gothic cathedral does relate to two very important aspects that suggest that the Temple of New Jerusalem is indeed located in Nova Scotia. First of all, from an aerial view the standard Gothic layout resembles the keyhole of an old mortice lock, one of the earliest locking mechanisms in the world.

The relevant suggestion here seems to be that, as Fulcanelli claimed, one of the keys to finding the secret textbooks of wisdom lies in the decipherment of the Gothic cathedral. But the answer may also lie in its application to a specific location and not to the basic layout of the Gothic cathedrals of France (remember the inclusion of the layout of the church of St. Sulpice within the four Rennes Parchments).

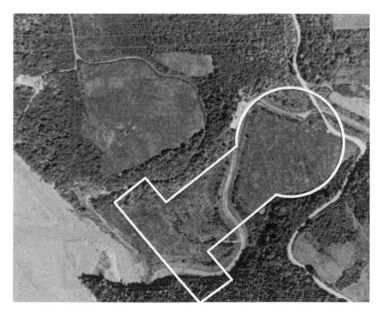

The standard Gothic layout fitted to the valley at Green Creek, Nova Scotia

If the standard Gothic layout is then fitted to the valley of Green Creek, with the altar positioned in the east facing the rising sun, the second aspect comes into focus. The inner sanctuary that is normally located to the north of the altar is, in actual fact, located behind a waterfall. In addition, all of the physical evidence at the Green Creek site suggests that a cave lies behind the waterfall—the symbolic veil of the temple. And, to spin the wheel one more time, Judaic tradition tells that the inner sanctuary or Holy of Holies was constructed with the bones of the sacrificed ram (Hiram?). Is it fair to speculate, therefore, that here is the final resting place of the architect of the new temple?

Another intriguing thing about Green Oaks, Nova Scotia is that when compared to Glastonbury Tor, there are a number of similarities from a physical and defensible point of view. Both hills are surrounded by marshlands and once had causeways that led to the water's edge. Both areas are indicative of extensive mineral deposits and mining activity. Both hills provide a commanding view of the surrounding countryside and are visually linked to other strategic high points in the countryside. And both at one time had sacred groves planted on their hillsides.

It certainly appears that Green Oaks, like Glastonbury Tor, was pos-

The bear's head

This photo taken by the author shows a close-up of the carved limestone outcrop depicting the bear's head drinking at the waterfall, at a location relating to where the holy well of a Gothic church is normally located.

sibly a prehistoric sacred area, a pagan-Celtic and Christian sanctuary and a certain chieftain's stronghold, in that order. In fact, it appears that Green Oaks was the reflection or mirror image of Glastonbury Tor. But while the Tor is known throughout the world as a mystical place, Green Oaks remains a refuge to those who possess the secret of the Grail.

George Young, a mystery writer in Queensland, Nova Scotia, recently claimed to have found the key to the lost Grail. While examining Poussin's *The Shepherds of Arcadia,* he realized that the hand signs given by the painting's figures are really Ogam signs. When Young first translated the writing into Latin, which is the custom with Ogam, the letters made no sense. But once he turned the painting upside down and read from right to left as if reading a mirror image, the letters *T, D,* and *D* quickly became *F, L,* and *L;* and, by inferring the only letters to make a word in Latin, the result became *fallo,* which translates into English as "to deceive."

To Young, this message relates to the theories of Baigent, Leigh, and Lincoln, that Christ somehow faked his crucifixion and was indeed married to Mary Magdalene. Yet, as we have seen, it can also relate to another deception. Under the rather formal dress of the shepherdess lies a child in the womb. In fact, the message suggests the "fallacy" or deception necessary to disguise the fact that the shepherdess is pregnant—a fact hidden by the *falla* or "showy dress." On the other hand, all of this could be pure folly.

Still, it is more than interesting that while the upper portion of the shepherdess's garment is yellow, the bottom portion of her dress is blue. This suggests that the veil that hides the deception is indeed a waterfall. When combined with the previous comparison of the four figures, it now appears that the Templar custodian or guardian not only supports the pregnant shepherdess, but also appears to be hiding behind a veil of some sort. Is it a dual-purposed veil of secrecy and deception that has also worked to the custodian's benefit?

On another level, if the colors of blue and gold are combined, the resulting color is copper or bronze. Were Prince Henry and his Templars and the ancient Celts after not only the gold and silver that lay in the mountains of Glenholm, but also the precious bronze which contains various metals, including copper and tin? Was this the private source of wealth that the Templars used to forge their superior weapons and to build their symbols of stone? Or did the Templar wealth just evolve out of three centuries of dedication, gifts, banking, and other Old World endeavors such as burning and pillaging?

THE ROYAL ARCH

Burning and pillaging was a normal way of life, not only for the Templars but also for those ancient warriors who came before them. However, within the indiscriminate and savage acts of the invading parties, several highly significant cross-cultural events also took place. Slaves and their local knowledge of ritual and custom were disseminated throughout the lands along with pillaged goods and livestock. An even greater event in terms of familial patterns resulted from the raping of the local women.

One such event occurred in A.D. 70, when Roman legions under Titus sacked and burned the Temple of Jerusalem. The famous scene of the treasures of the temple being carried away by Titus and his men is depicted on the Arch of Titus. But the temple contained more than the normal metallic treasure. It is probable that the temple housed official records pertaining to Israel's royal Davidic line. This meant that if Jesus was indeed "King of the Jews," then the Temple of Jerusalem would have contained proof of his heritage and other information directly relating to him.[15]

The suggestion of the arch or lintel being a sacred element of architecture has evolved from the Egyptian belief that the arch allowed the door to another dimension to open. For example, the axis of the Egyptian Temple of Ra-Hor-Ahkty, located just beyond the southeast end of the Great Temple of Amen-Ra, is oriented to the winter solstice sunrise. Here the sun is framed by the freestanding arched doorway of the temple and for the first time in the new year touches the inner sanctuary of the temple, found in the rear.

On a more subliminal level, this bursting forth of sunlight or illumination can be related to the moment a child is brought into the world. Thus, the female labia were seen as the pillars of the doorway to a "New World," while the upper pubic bone was seen as the arch or lintel. And in the case of any royal Merovingian princess, the doorway to the abyss would have been coined as "the Royal Arch."

Therefore, on one level, Royal Arch Masonry can relate to the notion that the secret initiate is the guardian of the hidden secrets of the royal descendants.

An arch can be seen to represent, on the one hand, a bridge that spans a river or a stream or, on the other hand, a bridge that spans time or wisdom. Yet, significantly, the one thing that has spanned the centuries is the concept of one true God—the concept that one spirit has power over everything in the universe. Within the Jewish faith, there is the ancient belief that this power has a secret name and to know the name was to tap its power.

In the Old Testament, God is referred to by various names such as Adonai or Elohim, and these are still used in the practice of occult magic. In the earliest biblical times, the personal name of God was considered so sacred that it was rarely pronounced aloud. It was known as the *tetragrammaton,* or word of four letters—*Y H V H,* which in Hebrew are *yod, he, vau, he* (notice that the symbol or letter *he* completes the square). The correct pronunciation is uncertain because there are no printed vowels in Hebrew, and because the word was spoken so rarely that there is no traditional pronunciation to follow. Judaic scholars prefer to write and say it as Yahweh, although the English Bible generally renders it as Jehovah.

Apparently even more powerful than the tetragrammaton was the Shemhamforash. It supposedly was the name of the seventy-two syllables that Moses is said to have used to divide the waters of the Red Sea to enable the Israelites to escape the pursuing Egyptians. In other words, this knowledge allowed the Israelites to "bridge" the waters of the Red Sea.

If the Masonic Jewel of the Royal Arch is examined, it can be seen that it too is made up of seventy-two elements, or right angles, that express the four elements and sphere of the universe, which are equivalent to the five regular Platonic bodies. Was Nicolas Poussin also suggesting through the depiction of the four elements, or figures, in his painting *The Shepherds of Arcadia* that, as the Platonic theory suggests, the universe itself, as well as its subordinate parts, were created by the deity from the four elements?[16] Is this the wisdom that allowed the Templars to span time, or did they possess something more tangible, such as the family tree of the House of David?

Time and motion are two of the most important clues to the philosophy of the Templars. We have already seen how this obsession allowed them to calculate longitude centuries before the general public had access to the information. And we have learned of their immense knowledge concerning astronomy and the movements of the planets and the stars. Their fixation with measuring time/distance patterns almost rivals Sherlock Holmes' fixation concerning train schedules. But there appears more to the Knights' ability to always be one step, or three steps (two moves one way and another at a right angle, as in a chess game), ahead of their enemies.

It is as if the Templars possessed some magical device to convey their thoughts telepathically, if this is the proper phrase, from one Fortress of Glass to another, from the Old World to the New World. It's an interesting thought. For the moment, let us just assume that the Knights Templar possessed the finest human communications and spy system that money could buy, and based a lot of their actions on "hidden" knowledge that was passed down through the ages by the Celts and other earlier explorers.

In support of this assumption, the Celtic contact with the northeastern Indians of the New World appears to have been a relatively long-standing one, since there is some indication of a Celtic presence among the coastal Indians that the Vikings encountered. It was recorded that the Indians told the first Viking explorers of a "white man's land." However, since these visits touched only upon the coasts, no great knowledge of the interior comes out in the Viking sagas. There are indications, however, of a Celtic presence of some significance among the Indians, for they tell of a land that lay inland from the coast, where the settlers walked in religious processions carrying banners.

Indeed, there could have been sporadic Celtic voyages to the eastern seaboard of North America from about 700 B.C. to at least A.D. 1000. And judging from the Celto-Iberian linguistic influence upon the Mi'kmaq, as presented by Barry Fell, there appear to have been a few Celtic settlements in Nova Scotia as well.

One thing remains absolutely certain. The Celts of the British Isles never lost their tradition and knowledge of some "blessed" and "fruitful" land to the west. It therefore appears logical to assume that the Celts must have carried this knowledge to Britain from their Spanish and North African phases of migration when they sailed with the Phoenicians and Carthaginians. This fruitful and almost magical land in the western ocean was sometimes called Iargalon, "the land beyond the sunset." Iargalon and Avalon indeed now appear to have been the same mystical place in Celtic myth, where demigods and heroes resided side by side, eye to eye.

This brings us back to the matter of the Celtic settlement at Green Oaks, Nova Scotia. The Celtic image first highlighted by Michael Bradley and now by the location of Green Oaks is just one of many of those confusing things found in the Celtic vocabulary. Just as *duir* simply means "oak" on one level, but "door" and "right-handedness" and even "divinity" in other and cryptic senses, Green Oaks has come to represent something that is right, or to the right, or at the right hand of a figure or an element.

Michael Bradley first discovered that there are two Oak Islands in Nova Scotia, and that their relationship to each other is very curious. In fact, there are at least three Oak Islands, and perhaps as many as six or seven in total. This indicates that by following the coded meaning behind the symbol of the Trinity, anyone traveling from the east within the inner circle would have known to keep to the right as he passed the "Island of Oaks" in Mahone Bay. Then, by following the Nova Scotia coastline around its southernmost point, the intrepid voyager would continue to the right as he passed the other Oak Island and its red oaks situated at the mouth of the Gaspareau River. This would have led him straight through Cape Split into Minas Basin with (coincidentally?) Glooscap's two camps, Cape d'Or (door?) and Cape Blomidon (below my den?) on either side of the passage. Could these be the "pseudo" Pillars of Hercules that Poussin was suggesting as he included two mountain peaks, one black and one white, in *The Shepherds of Arcadia*?[17]

Once into the Minas Basin, those who followed the Celtic signposts would have found the "green oak" door that leads to the inner temple by turning right into the Shubenacadie River at the headland of Minas Basin. Then, at Green Creek, anyone connected with the inner circle would have recognized that the grove of white oaks, this time located on the east bank of the river, signified that the door to the inner sanctuary lies in the Val d'Or (valley of the door?).

If we take this back to the tarot cards of the Devil and the Tower, not only is a male secured within a tomb or the ruins of a tower, but there is also his female partner.[18] This could relate to the *Chemical Wedding of Christian Rosenkreuz,* published in 1616, with its familiar alchemical symbols (note that the date is a reflection of tarot card number 16, the Tower, and also happens to be the year that Shakespeare died).[19]

Could it be that the tomb of Christian Rosenkreuz contains the remains of both him and his mate, and possibly the remains of a love child? Perhaps this is the symbolism behind the devil's chain that binds the male and female—the otherworld connection that has bound them to the devil's plinth (the keystone), which rests at the bottom of a rather majestic tree. If so, then does the holy treasure still lie in the shadows "behind the green door" of the destroyed stone tower, waiting to be released?

Round stone tower

This photo taken by the author clearly shows the remains of a circular foundation of what appears to have been a round stone tower, located on the crown of the bear's head at Green Oaks.

10

Out of the Shadows

———❖———

The key to the innermost door of the Grail Castle appears to derive from, among other things, a concept of utter despair and broken-heartedness. Could this concept be a mixture of earlier, more ancient, experiences? The Grail romances conceal within their depths ideas of the decline of all great civilizations. The key may also reflect the loss of faith that the Knights Templar experienced following the fall of Jerusalem.

Questions of this nature may never be answered but it is known with certainty that the Templars possessed something that allowed them to persevere and overcome even the darkest hour. Something of supreme significance sustained the Knights Templar beyond even torture and death. One suggestion is that the Templars possessed either a hidden knowledge or a seemingly direct conduit to God.

Was it a hidden spiritual knowledge that allowed Prince Henry Sinclair to overcome the greatest of odds, both spiritually and physically, to transport the Holy Grail to the New Jerusalem? Surely, it wasn't just the promise of the many riches that lay in the New World. It could have been the lure of immortality that the legendary Glooscap achieved, or perhaps it was the secret of life after death that the ancient Egyptians were said to have possessed.

In Egypt, from the earliest recorded times, there were two types of shrine or temple.[1] One was normally dedicated to the worship of the local deity, while the other would be the shrine of the dead king. In any study of Egyptian religion, the status and power of the pharaoh is of the utmost importance, for the monarch was considered to be God. And

169

because he was considered to be the giver of fertility and the preserver of all, all the land and all the people belonged to him.

In this manner, the pharaoh was considered to be both God and man. As God, he was the giver of all to his subjects and as a man he was to be like other men, the creation of his own God. To his Egyptian subjects he was the incarnation, the living embodiment, God in living form. Yet, the king himself worshipped the sun and it was the sun whose name he incorporated in the title of Osiris. It was Osiris who was the occupier of the throne and ruler of the Land of the Dead.

The king was also considered to be the divine victim who might be put to death to ensure fertility. The Pyramid Texts show that the sacrifice of the Osiris-kings was well known in the Sixth Dynasty. They also show that the sacrifice was in the nature of a talisman or charm. According to legend, Osiris was introduced into Egypt from a northern country. The Pyramid Texts show that the same rite was also used in southern Egypt where Seti I was worshipped.[2]

It was the custom, in the late Eighteenth Dynasty, for the blood of the sacrificial victims to be sprinkled on the field. It was then ploughed into the ground. Ploughing of the ground was part of a later ceremony whereby the Pharaoh preserved his own life when the time came for him to be sacrificed. In the temple of Medinet Habut, the king is shown ploughing a field with a yoke of oxen and later reaping the corn.[3]

The actual method by which the pharaoh was put to death seems to have traditionally been by snakebite. Legend has it that if the king did die from the bite of a snake, some part of the body would be buried in the fields before mummification.[4]

Seti I, of the New Kingdom dynasty, is generally considered to be the greatest military king of Egypt, although Rameses II is probably the best known of all the pharaohs. The record of the battles of Seti I fill a greater part of his life history, but there is one other achievement of Seti I that throws a significant light on Prince Henry Sinclair's knowledge of Egyptian history. This was the establishment of a water station on the way from the Nile Valley to the gold mines in the eastern desert. A well or cistern was dug according to the king's command, and water flooded it from the mountains.

In a similar manner, the legends of Glooscap speak of the man-god using his power to divert a stream in order to quench the Mi'kmaq's thirst. Prince Henry Sinclair may in fact have altered a stream's course so that it would prevent the Mi'kmaq from dying of thirst during the long summer heat. It also allowed them to irrigate their crops within the valley of Green Oaks.

It is recorded that Seti I was also a great restorer of ruined sanctuaries. Where he made such restorations he recorded the deed by only one line of inscription above the main doorway, merely stating the fact, with his name and titles. His finest work was the magnificent temple of the Seven Chapels at Abydus, dedicated to the memory and worship of the Osiris-kings who were buried in that ancient royal cemetery.[5] His own great tomb, however, was at Thebes in the Valley of the Kings and is considered to be one of the marvels of ancient Egypt, rivalling even the Great Pyramid. It is cut three hundred feet into the solid rock. The tomb's walls and most of the ceilings of the halls and passages are decorated with sculpture and paintings that depict the journey of the sun through the realms of night and the shadows of the dead.[6]

Some recent experts suspect that the mystery chamber of the Great Pyramid may be the final resting place for the treasures or the body of another great pharaoh, Cheops. Cheops built the Great Pyramid to achieve eternal life after death. No doubt, the mystery chamber had a major religious function within the pyramid and may have been linked in some way to the Egyptian goddess Isis.

According to calculations by the Belgian researcher Robert Bauval, it is probable that the upper passageway was built to point directly at the Dog Star, Sirius, which is the star held by the ancient Egyptians to be the heavenly incarnation of Isis herself. As well, other passages within the Great Pyramid appear to point to other heavenly bodies, including the belt of Orion and Polaris.

It is even possible that the mystery chamber acted, in ritual terms, as the resting place of Isis. This chamber within the Great Pyramid might also have acted as a royal treasury in the same manner that the heart of the legendary Chalice Hill of Glastonbury is reputed to be the Fisher King's secret treasury. Or perhaps this new inner chamber acts as the resting place of the king and queen's offspring. More specifically, the new inner chamber could conceal their male offspring, who would have assumed as exalted a position as his father.[7]

Through this connection, the inner chambers of the Great Pyramid can be likened to the inner circle of royalty and their relative position to one another. The king remains in the center, with the queen below him. Below her may lie the princesses, whose one purpose was to perpetuate the royal line. And, located at the king's right hand, within the mystery chamber, perhaps lies the son whose rising is signified by Sirius.

Sirius is the brightest star of the night sky and its appearance in the early evening is a sure sign that winter is coming. The brightness of Sirius might alone have given it special significance in the star lore of ancient peoples. But the coincidence of the helical rising of Sirius with the solstice and the annual flooding of the Nile prompted the Egyptians to base an entire calendar and timekeeping system on the star's behavior.[8]

Because of its historical lunar and seasonal relationships, the Knights Templar would have also attached a fair amount of significance to Sirius and its cyclical behavior. The Templars may also have perpetuated the notion that the son's chamber of any tomb must be aligned with Sirius and Orion, and even Polaris. In other words, the son (of God) would have been seen as a conduit or direct connection between earth and the spirit (God) of the heavens.

Knowing that the Templars felt that the Egyptians held an inner knowledge of the planets and the stars, then perhaps the reverse side of the Great Seal of the United States with its pyramid and all-seeing third eye can also relate to the notion that there was a direct stairway to heaven from earth. In addition, on the front of the seal is depicted an eagle with a serpent in its mouth.

If we again take this back to Sinclair's activities, it must be noted that the Shubenacadie River Valley is known for the eagles that nest along its shoreline. In fact, several lookouts have been provided for tourists to observe and photograph the eagle nests. Could it be that Sinclair/Glooscap actually found himself perched above the valley that contained the true red serpent/stream? Could this be what is meant by the cluster of arrows that are found in the claw of the American eagle? Could these arrows, in turn, confirm the notion that Prince Henry was reestablishing a settlement that had once paid homage to Apollo/Artemis—the dual archer-god?

Apollo/Artemis were said to have had numerous love affairs with both men and women and left a number of broken hearts.[9] Hence, the theme of the "brokenhearted" may have originated with the Greek myths, although the heart is one of the earliest symbols to be recorded by man.

In the story of Hero and Leander, the couple was united by an arrow shot by Cupid, or Eros, as he was otherwise known. Leander lived at Abydus, and Hero at Sestus, where she dwelled in a tower outside of the town. At a festival of Adonis, she met Leander and he vowed to swim to her by night, since Sestus and Abydus were divided by the sea. Sadly, Leander struggled with the waves and drowned. Hero, seeing Leander's body upon the rocks, became despondent and hurled herself over a sheer cliff to join her love in death.

The story of Hero and Leander is found among the folktales of all Europe as well as in an Egyptian love-lyric. The story may even provide the basis to the tarot card of the Fool who, while appearing in a love trance, is seen walking off a cliff into an abyss.

The casting of oneself into the sea was another popular theme that in fact symbolized the birth or rebirth of Aphrodite (Venus). Aphrodite's birth is depicted in Botticelli's famous painting, with Venus rising from the waves on a seashell. Aphrodite is in origin akin to Ishtar and Astarte in her incarnation of the maternal principle. Her birth supposedly proclaimed an end to the era of wanton destruction and introduced a new order and maturity of species. Accompanied by Eros and with his aid, tradition says that she was the irresistible force impelling procreation and production, who "strikes fond love into the hearts of all, and makes them in hot desire to renew the stock of their races." Eros was the son whom Aphrodite bribed with a ball of golden hoops or rings to shoot an arrow into Medea's heart, so that she would fall in love with Jason and help him recover the Golden Fleece.

On a physical level, an abyss is seen as a deep, immeasurable space or vast chasm that is bottomless. The internal regions of hell and the subterranean regions of the oceans are described as abyssal. The deep chasm of cascading water into which Sir Arthur Conan Doyle's characters, Sherlock Holmes and his arch-rival Dr. Moriarty, allegedly fell to their deaths was described as an abyss. Also, it is at the knight's tower on the circuit of the Divine Horseman of the Abyss that the White Lady of the Legends apparently lies, awaiting her gallant prince.[10]

Many of the legends surrounding Glooscap, as well, touch upon the related aspect that another world or abyss existed below the earth's surface. In the Mi'kmaq legend *Mooin, the Bear's Child,* an evil stepfather lured his small stepson into a dark and deep cave set in a rocky hill deep in the forest.[11] Then the stepfather took a pole and thrust it under a pile of huge boulders so that they tumbled over and covered the mouth of the cave completely. Only through the strength of Mooninskw, the she-bear, could the rocks be removed. From then on Mooinskw became the mother to the little Mi'kmaq boy.

In another Glooscap legend, *The Boy Who Worried Tomorrow,* we are told of the soul of the evil Chemoo, the giant wizard, that was kept in a locked box deep inside a mountain, with the key to the box hidden in another box deep at the bottom of the sea.[12] Could this suggest that the key (or one of the keys) to finding Glooscap's cave lies at the bottom of Oak Island below the sea?

Yet another Glooscap legend tells how Marten, the servant of Glooscap, met an elf-boy, Sabadis, who lived in a vast cave in another world and followed him to an inner cave where they met Sabadis's sister Welahe. It turns out that Welahe and Sabadis were actually spirits whose resting place is in the sky, where Sabadis shoots the arrows made by his sister. Obviously, this appears to be a direct connection to the constellation Sagittarius or the god Apollo.

Traditionally, the female twin to Apollo—Artemis, the goddess of the moon—was also to be found among the shadowy hills, dark caves, and windy headlands, sending forth her shafts of sorrow. She has also been likened to Isis, the Egyptian goddess of the abyss. In the *Book of the Dead,* one entire chapter is devoted to Isis's ability to bestow on the dead some of her magical powers, allowing them to travel the dark tunnels to the light.

SKULL AND CROSSBONES

The mystery as to who were the original builders of the dark labyrinth of shafts and tunnels found below Oak Island and Green Oaks will probably remain as elusive as the answer to why and how the pyramids were built. But there remain other clues that may apply to the larger story of how Oak Island relates to Prince Henry Sinclair's explorations and old habitation.

In 1930, a silver Spanish coin dated 1785 was found beside an old road running from a house built on the island by a former owner, Anthony Graves. In 1965, another Spanish coin was discovered at the same site, and this coin was dated 1598.[13]

Consequently, most Oak Island treasure hunters have used the dates of these coins to support their claims that the Money Pit was constructed just after the recorded dates by British military engineers or by the likes of the pirate Sir Francis Drake. What the intrepid hunters have failed to realize is that the coins may have been dropped intentionally, to both confuse and fascinate the uninitiated. At the same time, however, these "jokers," whether high-ranking British officers or pirates, were providing clues to the initiated and dating their own explorations.

The Spanish coins are silver, which traditionally represents the moon, and show the Pillars of Hercules and a royal crest.[14] From this, it is possible to theorize that Oak Island represents the starting point to a quest based, in part, on the twelve tests of Hercules and that, if followed correctly, the position and cycle of the moon leads the hero through a set of pillars to a royal settlement or royal treasure.

Another clue found on Oak Island is a large limestone boulder with four figures carved on it. The first figure depicts the symbol H, which represents Solomon's Pillar. The second depicts the symbol +, which is an ancient mark of enlightenment, while the third depicts a circle, which represents gold, sun, or light. The fourth completes the square. It depicts an equilateral triangle that, on one level, represents truth and wisdom. But the fifth element is missing! Is the hidden element the limestone itself?

Truly, over the centuries, Oak Island has become the depository of a number of bad jokes in the form of conveniently lost coins, tackle blocks, carved stones and boulders, and other "black" humor. As the old saying goes: "All that glitters is not gold."

Reason dictates that only a well-organized group of individuals committed to secrecy could have perpetuated such a hoax. Or does it? Many of the Oak Island speculators that have been duped were Masons. Names such as Frederick Blair, Gilbert Hedden, George W. Grimm Jr. (Hedden's New Jersey lawyer), Mel Chappel, and Reginald V. Harris all had Masonic connections. Obviously, they were not privy to an inner circle of truth and wisdom and failed to recognize a sign of ancient enlightenment when it confronted them.

The most unlikely group of confidants or keepers of the truth (and again, this is the beauty of the notion) were the English and French pirates and corsairs that plied their trade during the sixteenth, seventeenth, and to a lesser degree, the eighteenth centuries. Men such as Drake, Dampier, and Morgan all showed a certain disrespect for law and order, yet showed a remarkable allegiance to the crown and hatred toward the Spanish and Portuguese. In many cases, though, rather uncharacteristic acts committed by various pirates demonstrated an underlying spiritual and charitable nature toward common folk, especially women and children. In many other situations where the pirate was not a member of the inner circle, the pirate life was one of boredom, disease, compulsive gambling, and wild binges. *Treasure Island* is just a fantasy.

In the seventeenth and eighteenth centuries the ports of La Have and Cape Sable, Nova Scotia, were two of the favorite haunts and ports of refuge for the pirates and privateers that plied their trade along the eastern seaboard.[15] Even Sir Francis Drake, one of the first of the English "gentlemen" pirates, is known to have made several excursions in the vicinity of Nova Scotia and Oak Island around the early 1600s.

Francis Drake preyed upon Spanish Catholic treasure armadas. The Queen of England knighted him for his services. From all accounts, it appears as though the English crown was also financially involved in his private adventures. It is Drake whom the current owners of most of Oak Island, Triton Alliance, see as the most likely candidate to have deposited the booty gleaned from his second or third campaign against the Spanish. Triton's research hints that if there ever was an Oak Island treasure, it may have been recovered by its owners or others between 1602 and 1605.

Two other privateers, Captain William Kidd and Olivier Le Vasseur, have been credited with the development of the waterworks found on Oak Island. Although Captain Kidd led the longer and more fascinating life, his particular relevance to this story lies in the many artifacts and maps that were said to be left following his hanging on May 23, 1701.

As described in chapter 1, one of the most enigmatic pieces of evidence relating to the mystery of Oak Island is the legendary Kidd map found in the book by Harold T. Wilkins, *Captain Kidd and His Skeleton Island*. Although Wilkins eventually admitted to having made up the map, the relative distances and bearings found on the map have been determined to relate to the stone triangle found on Oak Island. However, no one has been fortunate enough to be able to relate the code "7 by 8 by 4" to the stone triangle or any other portion of the island. That is, until now.

If this code is related back to the idea that the stone triangle was in some way connected to the establishment of a longitudinal meridian, based upon a lunar calendar or the moon's cyclical movements, then perhaps the answer lies in the multiples of the numbers cited.

For example, 7 times 8 equals 56, and 56 times 4 equals 224 which, divided by 24 (hours in a day), equals 9.3, or the length of a minor lunar standstill in years. The same number divided by 12 (a relative number of hours between night and day) equals 18.6, which is the length of a major lunar standstill in years. The result is that the numeric code on the Kidd map not only gives the dimensions of the stone triangle and the relative dimensions to identify the Money Pit and other critical locations, but also supplies the background information required to predict a major and minor lunar standstill.

Furthermore, if we apply a little of the same reflective thought shown through the manipulation of the number 681 (found in the Rennes parchments, as shown on page 10), we find that 7 times 8 equals 56, plus 4 equals 60; and 7 times 4 equals 28, plus 8 equals 36. If we then multiply 60 times 36 we arrive at 2,160, which just happens to be the diameter of the moon in miles.

One last feat of hocus-pocus before we move on to the Buzzard. The number 224, divided by the average length of a lunar cycle (29.5 days), equals 7.5, which relates back to the angle of magnetic declination that was speculated upon by Furneaux and others. If we multiply by 2 then, we see that a magnetic declination of 15 degrees occurred around 1784 and 1604, both dates that correspond nicely to the Spanish coins found on Oak Island.

Olivier Le Vasseur was nicknamed "The Buzzard" and might just be considered the antithesis of Captain Kidd. Where Kidd was considered to be businesslike and almost timid, the French pirate from La Rochelle is described as a mysterious, swashbuckling, and gallant knight of the seas. The Buzzard's home base was Saint Mary's Island, off the coast of Madagascar, and it is here that it is said that his enormous treasure still lies. Yet the Buzzard can also be linked to the explorations of Prince Henry Sinclair and his application of Masonic ritual in Nova Scotia.

When the Buzzard climbed the scaffold to be hanged for his crimes, it is said that he threw a cryptogram into the crowd, shouting: "My treasure to him who can understand!" Unfortunately, it was said that the cryptogram could only be solved with the aid of *The Little Keys of Solomon,* two signed letters, and a will. These are all documents that have been shown to relate to the Rennes mystery.

Two other facts stand out concerning the life of Olivier Le Vasseur. First of all, the Buzzard insisted on calling his command ship *The Apollo.* Secondly, the Buzzard is known to have been a Freemason. The Buzzard was also involved in the attempt to establish an alternative Utopian society on the island of Madagascar. The society was to be known as Libertalia, where it was hoped that a community could be established without regard to race or creed. This relates in a similar vein to the community the Acadians hoped to establish in Nova Scotia.

THE ACADIANS

In 1604, the first historically recognized and successful attempt to establish a French settlement in the New World took place within those lands situated between the 40th and the 46th parallels. Rather conveniently, these lands, for which the French king Henri IV granted Pierre Dugua de Monts a monopoly, included those lands along the 45th parallel where it was rumored that the lost settlement of Prince Henry and his Templars was located. The tract of land that the Sieur de Monts received would come to be known as *La Cadie,* or l'Acadie. Generally, the boundaries of this territory included, in today's terms, Nova Scotia, New Brunswick, Prince Edward Island, and part of the state of Maine. De Monts's official task was to promote the settlement and cultivation of the land, to prospect for mines, and to convert the native peoples.

Acadie was the key to not only the trade routes and the fisheries of the North Atlantic, but the inland fur trade and mineral wealth. Thus, Acadie became a point of military and political struggles between

France and England and changed hands nine times between 1604 and 1710. It first fell from the hands of the French to the English in 1654.[16] As a result, no new Acadians, as they became known, were able to establish themselves in Port Royal until after the Treaty of Breda in 1667, when the colony was given back to France.

Following the loss of Port Royal in 1710, mainland Nova Scotia was once again ceded back to the British. The conditions of the subsequent 1713 Treaty of Utrecht allowed, however, for Île Royale (Cape Breton), including the original fort of Louisbourg, and Île Saint-Jean (Prince Edward Island) to remain French. On the other hand, the mainland Acadians did not fall prey to any British ill treatment until the founding of Halifax by the British in 1749. Up until this time they had peacefully continued to farm the "heartland," as it was known, and cohabitated with the Mi'kmaq.

For some inexplicable reason, the attitude of the British changed dramatically after the founding of Halifax. On July 28, 1755, an order was given to deport all Acadian men, women, and children, due to their refusal to sign an oath of allegiance to the king of England. The result was that after a century of relative peace and stability, thousands of Acadians were deported either to the mid-Atlantic American colonies or to the Carolinas. Many perished aboard the crowded ships and never saw their new homeland. And, with strange abandon, British troops torched and ransacked all of the Acadian settlements, even those individual homesteads in the outlying areas.

Aside from the obvious political manipulations on both sides, there may have been an underlying reason for the unusual level of cruelty and destruction on behalf of the British. One possibility is that the inner British circle had somehow confirmed their suspicions that within the land of Acadie lay an immense and priceless treasure that the Acadians either possessed or maintained the clues to its discovery. Folk songs of the Acadians either have always spoken of a lost Acadian treasure and in fact the Acadian flag depicts a golden five-pointed star on a royal blue background. This suggests that indeed a golden treasure had crossed the sea from the Old to the New World.

Two seemingly unrelated facts support this theory. First of all, among the British records of the expulsion there is a notation of seven families from "the River of the Old Habitation," including the popular family name of Saunière.[17] Yet, following an extensive search of all French records, although the small cluster of families has been identified, no actual location of the community is available. The curious thing is that since the Acadians were supposedly the first settlers in Acadie, how did there come to be an "Old Habitation?" The Acadians surely would have not labelled an Indian village as an old settlement.

Supporting this question is the fact that a map of Acadie was produced in 1757 "to serve as a general history of the voyages." This is unusual in that it was produced two years after the expulsion of the Acadians and therefore could serve no purpose other than to provide a document identifying the French settlements prior to the expulsion.[18] If this is the case, there are some very interesting aspects to the map. The most significant of these is the fact that the *Carte de L'Acadie* is based on a longitude measured from the Paris Meridian and shows Oak Island lying 66.6 degrees west of Paris. The map also shows the settlement of Shubenacadie, not in its current location but at the present location of Green Oaks.

Could Shubenacadie, therefore, have been the River of the Old Habitation? From what is generally known, the Mi'kmaq established both summer and winter camps. The summer camps would obviously be located along the shoreline and within the "heartland" of the land marshes where the natural clearings would have allowed the drying of fish and meat and rudimentary scattering and harvesting of grains. Logically, the winter camp would be located in the shelter of an upland forest. It therefore makes sense that a Mi'kmaq summer camp was located at the mouth of Green Creek where it meets the Shubenacadie River and that this camp would be associated with some sort of spiritual presence. All the better if the hill that overlooked the Mi'kmaq camp was the home of their guardian, Glooscap.

There is even the popular story that Oak Island was developed by the Acadians to enable them to hide most of their valuables and religious artifacts prior to the sacking of the British. But this seems implausible because, by all accounts, the Acadians seemed to feel, like the Templars before them, that they were immune to political interference. This notion may have sprung from some secret knowledge they possessed, some secret that was represented by the Templar belief that the soul lies within the head of the body.

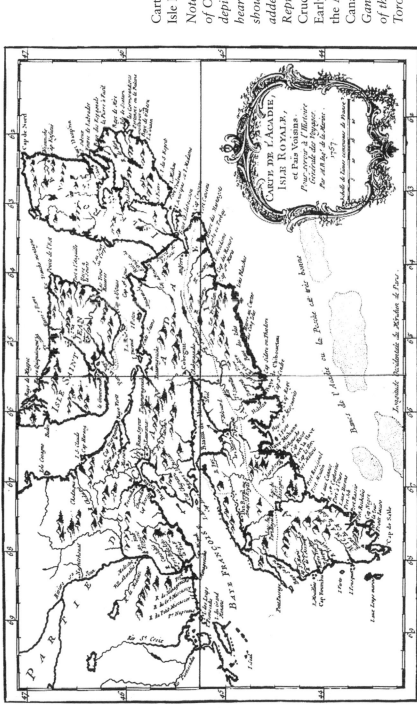

Carte de L'Acadie,
Isle Royale, 1757

*Note how the settlement
of Chubenacadie [sic] is
depicted at the very
heart of L'Acadie, as
shown by the cross
added by the author.
Reproduced from
Crucial Maps in the
Early Cartography of
the Atlantic Coast of
Canada by W. F.
Ganong, by permission
of the University of
Toronto Press.*

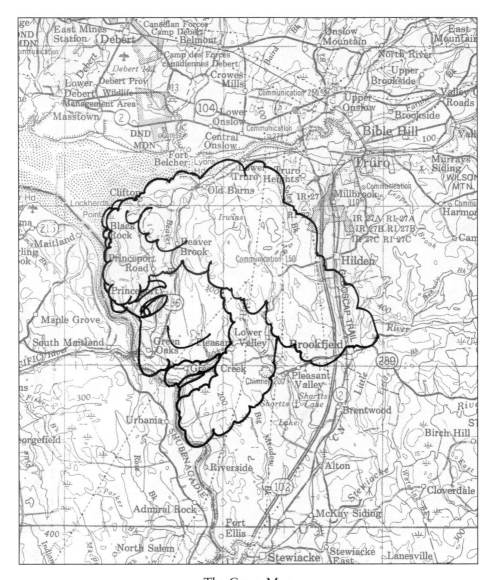

The Green Man

A Celtic figurehead as it relates to the headland of Minas Basin. Note how the mouth of the figure relates to the mouth of Green Creek. Is this but one example of the application of a Celtic spiritual belief to the physical landscape?

The notion of a headland at the gates of hell suggests that a similar notion may be reflected at the gates of heaven, within the Green Oaks area, and indeed there is! The clue lies where the mouth of Green Creek touches the Shubenacadie River. In profile, just north of the mouth of the creek lies an outcrop that is known locally as "Anthony's Nose." Just below Anthony's Nose, between the nose and the mouth, is the hillside of planted white oaks that turn gold and red in the autumn. Could this be the start of a reddish golden moustache to our Celtic figurehead?

In addition, just north of Anthony's Nose lies the small community of Princeport (where an eye would be positioned within a skull). Conveniently, across the river lies the other eye, South Maitland. What the relative positioning of these two "eyes" may be suggesting is that by following the inner knowledge of the third eye, or the Shubenacadie River, Prince Henry Sinclair's port may be found. Further to the north we find the forehead at the start of the Shubenacadie River at an area known as Black Rock. This is again conveniently placed where the imaginary hairline would start.

The location of Black Rock at this point also suggests another relationship to Poussin's shepherds of Arcadia. If the relationship between the painting's foreground, middle ground, and background is applied to the actual headland of the Shubenacadie River, then indeed a black rock is positioned in the background of Poussin's painting. In fact, if one looks closely one can almost detect some facial expressions in the black rock of the painting.

Directly to the north of the tomb or temple at Green Creek lies the small community of Green Oaks and, remarkably, green oaks are depicted directly behind the tomb of Arcadia shown in Poussin's painting. To the west across the Shubenacadie River from Green Creek and Green Oaks lies the small community of Urbania. Can this possibly suggest that within the tomb is the one known as Ursus, the Bear of Arcadia?

To complete the analysis, we have already seen how the guardian within Poussin's painting rests his foot on a rather large rock. Knowing that the Grand Master of the Priory of Sion was known as the Navigator, or Admiral, it should come as no surprise that the small community of Admiral Rock is found just south of Urbania and Green Creek.

It's truly amazing to think that Poussin could have related his masterpiece of 1640–42 on so many levels to a landscape that only officially had been explored for the first time in 1604 by the French explorer Samuel de Champlain. Or is it? Was Champlain part of the same secret society that perpetuated the secret inner knowledge that the holy tomb lay in Arcadia (Nova Scotia)? Given the relative dates, perhaps Champlain actually discovered the Arcadian tomb. But was the tomb empty? Is it possible that the contents of the new Temple of Solomon had been moved once again by the Knights Templar?

Within the seventeenth and early eighteenth centuries, a feeling of melancholy spread throughout the esoteric and occult circles of Europe. The great European monarchies had lost all hope of recovering past glories, due in part to the French and American revolutions. It was as if an inner light had been lost. It was as if the usurpers had gained a foothold in the New World, thus forcing the abandonment of yet another secret refuge.

11

Into the Light

-----◆-----

Do the Grail romances only represent a physical quest in search of some hidden treasure, or, to a more sublime degree, do they represent a spiritual awakening of the unconscious? Surely, the romances were not developed only as support for courtly love, but as a pathway to an inner search for truth.[1]

It was determined that there exists a secret code in a number of the Dead Sea Scrolls that the Templars may have learned during their time in the Holy Land. Indeed, a noted expert on early Christianity, Dr. Hugh Schonfield, demonstrated that if the name Baphomet was written in this code and then translated, the result would be the Greek word *sophia* (meaning wisdom).[2] From this, it can be concluded that when the Templars worshipped Baphomet, what they were really worshipping was the principle of wisdom and not some form of Satanism. Recognizing wisdom is exactly what the ancient Egyptians had done when they worshipped Thoth and his hidden works as "the personification of the mind of God."

By this analysis, one fact that comes to light is that the earliest Freemasons regarded Thoth as their original patron, instead of Saint Anthony. According to old Masonic tradition, Thoth played a major part in preserving the earliest knowledge of Masonry and transmitting it to humankind after the Flood. This so-called Thoth connection sets those links in the ancient and enduring context of a "royal wisdom" tradition stretching back to pharaonic times. This brings us to the question as to who, through the ages, might possibly have been initiates in the same wisdom tradition?

One likely candidate is Sir Isaac Newton, who is listed as a Grand Master of the Priory of Sion. He once stated his view that the Egyptians concealed mysteries under the veil of religious rites and hieroglyphic symbols, beyond the grasp of common man.[3] Among these mysteries, he believed, was the knowledge that the earth orbited the sun and that the sun remained at rest.

What is much less well known about the great scientist is that he spent a significant part of his adult life deeply immersed in hermetic and alchemical literature. In addition, he supposedly was obsessed with the notion that a secret wisdom lay concealed within the pages of the Bible. Daniel of the Old Testament and John of the New Testament especially fascinated Newton because he believed that a radically different method of interpretation could lead to the true meaning of the Holy Grail.[4]

Yet of all those whose work is associated with the spiritual pursuit and understanding of the ancient wisdom, the theories of C. G. Jung remain the highest. Jung's work in the fields of psychoanalytical studies was very different from that of his contemporaries, since he recognized inner spiritual truth as being present within the psyche of every individual.

In reality, Jung's search for the inner spirit represented a more direct experience of the psyche. He felt that the accepted theoretical viewpoints available at that time failed to encompass the complexity of the human psyche as a whole. Instead of speaking about the psyche, it became his intention to let the psyche itself speak. Thus, in his work with his patients, he limited himself to helping them understand their own dream images. His working hypothesis was to regard dreams of the unconscious as self-representations of objective psychic processes, which the conscious personality should confront directly.[5] In simpler terms, through one's dreams one's inner self is trying to tell one's outer self of one's fears and desires.

From an historical point of view, it is this personal quest for the original experience of the creative spirit in the unconscious psyche that brings Jung close to the spiritual movements that began to appear in the West in the twelfth and thirteenth centuries. These spiritual movements not only included alchemy but also the Holy Ghost movement of Joachim of Flora.[6] All of these movements had an important common element in that they followed the prompting of the inner soul and sought for a more direct, inner experience of the Divine, without the help of an intermediary such as a priest.

The Grail romances also have a spiritual affinity with these movements. For example, one of the romances tells that whenever Joseph of Arimathea listens to the counsel of the Grail he hears the voice of the Holy Spirit speaking to him in his heart.[7] The Grail is therefore seen as a direct and distinct conduit to the voice of God and therefore to God himself. Consequently, when Perceval sets out on his quest, the journey can be interpreted as the seeking of knowledge that can only be achieved through an inner, individual experience of the Holy Spirit. By associating the Holy Spirit with its earliest form, Mother Earth, it is soon realized that Perceval was looking to become, in essence, "one with nature."

This became the start of an idea that was further developed by alchemy in the concept of *lumen naturae*—"the light of nature." This light of nature is considered a kind of intuitive knowledge of all that is good and rich, enkindled by the Holy Spirit in the heart of humankind. For the alchemist, the *lumen naturae* was a source of knowledge or attainment of wisdom equal to the highest spiritual revelation.

In alchemy, there certainly exists the need to search for an experience of the Divine. The most important symbol for the Divinity therefore became the philosopher's stone, the *lapis,* which is described as something that could be found everywhere. At the same time, the stone became a symbol of eternity and the inner wisdom of man. Hence, the philosopher's stone was considered by the alchemist to have all the attributes of the Trinity, and became nothing less than the exact image of God. For the mystical adept of the Middle Ages, the Grail was therefore a symbol of one's inner soul or spirit. Accordingly, the great secret, which Jung felt was hidden behind the stories of the Grail, is the mystery of the transformation of God in the soul of man.

Freemasonry and the spiritual psychology that has been derived from Craft Masonry's symbolic structure have also been likened to this quest to identify the divinity that exists in all men. Masonic tradition sees the complete human being as having four levels: flesh, a psyche/soul, a spirit, and a direct contact with the Divine Source. It proposes that the human psyche also contains four levels that reflect a larger four-level structure. Specifically, that structure is represented by the Temple of Solomon, which is described as a three-story temple within which one can be conscious of a fourth and higher level, the omnipresence of the Divinity.

Using this analysis, a parallel can be drawn between the three stories of the Temple of Solomon: the ground floor, the middle chamber, and the holy of holies, and the three levels of awareness in Jung's psychological model: the individual consciousness, the personal unconscious, and the collective unconscious. When the three levels are achieved, the fourth level becomes apparent. This is yet another association with the concept of completing the square.

This four-level framework within which Freemasonry operates also reflects the metaphysical system that was embodied in the plan of the Gothic cathedral. It describes the geometric progression that starts with a point as the fundamental element. The point moves, and in doing so generates a line; the line moves, in a perpendicular or right-angled direction, and generates a plane (or a two-dimensional square); then the plane, moving in a similar way, generates a solid (or three-dimensional cube). The geometric succession of figures is such that each action brings a new object into being that has its own characteristics, but that also includes the characteristics of the object that generated it. For example, the solid cube, which is defined by the rules of three-dimensional geometry, contains the plane from which it was generated.[8]

This so-called projection is the same metaphysical interpretation that can be found in the dimension of consciousness that was the basis of almost all that was envisioned by the Renaissance scholars.[9] The startling resurgence of art and intellectual activity that occurred during the Renaissance was thought to be the result of the interaction of two schools of thought—Scholasticism and Humanism.[10] But it is only during the last fifty years that some historians have suggested that the popular revival of Western mysticism in the late 1400s, the hermetic/kabbalistic tradition, was a third major influence. It is this third stream of thought (or third dimension) that is largely significant to this book's story, both from a historical point of view and because some of today's Masonic material refers to the literature of this tradition.

It is a fundamental principle of hermetic philosophy that certain deep inner truths lie hidden behind symbols in art, music, literature, and configurations in the landscape and the sky. As suggested earlier, it was even believed that a message intended for generations yet unborn might be preserved in the layout of ancient streets and roads that reflected the messages of the constellations.[11] In ancient words: "As above, so below."

Similarly, the *Hermetic corpus*—the *Hermetica,* supposedly originating from Hermes Trismegistus, the "Thrice Greatest," can be divided into two categories. The writings that make up the first group date back to the third century B.C. They are comprised of tracts of astrology and astrological medicine, alchemy, magic, and the system of occult contacts that purports to reveal secret links between unconnected parts of the universe. The second category dates from about the second and third centuries A.D. It consists of a body of religious philosophy that has ties with the more popular writings on magic and alchemy.

It is from the magical, astrological, and alchemical theories of the *Hermetica* that most of the later European theories of magic and alchemy are derived. Descriptions such as those that unite a particular star or sign of the zodiac to a part of the human body or connect the part of the body with a certain precious stone had their greatest diffusion in the *Hermetica*.[12] The complex cosmology described by the *Hermetica* involves various degrees of creation, principalities, and powers of the universe, including rituals for the summoning of spirits.[13] For it was felt that the greatest practical magic consisted of the perfecting of humankind, the making of man as God.

Could it just be that the survival of hermetic thought and all it encompasses is a hint to the philosophy of the Templars and a hint to the basis of their Christian beliefs? By adopting the Christian saint, Saint Anthony the Hermit, the Templars provided a reminder of the earlier principles outlined by the *Hermetica* (of the Hermit?) and their belief in its proposed source, Hermes Trismegistus.

How far any believer in Hermes, including the Templars, actually carried practical magic is still essentially a matter of speculation. However, it does seem that particular methods of inducing a hermetic revelation, and thus attaining a gnostic state of mind, were advocated in all of the mystery cults. In the historic text *The Secret Sermon on the Mount,* Hermes is represented as teaching his son Tat, who has been unable to achieve the necessary state, to obtain the knowledge he seeks.[14] Hermes advises his son to withdraw into himself, to eliminate the body's senses and to purge himself of the torments of his material surroundings. Having done this, Tat declares that he no longer sees with his eyes but with an inner energy that transports him to ecstasy and to heaven.[15]

Prior to Christ, the only true biblical encounters directly between God and man are when Moses received the Ten Commandments on Mount Sinai, when he received the plan for the Tabernacle from God in the desert, and when Noah received God's instructions to build the Ark. It is said that Moses taught the Jews the knowledge of the God of the Universe and how to recognize his spirit. It was Moses who ordained the times of the setting up of the sanctuary and who interpreted the word of God so that the Ark of the Covenant could be constructed to hold the Ten Commandments.[16]

Significantly, the Old Testament also states that the spirit of God buried Moses in a valley in the land of Moab. Hence, we find the spiritual meaning behind the Masonic lodge being located in the Vale of Jehosophat, implying thereby that the principles of Freemasonry are derived from direct knowledge of, or contact with, God.

Did Moses and Hermes both have the "magical" power to contact the spirit of the Lord? Or did Moses achieve his state of inner peace just by isolating himself in the wilderness for forty days? It is said that both Moses and Hermes were initiated in the secret mysteries of Egypt, where the snake was venerated as knowledge and wisdom. It was Moses and Aaron who were able to make a snake become as rigid as a staff. Another important symbol of the ancient mysteries is the *caduceus,* the intertwining of two snakes and a staff, which represents the art of healing and medicine that Hermes, as well as Christ, possessed.

In a similar manner, did Prince Henry Sinclair achieve the same level of inner consciousness that allowed him to directly communicate with God? Or was it in a state of euphoria that he felt, after spending twenty-eight days at sea, that the Annapolis Valley was a spiritual resting place "fit for a king?"

There is one clue that links Hermes, Moses, Prince Henry Sinclair, and even Christ to the earthen burial grounds at Green Oaks. The link is the serpent. The serpent shape is a well known symbol that many great religions, including those of the Greeks, Egyptians, Celts, Phoenicians, and native North American Indians, were all known to revere through altered landforms. In many cases, it was assumed that the serpent depicted in the landform is in the act of swallowing its own egg. In reality, the egg turned out to be, in most situations, the earthen burial mound of a great chief.

Prince Henry Sinclair, or those before him, may very well have marked the position of a great earthen tomb through the redirecting of a tidal stream to resemble a snake. This means that at the mouth of the "red serpent" lies the stone or egg that the alchemists have so long sought to achieve.

As the inner wheels of the clock turn once again, it is no coincidence that one of the most influential writers on alchemy whose work was rediscovered in the library in Alexandria was Aristotle. According to his writings, the basis of the entire material world was something he called "prime" or "first" matter. This was not, as it may sound, some red sludge from which the world gradually evolved but was considered to be the one unchangeable reality behind the ever-changing material world. Alchemists such as Aristotle believed that to give this matter a physical identity and individual characteristics, various stages of form are required.

The main interest of Aristotle's theory of the four basic elements from the point of view of alchemy is the idea of change or spiritual progression, which is also the main basis of hermetic thought. According to Aristotle, each element can be transformed into another element through the quality they possess in common. In this manner, fire can become air through the action of heat; air can become water through the action of moisture; water can become earth through the action of coldness; and earth can become fire through the action of dryness. It is also possible under this theory for an element to gradually complete the circle of change and go from fire to air, from air to water, from water to earth, and from earth back to fire.

The next stage in Aristotle's theory was that all physical manifestations in the world are composed of all four elements in different proportions and combinations. Therefore, it is the varying amounts of each element in the composition that account for the infinite variety of things in the world. Because it was believed that elements could be transformed into other elements, it was only a small step to the assumption that all substances could be transformed by altering the proportions of the elements that constitute them. Based upon this theory, it is easy to see how alchemists adopted this idea. If, as they believed, both lead and gold consisted of different proportions of the same four elements, then there was little to prevent the one from being transformed into the other.

The number of basic elements (four) is extremely important because it is connected with the simplest solid figure, the cube. Therefore, the number four is of solidity and matter, of the construction of things and especially of the earth itself, a solid body bounded by the four cardinal points.

In numerology, many of the characteristics of the number four derive from a vision of lifelong backbreaking toil on the earth's surface for uncertain and often minimal returns. In other words, individuals who find themselves burdened by manual labor often wish to have the yoke removed. Following this manner of logic, could it be that an oxbow still suppresses whomever or whatever lies beneath it in the watery grave that Prince Henry and his men constructed out of the earth?

Tarot card XXI, the highest numbered card, shows a woman, a bull, a lion, and an eagle, which obviously symbolize the four elements of alchemical theory: water, earth, fire, and air, respectively. A related clue may also lie in one of the carvings that Saunière placed inside the church at Rennes-le-Château. At the base of the carvings is the demonlike Rex Mundi. Just above his head is a pool of water. Two salamanders, otherwise known as fire creatures, flank the pool of water and above, four angels, whose domain is the air, complete the sign of the cross.

Again, the four elements. But it must be remembered that a combination of the four elements also produces a fifth central element. It was, significantly, the Pythagoreans who first believed in a fifth element, the quintessence, or spirit, that was produced as a result of a perfect combination of the four basic elements. They believed that the fifth element was something purer and more subtle than Fire or Air and was something that always seeks to leap upward toward the stars and heaven.

As it all starts to come together, it makes complete sense that Prince Henry Sinclair applied the alchemical squaring of the circle to symbolize the heavenly combination of the four basic elements. This would have symbolized the union of man and woman that was deemed necessary to create the fifth element, the spirit or essence of being, the child or product of God. As Saunière intimated through his construction of the Tour Magdala, this birth would be shown to us by the dwellers of the tower suspended in the air. In this case, the "guardian angels" just happened to be Prince Henry Sinclair, his Knights Templar, and, possibly, the direct descendants of Jesus Christ.

REVELATIONS

By now, the connection between the modern-day Freemasons and the medieval Knights Templar and their ancient beliefs cannot be argued. Still, there remains to be discovered the direct connection that confirms that the very essence of Freemasonry was reflected in the personal quest and explorations of Prince Henry Sinclair in Nova Scotia. The philosophy of Freemasonry should be explored even further for this elusive connection.

The four ancient virtues—Justice, Fortitude, Temperance, and Prudence—are the cardinal elements upon which the basic principles of Freemasonry are based. In fact, the four virtues are referred to as the "furniture of the Lodge."[17] A combination of these four virtues is considered within Masonic tradition to be the guide to the "Blazing Star," which on one level is seen as the star that proclaimed the birth of the Son of God.

Prudence (Wisdom) is the most exalted and is considered within Masonic circles to be the ruler of all the virtues.[18] Reflecting the tarot card of the Hermit, Prudence is seen as the path that leads to every degree of enlightenment. In many ways, Prudence is considered to be the golden apple, the reward, that awaits the one who has observed the cardinal virtues throughout his or her lifetime.

The following of the four virtues, for all intents and purposes, constitutes the spirit of Masonry.[19] By following a path that is lit by the light, or knowledge, of the Blazing Star, the Mason arrives "on the square," which then demonstrates the fifth element—the essence or spirit of God. On a more physical level, by simple deduction (once all the facts are known), one now realizes that the path that Prince Henry and his men "blazed" across the wilderness of Nova Scotia leads to a point where the spirit of God awaits a rebirth or release.

What represented the spirit of God to Prince Henry and his Templars? Suppose Sinclair possessed undeniable proof as to the union of Jesus Christ (spirit) and Mary Magdalene (matter) and their offspring.

Or that the Templars of Scotland possessed the knowledge and wisdom passed down from the Egyptians through Moses as to how to directly contact God. Or, more simply, Prince Henry considered the fruits of the earth to be the spirit of the Goddess.

Another theory that has recently surfaced is that there remains a fifth gospel, which can be attributed directly to one who experienced firsthand the life and teachings of Jesus Christ. Whether this person is Joseph of Arimathea, Mary Magdalene, the disciples Thomas or Peter, or Jesus Christ himself, we may never know. This theory is based, in part, on the notion that the New Testament is a much-edited version of Christ's actions and words. Coupled with the facts presented by the Dead Sea Scrolls, the Gospel of Thomas (a collection of 114 sayings and parables discovered in Egypt in 1945), and a library of first- and second-century materials written by the Gnostics, it certainly appears to be true.

The authors of this theory proclaim that somewhere lies a fifth gospel that tells the authentic words of Jesus and that does not present Christ in the typical archetypal manner. From this, it could then be deduced that Christ portrays more of the spirit of God than actually being the Son of God.

In support of this notion, the Golden Arms of the Antient Grand Lodge of the Masons display the four cardinal elements: Man, the Eagle, the Lion, and the Bull. These elements were derived from Ezekiel's vision as proclaimed in the gospels. These symbols figure prominently in the Jewish mystical tradition, where they are considered archetypes of the inhabitants of the four worlds. Among the Antients' most revered beliefs was the notion that a supreme level of consciousness could be attained through an ascent of the various levels along an east–west axis to where a vision of the Deity was possible.

The notion that visions of the four living creatures can be found within a paradise on earth is enhanced by what we already know concerning ancient sculpting of the natural landscape. Across Britain there are several fine examples of carved hill-figures, primarily of the horse (or dragon), but including figures of man and other symbols.[20] From the earliest times, we seem to have been fascinated with the notion that giant landmarks that faced the sky could bring us closer to the heavens and God.

A curious factor that has more than a passing significance for Prince Henry's Nova Scotia site is the number of British sites where an earthwork is found on the hilltop above a chalk-cut figure. That these hill-forts were, in fact, defensive positions is open to speculation. A possibility that appears not to have been considered is that they were sacred enclosures.[21]

Even the Glooscap legends speak to the tradition of altering the natural landscape. Glooscap was seen as the man-god who knew nothing that was beyond his power. It is said that Glooscap could build mountains out of plains (perhaps stone towers from the rocks taken from the fields) and change the course of rivers and streams if it suited him. It is also said that animals and people could take any size or shape that Glooscap wanted for them.

As Prince Henry Sinclair, Glooscap was realistically a little less ambitious. Perhaps Prince Henry just enhanced the natural features that were already present in the valley at Green Creek. By altering the course of the stream from its original meander and by relying on the surging tides of the Shubenacadie River (the Shamir?) to cut its path, Sinclair was able to depict the plan view of the Eagle, the Lion, and the Bull to the sky above. The positioning of the altered stream also portrays the yoke or ox-bow of the Bull, reflecting the geological terminology of a natural river course.

Prince Henry Sinclair knew that by reflecting the four spiritual figures of God—by completing the square, so to speak—a fifth element, or the essence of God, would be reflected to those who viewed them not only from the skies above, but also from the hilltops overlooking the valley. In essence, the figures that lie in the valley to this day represent a mosaic or fabric of life that can be woven by following the path of the four virtues. In simpler terms, through the knowledge and wisdom that allowed Prince Henry to alter the physical landscape, he was able to achieve a higher level of understanding of nature and its processes. Thereby Glooscap/Sinclair achieved the ultimate balance between man and nature, between good and evil, and between ancient pagan ritual and later Christian practices.[22]

In Kay Hill's book *More Glooscap Stories—Legends of the Wabanaki Indians* there is one particularly intriguing story, "Glooscap and the Seven Wishes."[23] In this legend, Glooscap announced that he was moving his lodge to the north (from New Ross to Green Oaks?)

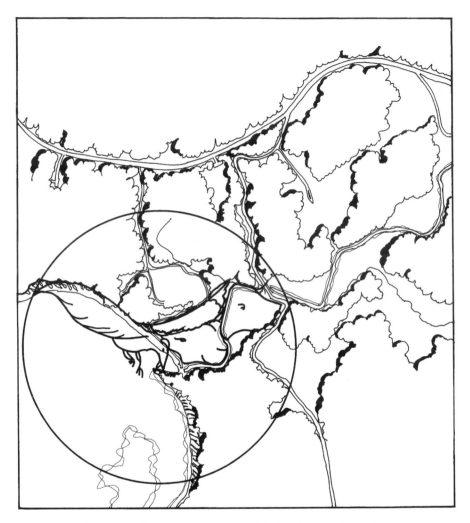

Plan view of the Eagle, Lion, and Bull of the Golden Arms
of the Antient Grand Lodge

Compare this sketch to the air photo of the Green Oaks site and see if you can decipher the figures in the landscape.

and the way to it would be very hard and dangerous. Yet whoever came with him would receive his heart's desire and would be allowed one wish. The story goes that seven of the strongest and bravest young men made the attempt.

Through cooperation and application of the four virtues, the seven young braves finally made it to Glooscap's lodge and imparted their individual wishes to him. The telling of the complete story of the first six wishes is not necessary other than to say that the honest and diligent were able to fulfil their desires, while the unfaithful and vengeful lost their wishes. However, it is the seventh wish that presents an interesting notion that must be examined further.

Once the seventh young man, whose wish was to outlive everyone, had come to the top of a high hill, he then reasoned that ordinary rules did not apply to him. The story tells that he opened the box that contained his wish and at once became a cedar tree, all bent and twisted by the hill's high winds, too knotty for lumber, too hard to burn, safe to outlive everyone but Glooscap.

This must tie back to the story of how Glooscap and Kuhkw buried one of the seven visitors, "who was wonderfully enamored of a fine country." The amazing reality concerning this story is that Prince Henry Sinclair possessed the silvicultural knowledge that allowed him to reason that a knotty, twisted cedar tree would not be of any practical use except to provide a beacon to those who knew what they were searching for. Equally amazing is Sinclair's knowledge that some cedar trees, if fed by the right composition of limestone and other minerals, can live for a period of two thousand to four thousand years or more.

The aspect that the seventh ascended to the top of a high hill following a series of adventures or trials is significant when compared to the basic initiation rites of Freemasonry. Within the rites, there is continual reference to the pathway from the west to the east, which is known as the direction of the "dimension of consciousness."[24] Even as far back as ancient Greece, the process of understanding the psyche or philosophy of awakening was set out in the *Odyssey*, which records a series of dangers that Ulysses was required to overcome before he was able to complete his quest. But in Greek myth there is also the warning of what comes of those who, once they initiate the quest, fall victim to the dangers along the way.

In the legend of Prometheus, Hermes asks Prometheus to withdraw his threat to Zeus, but the demand is refused. Upon the declaration of Zeus, Hermes splits a rock with lightning, entombs Prometheus in its midst, and sends an eagle to feast all day long upon Prometheus's liver.[25] It is said that Prometheus will have no release until a god is found who will take his pains upon himself and of his own free will descend into the dark Tartarus (Hades). The story ends with Prometheus and the daughters of King Oceanus sinking from view into the mire.[26]

This theme of the rescue from water or mire within a garden or fertile valley can also be found throughout the pages of the Old Testament. There is the story of Jonah, the prophet who was swallowed alive by a giant fish or whale and three days later regurgitated onto dry land so that he could preach the Word of God to the citizens of Nineveh. Even more familiar is the story of Noah, whose sons, after the floodwaters receded, heard God's command and went forth and multiplied.

By far the most famous Old Testament figure to be saved from water was Moses, who later went on to lead the Jews into the Promised Land—though it was Jesus Christ, through his own baptism and sacrifice, who allowed the salvation of all the people on earth.[27] Is it possible that the Templars wished to reenact the casting of the child into the water until such time that the entire world was prepared for confirmation of Christ's baptism and sacrifice?

Leonardo da Vinci painted many versions of the Madonna and Child. In one of his most popular versions, *The Virgin of the Rocks* (1482–83), twin children are shown next to a pool or stream. In his later painting (c. 1505–07) of *The Virgin and Child with Saint Anne and Saint John the Baptist,* once again twin children are shown with the virgin, whose feet rest in a shallow pool of water. A slightly different twist is found in Leonardo's 1508–10 *The Virgin and Child and Saint Anne.* Although the three figures are shown with their feet in water, a fourth figure representing a "Lamb of God" is also shown being plucked from the watery depths. Could this be another of Leonardo's references to the Christ-child, the Lambspring of God, needing to be rescued from the watery grave?

A valley with a river running through it and walled by rocky cliffs appears in most of Leonardo's landscape settings, including the *Mona Lisa.* In many ways, this generic scene can be likened to the walled garden that enclosed the outer court surrounding the tabernacle or temple or the walls of the Garden of Eden. In many other ways, it can represent the border that holds the mosaic together or the frill that outlines the Mason's lambskin apron.

Today the apron's design indicates the Mason's rank within the lodge, but the original aprons contained more of the symbols that were meant to lead one to the inner Holy Spirit. Symbols such as the skull and crossbones, mosaic, square and compass, sun and moon, the third eye, and two pillars were most prevalent. On occasion, a third broken pillar was also illustrated.

The third broken pillar was meant to symbolize the loss of innocence by the Blessed Virgin and the condition of humankind after the expulsion from the Garden of Eden. Similarly, it can relate to the broken hearts of the exiled Benjamites and, for that matter, the vanquished Acadians. In Masonic tradition, hope of relief from a loss of this nature is promised by the sprig of acacia and by the workings of time. Again, we are confronted with the compelling concept of establishing a new beginning.

The recovery or rebuilding of a New Jerusalem or Temple of Solomon is as much an ideal as it was a reality. Blake's poem "Jerusalem" speaks of a time when there is freedom for everyone tempered by responsibility and compassion. In *The New Atlantis*, Francis Bacon spoke of "Solomon's house . . . whereby concealed treasures which now seem utterly lost to mankind shall be confined to so universal a piety."[28]

In alchemy, the Heavenly City or New Jerusalem described in Revelations represented the sparkling stone or holy city; the heavenly marriage (of the Lamb); the mysteries of paternal incarnation; the conquest of death; the water of life and its fountain; the tree of life and its fruits; and the God of the end and the beginning—all rolled into one. It also became the philosophers' rose garden through which flowed the hermetic river to its spring.

To Prince Henry Sinclair, his Garden of Eden was a much simpler one that supplied his needs abundantly: ample water and food, good companionship, and, the exhilaration created by the knowledge that its secret was secure. It would remain a secret known only to those within the inner circle, masked in overwhelming layers of geometric manipulation, hermetic thought, ancient mysteries, tradition, folklore, myth and legend, biblical reference, and pagan ritual.[29]

12

On a Golden Wing

As the end of this book grows near, at least one thing has been unveiled. Amidst the mystique surrounding the Order of the Temple, numerous traditions, echoes, and images became fused. For instance, the Grail knights surely merged with many historical and/or legendary antecedents, including the Arthurian Knights of the Round Table. But it is just as evident that the Templars were only too eager to reinforce their image as adepts, wizards, and sorcerers, as alchemists, and as sages of the ancient and sacred mysteries. Hence, many of the clues that at first appear to have no meaning whatsoever become part of a larger understanding of the basis for the Order's mystical and esoteric activity.

Yet when all of the evidence is summarized and analyzed, it seems to suggest quite strongly that the Templars were far from embracing paganism, demonology, and black magic. In actuality, the Templars did nothing worse than promote a philosophy of wisdom and truth that reconciled ancient teachings with a belief in the Supreme Being and the spirit of God, as exemplified by Jesus Christ.

This philosophy even took on a special kind of reverence for the Virgin Mary and all mothers, for their ability to bear children; all the angels and saints, who were viewed as representatives of the Divine on earth; and the lowly priest and hermit, who through observation of the four virtues reflected the spirit or essence of God in everyday life. What the Templars were looking for was a way to strip away all the trappings of the Church and "to get to the heart of the problem." The Templars were looking to interpret the divine Logos (Word) for themselves. In alchemical terms, the Templars were looking to discover the true philosopher's stone.

Rather figuratively, the idea that the Order of the Temple adopted countless beliefs and modified them to suit their own purposes has been likened to the relationship that exists between a dog and a flea, or, on a more esoteric level, between the oak and mistletoe. In essence, the belief that the life of the oak was in the mistletoe was probably first suggested by the fact that in winter the mistletoe growing on the oak remains green, while the oak itself is leafless. Ancient legend tells that the mistletoe was not allowed to touch the ground because its healing power would be lost. Therefore, in some circles it became what is still known as the "golden bough." Indeed, many are still of the opinion that the Golden Bough was the mistletoe because at times mistletoe appears to be blazing with reflected winter light. Of course, the yellow color of a withered mistletoe bough has a natural similarity to yellow gold.

In *The Golden Bough,* author James Frazer concluded that the priest of the Arician grove, the King of the Wood, personified the tree on which grew the golden bough.[1] Therefore, if that tree was an oak, the King of the Wood that became a popular Old European symbol, it may well have been a personification of the Oak spirit.

Among the ancient Celts, Germans, Greeks, and Romans, it was thought that whoever cut a bough would suddenly die or lose the use of one of his own limbs. According to Frazer, in the ancient sanctuary of Aesculapius in Greece the cutting of any limb or tree was even punishable by fine or death.[2] This may explain the references to the severing of the hand in many of Poussin's paintings. On another level, Christ and his sacrifice has also been compared to the cutting of the limb of a tree or of a vine (remember the severed limb of the oak on Oak Island).

The development of the concept of a human sacrifice being required to ensure a successful rebirth or regeneration may well have developed from the ancient myth of the worship of Diana of the Wood. This worship occurred at the woodland lake of Nemi, "Diana's Mirror," as it was called. The ritual was instituted by Orestes, who, after killing the Tauric king Thoas, fled with his sister to Italy, bringing with him the image of the Tauric Diana hidden in a bundle of sticks. After Orestes' death his bones were transported from Aricia to Rome and buried in front of the temple of Saturn on the Capitoline slope, beside the temple of Concord.[3]

Classical readers will be familiar with the bloody ritual that legend attributes to the Tauric Diana. Tradition says that every stranger who landed on the shore was sacrificed upon her altar. But the rite assumed a milder form once transported to Italy. Here, within the inner sanctuary at Nemi, legend has it that a slave, if he dared, could break off a bough of a sacred tree. If successful in the attempt, the slave was then entitled to fight the priest of the sanctuary in single combat, and if he slew the priest he reigned in his place with the title of King of the Wood (Rex Nemorensis).[4]

The Tauric Diana's successor, the Roman Diana, was generally considered to be a goddess of fertility similar to Artemis and was evoked by women in childbirth. As such, like her Greek counterpart she needed a male partner. According to Roman legend, that partner was Virbius. In his character as the founder of the sacred grove at Nemi, Virbius was clearly the mythical predecessor or archetype of the line of priests who served Diana under the title of Kings of the Wood. Like Virbius, the first King of Nemi, they were also sacrificed.

It is natural, therefore, to conclude that the King of the Wood related to the Goddess in the same manner in which Virbius related to Diana. In short, the mortal King of the Wood would figuratively take Diana of the Wood as his queen. Over time, the priest of the sanctuary came to not only worship the sacred tree as his goddess but to embrace it as his "wife."

This union of a royal title with priestly duties was common in both ancient Italy and Greece and became known as the Divine Right.[5] Over time, the sacrificial kings came to be revered not merely as priests, but as intercessors between humankind and God. Thus, the ancient kings were often expected to provide rain and sunshine during the appropriate season and to make the crops and trees grow.

Similarly, there are several common points between the northern European personages such as the May King, the Grass King, the Jack-in-the-Green, the King of the Wood, and other folktale kings. The northern representatives of the tree spirit, like the King of Nemi, die a violent death and are brought back to life time and again.

This raising of the spirit, or spirits, is believed to have as one of its origins various esoteric documents attributed to King Solomon. The first, the *Testament of Solomon,* is supposedly Solomon's own story of his acquisition of magical powers. The second, the *Key of Solomon,* is supposedly the original and most celebrated "book of magic," again written by Solomon himself.

According to occult tradition, the engraving on the magical ring of Solomon was a pentacle. It was Solomon's ring, therefore, that allowed him to control the demon-god Asmodeus, and to make him build the original temple. Although there is no mention of the magic circle in the *Testament of Solomon,* it was suggested that the ring itself was symbolic of the circle. Accordingly, in magic it is the circle that protects the magician during the ceremony. Hence, it is to the northeast of the circle that the magician draws a triangle to confine any spirit that he might evoke (remember the triangle that was drawn to the northeast of Prince Henry Sinclair's magic circle).

Exploring this background behind Solomon's reputed magic, it now seems even more logical that the geometric progression across Nova Scotia was developed along the lines of an ancient quest that allowed only the truly initiated to find their way from Oak Island to Green Oaks and that is based on the figures or symbols represented by *The Little Keys of Solomon.* Only through the proper application of the Keys could the magician, alchemist, or hero hope to achieve the necessary unity and harmony to not only defeat the demons of one's own unconsciousness but to raise the spirit of the Almighty.[6]

It now also appears that Prince Henry, in all his wisdom, felt that it was best to hide the holy treasure until such time as it could be returned to its rightful owner and place. Remember that the Rennes Parchments tell that: "This treasure belongs to Dagobert II King and to Sion and he is there dead."

But Dagobert II is dead. The message might then be interpreted to mean that the treasure was hidden by the inner circle of the Knights Templar until such time that it may once again be returned to Jerusalem (Sion) and the Temple of Solomon.[7]

According to Baigent, Leigh, and Lincoln, the modern-day Priory of Sion claims to already be in possession of the "Treasure of Jerusalem" and has vowed to return it to its rightful place when the time is right. But doesn't it make sense that, if the hiding place of the treasure remained undiscovered for over six hundred years, there is no better place to store the treasure than to "leave it be?"

If Sinclair/Glooscap actually established a "castle" or settlement at

Green Oaks, then there must at least be some carved stones remaining from its construction. In fact, there is! Recovered from a position atop of the "bear's skull" is a stone that is 18 inches by 8 inches and 5 inches high that remarkably looks like a "cap" stone. The most remarkable aspect is that the capstone has been carved to a peak with ends that

Carved stone recovered from a position above the waterfall at
Green Oaks, Nova Scotia
Note the various angles of the carved stone and the tripod incised into both sides of the stone. Photographs by William F. Mann.

reflect 45 and 30–60 degree angles, with both of its longer sides reflecting an exact 45-degree angle.

The biggest clue, however, is the carved symbol of a tripod that is quite evident on both sides of the capstone.[8] The tripod was a symbol first associated with the Egyptians, then Artemis and her maidens, then Apollo, and then the Masons. It is also a symbol representative of Christ and of man. Yet, this is not all. A capstone with similar features is depicted in the foreground of Poussin's *The Triumph of David.*

The Triumph of David, Nicolas Poussin, circa 1632–33
Note the angled stone found in the lower left-hand corner of the painting and how the angles reflect those of the carved stone found by the author among the stone ruins at Green Oaks. By permission of the Trustees of Dulwich Picture Gallery.

The concept of achieving a higher level over the material world even following death corresponds to the Templar belief that time and motion can be applied for one's own benefit. The relative theory of synchronicity suggests that noncausal events are not mere accidents or chance but are a significant part of reality that may provide the clue to some of the ultimate mysteries of life. Maybe this explains why the Templars under Prince Henry Sinclair believed that all was not lost when they had to suddenly bury their holy treasure and return to a certain death in Scotland. Why? They believed that the real truth about such things would become known at the proper time.

Robert Graves, in *The White Goddess,* claimed that at one time there was a maternal, Goddess-oriented society where both sexes had their proper status, and the society had a basic balance and rightness.[9] According to Graves, this was changed by the advent of a patriarchal, male-dominated age of gods. The point being made is that both the Grail romances and Arthurian legends speak to an earlier period of sexual equality that was lost.

This lost society was referred to as the Golden Age. It is not the Elizabethan Golden Age, but a more prophetic time during the mythological Arthurian era when the king stood for everything that is right. The philosophy behind this notion of utopia also included the idea of a long-lost glory and promise of a fresh start. Other legends express the same dream, but the Arthurian Golden Age has one added dimension (a fourth dimension?). Like the story of Christ, the king is gone, but not gone forever. The Arthurian legends tell that Arthur is suspended in his cave on the magical island of Avalon, and one day will return with his queen at his side.[10]

Once again, herein lies the notion of a seed being planted and awaiting the time when the plant bursts forth from the ground. For a forester such as Prince Henry Sinclair, the Celtic myth of a banished god sleeping in a cave on a western island must have added a spiritual meaning to every acorn that his followers planted. On the other hand, he too must have felt the spiritual inspiration gained from the knowledge that he was instrumental in perpetuating the wisdom of the Holy Grail until the return of the Golden Age.

In reality, Prince Henry Sinclair was only one of many knight/guardians of the Holy Grail and the Divine Right. If one considers the Grail to be the royal Merovingian line and direct descendants of Jesus Christ, then the Merovingian princesses and matriarchs were the ones directly responsible for the perpetuation of the family tree. Like the Celtic princesses before them, the Merovingian princesses were once venerated as the Ladies in White, the human goddesses who could bring forth life. They, including Marie de Blanchefort, were the true keepers of the "seed" of the Golden Bough.

MERIDIANS

Although the ultimate truth may never be revealed, over the centuries many writers, artists, and philosophers perpetuated the basic underlying facts that relate to the larger story of where the Grail was hidden and why. Some of the more notable names include Arthur Conan Doyle, Jules Verne, Francis Bacon, J. R. R. Tolkien, C. S. Lewis, George MacDonald, Charles Williams, and even Hans Christian Andersen. Still, there is no other figure as controversial and enigmatic as Francis Bacon, who may well have had the greatest inkling as to where the Holy Grail lies.[11]

The most remarkable suggestion made about Bacon, other than the "Bacon-wrote-Shakespeare" theory, is that he was the illegitimate child of Queen Elizabeth. Regardless, or partly because of this story, as Francis grew up he was immersed in psychic phenomena as well as in more orthodox philosophy and science. In his treatise *The Advancement of Learning*, Bacon suggested that his idea of knowledge, or wisdom, is like some kind of precious liquid—a wine or an elixir—all of which ties in with many of the mysterious references to wine and grapes made by Poussin, a contemporary of Bacon.[12]

Francis Bacon may well have resurrected the dormant underground remains of the Templars or the Priory of Sion to satisfy a longing for the divine right that he believed was his. But at least one thing is known for certain. Aside from Bacon's literary and political manipulations, there is overwhelming evidence that he was part of a secret society, whether the Rosicrucians or another, that was fascinated by codes and ciphers and that initiated the use of watermarks on paper.[13] When one considers that a majority of the watermarks suggest the Holy Grail is hidden beneath a pool of water, Bacon's involvement becomes even more significant.[14] Could it be that Bacon's spiritual New Atlantis was in fact Sinclair's New Jerusalem?[15]

A contemporary of Francis Bacon, Samuel de Champlain, was certainly familiar with the shores of Nova Scotia.[16] Champlain, of course, is known for his explorations throughout "New France" and

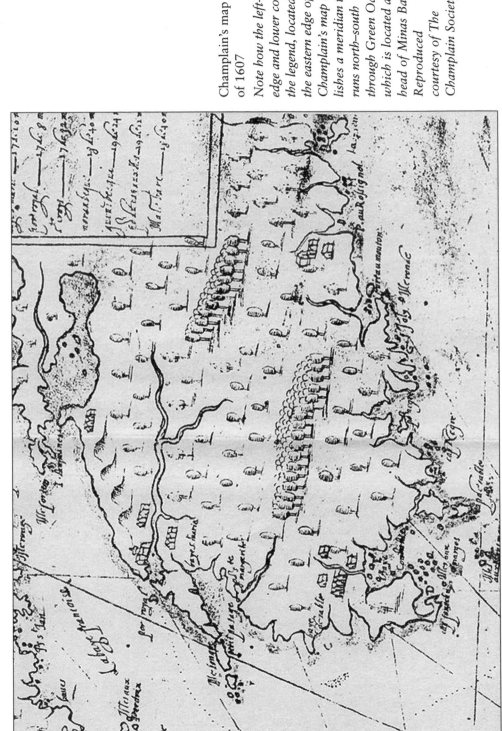

Champlain's map of 1607

Note how the left-hand edge and lower corner of the legend, located along the eastern edge of Champlain's map estab-lishes a meridian that runs north–south through Green Oaks, which is located at the head of Minas Basin. Reproduced courtesy of The Champlain Society.

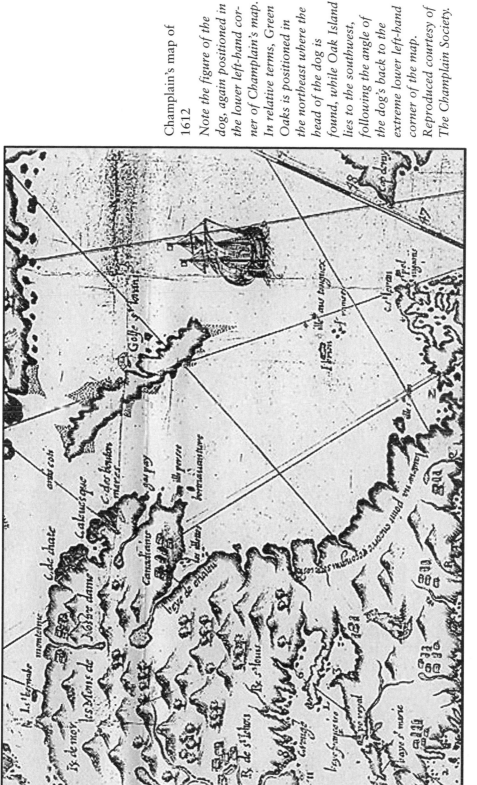

Champlain's map of
1612

*Note the figure of the
dog, again positioned in
the lower left-hand cor-
ner of Champlain's map.
In relative terms, Green
Oaks is positioned in
the northeast where the
head of the dog is
found, while Oak Island
lies to the southwest,
following the angle of
the dog's back to the
extreme lower left-hand
corner of the map.
Reproduced courtesy of
The Champlain Society.*

"Acadia." Champlain first came to Acadia in 1604 as a member of the de Monts expedition; it was from 1604 to 1632, during his early explorations, that he produced a number of curious maps that hint at a reluctance to disclose certain information that concerned very strategic landfalls or harbors such as Oak Island and Mahone Bay, Minas Basin and Cape d'Or, and the Shubenacadie River.[17]

In particular, neither his map of 1607 nor of 1612 shows Mahone Bay.[18] The map of 1607 starts at the small community of La Have located on the South Shore of Nova Scotia, to the west of Mahone Bay. By simply making his map begin immediately west of Mahone Bay, Champlain easily disguised any knowledge of those lands that lay to the east, including the headland of Minas Basin.[19]

Maybe it is not specifically what Champlain failed to include that is the clue but exactly where he chose to show the eastern boundary of his map. Conveniently, the north–south meridian dictated by the border of the map's legend falls exactly in line with the headland of Minas Basin. Was this one of many sly references hinting at a special "roseline" established by the ancients to demarcate secret settlements around the world? In this case, was the refuge situated at the headland or source of Minas Basin?

In the opposite manner, the map of 1612 shows all of Nova Scotia. Most curiously, in this map a dog is shown resting along the very same meridian as depicted in the 1607 map. Its face and head are positioned roughly where Green Oaks lies and by following the angle of its back (66.6 degrees?) in a southwesterly direction one is directed toward Mahone Bay and Oak Island. At this point, one has the tendency to be reminded of the "tail that wags the dog."

In ancient Egypt, the dog was seen as one of the four figures that prepares the body of the dead for its trip to the afterlife or Otherworld. Remember that the Lower World of Egypt was located in the north, at the mouth of the Nile. Likewise, the head of Champlain's dog is located to the north and at the mouth of Green Creek.

One may also be reminded that the word dog has remained the same and has kept relatively the same meaning through centuries of time and change. The use of the slang term "dog" to denote an old, ugly, or unclean woman has also existed for centuries. Therefore, by relating the head of the dog to the headland of Minas Basin, then maybe, just maybe, the watermarks of Francis Bacon and the secret societies of Champlain's time shed a little light on their objective.

There is the remaining question as to whether Champlain's real objective was to recover the holy treasure, or to purposely dissuade people from investigating both the Oak Island and Minas Basin areas. Was Champlain suggesting that he was aware of where the mysterious Land of the Dead lay and that a female who was considered less than clean in the Church's eye lay there? Or was he suggesting that in many Greek myths Artemis was a deity of the Lower World akin to Hecate, the guardian of the doors to the Land of the Dead, or Persephone, Mistress of the Dead.

If Samuel de Champlain was in fact an "agent" for the Holy Bloodline, it may be that he actually rediscovered the lost city of Norumbega. It seems from the available clues that Champlain possessed the hidden ability to establish longitudinal meridians, as did Prince Henry before him. It also appears that Champlain had at the very least an inkling as to where the lost habitation of Prince Henry Sinclair was located.

As touched upon earlier, if the Templars and those before them possessed the ability to establish longitudinal meridians long before it became standard practice, then they could have completed a known circuit of the world. A hint of this ancient knowledge can actually be found in the Roman story of *Pennant's Voyage to the Hebrides:*

> In the plain of Tormore, in the isle of Arran, are the remains of four circles. By the number of the circles, and by their sequestered situation, this seems to have been sacred ground. These circles were formed for religious purposes: Boetius relates, that Mainus, son of Fergus I, a restorer and cultivator of religion, after the Egyptian manner, (as he calls it) instituted several new and solemn ceremonies; and caused great stones to be placed in form of a circle: the largest was situated towards the south, and served as an altar for the sacrifices to the immortal gods. Boetius is right in part of his account: the object of worship was the sun; and what confirms this, is the situation of the altar, pointed towards that luminary in his meridian glory.[20]

What this suggests is that even during civilized Roman times, ancient stone circles and menhirs were used to track the sun's movements to establish longitudinal meridians. Indeed, if the four circles referred to were actually located on the "isle" of Nova Scotia, then all that needs to be established is that some ancient body had the ability to time the same eclipse in both the Old and New World.

If a typical diagram for solar eclipses in the Northern Hemisphere is examined, an interesting relationship becomes apparent. The path of the total eclipse charts a path across eastern North America that follows Satan's Axis. Could the ancients have established longitudinal meridians throughout the world by following the known paths of the eclipses of the sun? This is one notion that can be supported by the ancient wisdom of following the "lighted" path. It may, as well, be the basis for the medieval tradition of gathering around the Maypole.

There are some very strange places and objects on the Paris Meridian that support the notion that the ancients knew of such strategic lines on the world's surface. Officially, the Paris Meridian was established in 1666 (notice the number 666) following the building of an observatory that was designed by Claude Perrault, the elder brother of the more widely known Charles Perrault, the writer.[21]

Just as fitting, the Paris Meridian stops within the southern border of France at the village of Py. By following it from pole to pole there are bound to be countless other examples of symbolism relating to geometry or moral allegory. But by stopping at the suggestion of a relationship between a north–south axis and the circumference of a circle and its diameter, the notion that Green Oaks may be the location of the four circles on the plain of Tormore becomes even more tangible.

It especially becomes clear when the air photo of the area unveils the intertwining of four underlying circles on top of the hill at Green Oaks. The diameter of each of these four circles is exactly 144 feet (the square of 12 feet by 12 feet) and some very large boulders remain, albeit on their sides, in the positions of several astronomical alignments.

Amazingly, the north–south alignment defined by the circles runs through the eyes of the symbolic bear, serpent, and bull. Three eyes. Bull's-eye! At the eye of the oxbow lie the muddy pool and cave that a cascading waterfall or veil of water has hidden for over six hundred years.

One last side note pertaining to the mysterious explorations of Champlain in Nova Scotia concerns Champlain's long-term friend and business associate, the Sieur de Monts, who also had Templar and

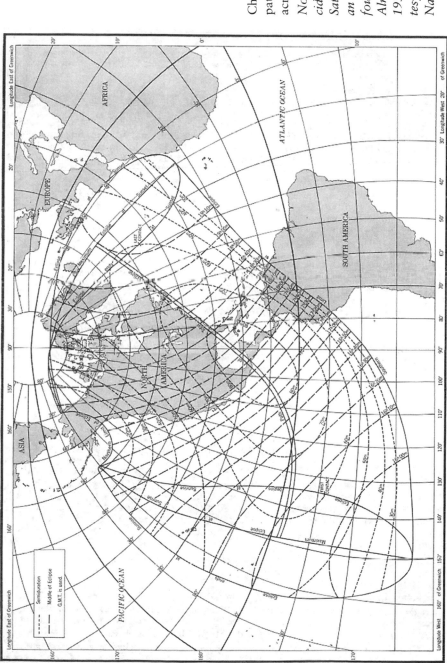

Chart showing typical path of a solar eclipse across North America *Note how the path coincides with the so-called Satan's Axis. Based on an original drawing found in the Nautical Almanac for the year 1938. Reproduced courtesy of the United States Naval Observatory.*

Knights of Malta connections. After his explorations in the New World, de Monts retired to the castle of Ardennes, which just happens to be one area that continues to this day the age-old tradition of the Corn-spirit conceived as a dog or wolf.

THE CROWN

Corn would certainly have been one of the main staples of the Mi'kmaq who followed Glooscap to his secret lodge at Green Oaks, which, like the Ardennes, lies in the northeast. Corn is depicted in great detail within Rosslyn Chapel. It may also just be beyond coincidence that Glooscap was said to possess a dog and a wolf, named Night and Day respectively.

Many other animals whose forms the Corn-spirit was said to take are the hare, fox, goose, goat, ox, and pig. All of these animals play major parts in the legends of Glooscap among the Mi'kmaq. The killing of the Corn-spirit also finds as its prototypes the Greek myths concerning Demeter and the death and resurrection of her daughter Persephone.

It is this incident that, when coupled with the nature of the Goddess as a deity of vegetation, links the myths of the Corn-spirit or Corn Mother and Harvest Maiden with the mystery cults of Osiris, Dionysus, and Mithras. This in turn brings us back to the connection between the Templars and the Holy Grail and the ideas and beliefs of the Kabbalah.[22]

Kabbalistic initiation entails a series of rituals or structured sequence of experiences that lead the practitioner to ever more radical modifications of consciousness and recognition, very similar to the stated purpose of Masonic ritual.[23] Among these "stages," one of the most important is known as Tiferet. During the Tiferet ritual, the initiate passes beyond the world of form into a formless world that, symbolically speaking, consists of a kind of sacrificial "death" and "rebirth," or resurrection. In Christian adaptations of the Kabbalah, Tiferet would have been associated with Jesus Christ and the resurrection of his body.

For medieval Kabbalists, the initiation into Tiferet was similar to the journey expressed within the Major Arcana sequence of the tarot cards, and it was associated with certain specific symbols that included a hermit or guide or wise old man, a majestic king, a child, and a sacrificed god. Over time, and more specifically during the Renaissance, other

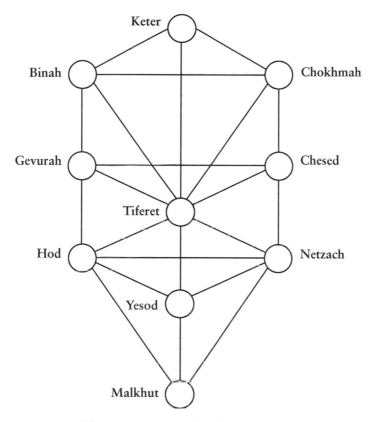

The twenty-two paths of the Tiferet

Note how the number 22 is made up of the esoteric number 11, which signifies a mirror reflection of one's self, and the number 1, which represents Keter, the Crown.

symbols were added as well, including a truncated pyramid, a cube, and a rose cross.

The relation of these symbols to the Grail romances and Arthurian legends is quite apparent. In every Grail story there is a wise old hermit who acts as a spiritual guide. In Wolfram's poem, the Grail as a "stone" obviously corresponds to the cube. In *Perlesvaus,* the various manifestations of the Grail and Grail quest correspond almost precisely to the symbols of Tiferet.[24]

The ten *sefirot* of the kabbalist system have come to represent the construction of the universe and of humankind, both of which are in the image of God. The twenty-two paths connecting the ten sefirot to each other are, in contrast, seen as the forces behind man and the universe. The ten sefirot, each of which has its own name, are linked to the numbers 1 to 10, and the twenty-two paths are linked to the twenty-two letters of the Hebrew alphabet. Therefore, the circles and lines respectively in the Tree of Life usually depict the sefirot and paths. This Tree embraces and classifies everything in the universe, which is to be revealed by God.

This idea of the Tree of Life has a great deal in common with the widely held belief in the construction of the universe that existed from classical times up to the sixteenth century. This belief stated that the universe was made up of nine concentric spheres. God was identified as the outer sphere, the stars made up the second sphere, and each of the planets then known was allotted one of the next seven spheres. Of these, the moon was the innermost sphere, which suggests that the moon occupied a rather more important symbolic position than it does today. Most importantly to the perceived relationship of the moon's effect on the earth, the inner circle also contained the earth, which was not considered a separate sphere. Therefore, the Cathar belief in dualism was supported by the science of its day.

Kabbalists were also influenced by Pythagorean theories based on the numbers 1 to 10. Thus, in order to make the planetary spheres correspond with the ten sefiroth and the first ten numbers, they increased the spheres in this scheme to ten, making the earth a sphere on its own to correspond with Malkhut on the Tree of Life. The seven sefirot above Malkhut correspond with the seven planets; Chokmah, or Divine Wisdom, with the sphere of the stars or zodiac; and Keter, the Crown, with God.

Keter, the Crown, is known as the first emanation and corresponds with the number 1. Hence, the theory is that the soul that reaches this sefirot achieves union with God. As might be expected, this plane is said to be guarded by the four creatures described in the first chapter of Ezekiel: "and every one had four faces, and every one had four wings." Significantly, its symbols are the Point, which stands for 1, and the Crown.

If one follows this logic, then a mixture of Cathar dualism and kabbalistic tradition tells us that the basis of life or the start of the pathway of the soul to understanding the spirit of God is the Crown and the

Point. Hermetic thought carried this tradition further and declared that the aura of light surrounding Christ, the halo, was the Crown. Therefore, as Freemasonry and kabbalistic principles suggest, the message is now clear: Christ will be revealed in Arcadia through the four visions of Ezekiel, thus providing the cornerstone for the establishment of a New Jerusalem.

13

A Fool's Discovery

The purpose of this book is primarily to entertain. However, I believe that within the last twelve chapters enough evidence was presented to convince even those who only believe in what can be seen to think beyond those lines. Did Jesus Christ survive his crucifixion? Was a Holy Bloodline created through the partnering of Jesus and Mary Magdalene?

These concepts challenge some of the basic tenets of Christianity. The absolute solution to either question may never be achieved, even if overwhelming physical evidence is uncovered. What is certain is that the Templars and the Merovingians before them repeatedly conspired to regain their "rightful" place as guardians of the mysteries of Christ through a number of interrelated but essentially distinct strategies.

Of the many strategies, perhaps the program that was most intended to erode the spiritual foundations of both the crowns of Europe and the Church of Rome was the creation of the "spirit" of the Holy Grail. Here was a tradition that subsequently found expression in the Rosicrucian manifestos and similar practices, in certain rites of Freemasonry, in the hermetic and esoteric rituals of the eighteenth and nineteenth centuries, and in the symbols of Arcadia and the underground stream.

For centuries a doctrine of archetypal chivalry based upon one of the most resilient of archetypal symbols—that of the Lost King—was promoted. Like King Arthur, the Lost King was seen as the mystical monarch who does not quite die but retires into some other dimension until such time as he rises again.[1]

Certainly, the tradition of Dagobert II, the last effective Merovingian king, conforms to the same archetypal pattern in such a manner that his image becomes fused with that of Jesus Christ himself. And once this connection was established, the notion that Dagobert was a literal and historical blood descendant of Jesus and Mary Magdalene became that much easier to propagate.[2] This also means that the "he" who is referred to within the Rennes Parchments is most likely Christ himself. And, like the forever-lingering story of Jesus Christ, it is by the same technique of psychological association that the mystery attached to Rennes-le-Château was and still is promoted.

Coincidentally, the Rennes Parchments were discovered at a time when the power of the Church of Rome was waning and a new wave of esoteric thought was once again spreading throughout Europe. Was this just another noncausal or historical circumstance? It is unlikely. It now seems that some secret society wanted to recreate an air of mystery surrounding Rennes-le-Château.

From repeated references to the four gospels and other biblical allegory found within the *Dossiers secrets,* it appears that someone was trying to reconcile pagan and Christian ritual for the time when the truth of the Holy Bloodline would be exposed.[3]

The gospels of Mark, Luke, and Matthew are similar enough to suggest that they derived from a single source. The common wisdom is that these three gospels were derived from either an oral tradition or some other document subsequently lost.[4] Yet, this common bond distinguishes them from the Gospel of John, which suggests significantly different origins.[5]

Nothing is really known about the author of the fourth gospel. The fact that it was attributed to a man called John is generally accepted as later tradition. What is known, or at least suspected, is that the fourth gospel is the latest of those in the New Testament and was composed around A.D. 100 in the vicinity of the Greek city of Ephesus (remember that Ephesus was the place of many mystery rituals).[6]

It is the Gospel of John that may relate to Poussin's shepherdess and the notion that she appears to be standing in water, as though she were the anointed one. Once again this is only speculation, but the point remains that both John's gospel and the shepherdess have something to hide. Could it be that the Templars possessed the original unedited version of John's gospel, which confessed in far greater detail to the life and times of Jesus Christ? Could it be that the fourth gospel is an edited text of an earlier version that can be attributed to Mary Magdalene herself or to Joseph of Arimathea, who was another witness to Christ's wisdom? Could it be that, by combining the events of the fourth gospel and the secret element hidden by the shepherdess, the truth is that the Magdalene was venerated on a higher level by the inner circle?

Whatever the answer, now is the time to synthesize and interpret the wealth of information and clues that were uncovered. As Sir Arthur Conan Doyle's character Sherlock Holmes discovered on numerous occasions, no point of departure should ever be discarded until such time that all of the facts have been collected and analyzed.

Francis Bacon, in his *Wisdom of the Ancients,* warned against this very same idea: "the commodity of wit and discourse that is able to apply things well, yet so as was never meant by the first authors."[7] In other words, many people look to provide meaning when no meaning ever existed. Nevertheless, Bacon himself, as a self-described "latter-day symbolist of pagan mysteries," deduced from the myths an extraordinary abundance of "concealed instruction and allegory," since "parable has ever been a kind of ark, in which the most precious portions of the sciences were deposited."[8]

Following the philosophy of Sir Francis Bacon, let us reexamine *The Legend of the Shubenacadie* for hidden messages and symbolism that may relate to the mystery of Prince Henry Sinclair and the Holy Grail.

The Legend of the Shubenacadie [River] is clearly a metaphorical allegory based on the Greek and Roman myths of Artemis and Orion, Medea and Eros, Diana and Aktaeon, and possibly others. The story line is essentially a classic tragedy where the younger Acadie loves an older, wiser Shuben. As in any good tragedy, she eventually breaks his heart. Or, in this case, she pierces his heart with a well-aimed arrow because she mistook him for a rare snow-white deer.

Although Acadie was the hero of the legend (in Anglo-Saxon *Heorot* means "stag" while its derivation in English is "hart"), he failed to complete his quest because he was foolish enough to succumb to the temptations of the goddess.[9] What results is that Acadie was buried in a watery grave and Shuben, who also died brokenhearted, was entombed where the weeping willow grows.

In reality, the location of these tombs must be relatively close to a stream, pool, or river, because willows only grow where there is abundant groundwater. In fact, there is a species of willow known as the "golden weeping" willow, which can be likened to the Golden Bough whose tip, it is said, points to buried treasure or graves.

Yet there is a rather more interesting stanza within the poem that relates the legend directly to Prince Henry. It reads:

> *He thought (alas his thought was vain)*
> *To meet with Hooran in the dale,*
> *Hooran was chief of Avon's plain*
> *And milder than the summer's gale.*

From all of the background evidence that was presented, this must certainly refer to Prince Henry as chief of the Avalon Plains or Elysian Fields. It may also refer to the Templars' penchant for vanity. The last stanza also tells of the exact location of the graves:

> *For them still flows in stream of tears*
> *The troubled waters that you see,*
> *Their memory still the river bears,*
> *The river Shubenacadie.*

Could this not suggest that, where the two bodies lay, a waterfall perpetually cascades in their memory in a turbulent tidal rip?

In a different manner, the images depicted by the tarot cards also relate to the images portrayed within *The Legend of the Shubenacadie*. The conflict between the older woman and younger man is found in the tarot card of the Lovers. The entombment of Shuben "amid a baleful hemlock bower" can be likened to the tarot card of the Hanged Man. The frolicking of Acadie in the copsewood dell (a small wooded valley), "where foxes frisk with wanton glee," may be likened to the dancing children depicted on the tarot card of the Sun.

Did Prince Henry, in his assumed guise as Glooscap, deliberately teach this allegorical poem to the Mi'kmaq so that its hidden truth could be preserved, given that the Mi'kmaq had no written language? Plato, similarly, was one of the first to use allegory so that his myths could be interpreted on many levels. Hellenistic Platonists and Stoics also used allegory as a weapon for the preservation of traditional authority, and Jews and Christians have always declared that the Old Testament contains hidden meanings as well as its surface truth. Therefore, it is quite possible that the legend holds many more levels of truth than were interpreted thus far.

This is also a good time to reexamine the military effigy of the knight found on the rock ledge outside of the small village of Westford.

Of the drawing produced by Frank Glynn (see page 51), the first thing that is immediately striking is the square hinge adjacent the knight's right eye. But the fourth side of the square is missing or replaced by the eye itself. Can this possibly suggest that only by following the "light of the eye" will the square be completed? It may also suggest that only by tapping into the "all-seeing third eye," or knowledge and wisdom of the ancients, will the square be completed.

This makes the positioning of the knight's claymore all the more interesting. Usually a knight carried his sword at his side, but in this case it is positioned to act more as a phallic symbol, with the pommel and hilt positioned around the groin. Was this a suggestion that the knight's duty was to protect the "seed" of the Grail family along with the womb that "bears" the descendants?

In Glynn's drawing, at the edge of the knight's skirt, a circle with two parallel bars is shown, along with a large five-pointed star. As described earlier, these symbols suggest that the Templars possessed the knowledge of astronomy and the ability to fix and guide their position by the stars, sun, and moon. As the claymore is positioned between the stars and the sun and the moon, in a north–south direction, perhaps the trinity can be located along or around a north–south meridian.

The Westford Knight is also shown holding in his right hand what appears to be a rosary or rose. Although throughout the centuries the rose has been seen as a symbol of many levels of secret esoteric thought and society, the rosary (the hidden knowledge) belonging to this knight may be suggesting that one should recall the twelve stations of the cross.

Above the pommel, or "apple," of the knight's claymore is a figure that in many ways represents a bird, such as an eagle, dove, or the mystical phoenix, the symbol of the Holy Spirit that rises from the ashes.

The pommel of the sword is also conveniently positioned where the knight's navel would be located. Could this suggest that the "garden of roses" lies at the navel or the one point on earth that acts as a gateway to another dimension, or possibly to heaven itself? Can the temptation provided by the apple be seen as the reflecting rose windows of many Gothic cathedrals, which though stained, allow a glimpse into the inner circle?

Many more questions remain to be answered. Could the Westford Knight be the key or could he represent the Triple Tau that leads to the Royal Arch jewel? Was the Holy Trinity, or a representation of what it stands for, entombed like Shuben and Acadie in a physical grave, or is it entombed by a spiritual key?

The question also remains: to what secret organization did the guardians of the Grail actually belong?

The answer to this question is not so simple, since the Templars were identified as a far-ranging group that included within their circles the Priory of Sion; the Order of St. Sulpice; the Rosicrucians; the Knights of St. John, Hospitalliers; and the Knights of Malta. Certainly, at one time or another, the protectors of the Grail assumed different associations or disguises whenever it suited their purpose.

The Templars may have acted independently of all the known groups and formed a super-secret organization of their own. This may explain why modern-day organizations such as the Priory of Sion appear to be disseminating information at an ever-increasing rate, as though the final piece of the puzzle has yet to be found.

The Rennes Parchments were to be found and deciphered, but for what ultimate reason? To answer this, the unraveled message bears repeating:

SHEPHERDESS, NO TEMPTATION, THAT POUSSIN, TENIERS, HOLD THE KEY; PEACE 681. BY THE CROSS AND THIS HORSE OF GOD, I COMPLETE—OR DESTROY—THIS DAEMON OF THE GUARDIAN AT MIDDAY. BLUE APPLES.

Is it now possible to interpret the code in relation to what was learned of the hidden inner knowledge that men such as Prince Henry Sinclair possessed?

SHEPHERDESS. The shepherdess depicted in *The Shepherds of Arcadia* was seen as a conduit to a higher level of understanding. In her guises as the goddess Artemis/Venus/Diana, she portrayed a balance of wisdom and understanding, a balance that comes only from the ability to explore and to open oneself up to accepting knowledge other than that promoted by the Church.

The shepherdess also represented the pagan Corn-mother and Harvest-maiden, Demeter/Leto/Gaia. These, in turn, present another path that leads to Prince Henry Sinclair and the Mi'kmaq. But, as we have seen, the shepherdess is hiding something else. With her feet in the water and the fact that she appears to be pregnant, Poussin may just be conveying the notion that the princesses of the royal Merovingian line were indeed the ones who carried on the "royal tradition," including the hidden Mystery of Christ.

NO TEMPTATION. This phrase links Teniers, the Flemish painter, with Saint Anthony the Hermit, but as there are numerous versions of this painting, there appears no way of being certain which might be the relevant one. Regardless, there are some specific facts relating to the life history of Saint Anthony that Prince Henry must have personalized for his quest.

Saint Anthony was seen as being tormented forever by demons and visions that Satan cast before him. As such, it makes a great deal of sense that Prince Henry would employ a symbolic talisman, the Seal of Solomon, to control the demons and visions that lay right under Anthony's nose.

The biggest temptation, as it relates to the underlying story of Mary Magdalene and the continuation of a Holy Bloodline, may figuratively be what lies in the womb. In some ways, this figurative womb provides no temptation to a saint who declared that celibacy was one path that led toward a higher realization of God. On the other hand, the comfort and warmth of the womb could represent the ultimate spirit or essence that the hermit was seeking by shunning all earthly pleasures.

More realistically, Prince Henry most likely related the caves that exist under the hill at Green Oaks with the caves of the hermit. Through Henry's knowledge of the classics, the caves also related to the caves of Apollo's temple at Delphi, the labyrinth of the Minotaur, and the gates to Hell.

Another theme that fascinated the Templars was the burying of Saint Paul in the desert by Saint Anthony with the help of two lions. Since Saint Anthony was seen as a strong connection between the emergence of Christianity and ancient Egyptian mysteries, this theme supports the premise that Prince Henry, as the lion or guardian of the Grail, was attempting to reconcile the connection between pagan and early Christian mysteries.

THAT POUSSIN, TENIERS, HOLD THE KEY. Poussin, Teniers, Champlain, and Bacon were all contemporaries in the late sixteenth and early seventeenth centuries. During this time a wealth of esoteric thought flooded into society by way of several secret organizations that sprouted on either side of the British Channel. Much of the resulting hocus-pocus should be considered just that. But the underlying key to all their manipulations was that a holy treasure could be found through an application of sacred geometry and moral allegory.

Poussin's painting *The Shepherds of Arcadia* supports Bacon's idea that "parable is an ark," which can be interpreted on many different levels. The strongest "key" of all appears to be that only God and his appointed guardians know exactly where "in the arc," or where at the point of concentration of light (again, hidden knowledge), the entombed treasure lies.

Many of Poussin's other paintings present further pieces to the puzzle. One of the most disturbing clues relates to a series completed by Poussin called *The Four Seasons*. In the most fascinating manner, the four shepherds of Arcadia can be seen, in terms of their mood, color and symbolism, to each represent one of the four seasons. For example, *Winter, The Deluge* and the Christ-like shepherd are both presented in a dark, spiritual character that is mysterious and secretive, yet attractive and forbidding. All the while there is the suggestion that out of God's flooding of the earth and Christ's sacrifice, good will triumph over evil.

There is also the suggestion that, within each painting, a time capsule of sorts, whether it is an ark or a tomb, is awaiting one who possesses the keys of wisdom and understanding. Poussin also provided the notion of what these keys are. In his painting *Christ Handing the Keys to Saint Peter*, there is a strong connection between the formalization of the Christian Church and the Keys of Solomon, which attest to Solomon's magical ability to control the pagan demons. Both Poussin and Prince

Winter, The Deluge, Nicolas Poussin, 1660–64

Note how one of the survivors is clinging to a horse's neck. Is this a Horse of God? Note also how the ark is positioned between what appears as two pillars and a lintel. Could this not suggest that those mysteries and secrets that survived the Flood relate to the Temple of Solomon in some manner? Reproduced courtesy of the Louvre.

Henry Sinclair certainly possessed concrete evidence that Jesus Christ had indeed existed and had possessed the "magic" of Solomon.

PEACE 681. This enigmatic clue reveals the *raison d'être* for Prince Henry's journey. It is now clear that Sinclair's objective was to conceal the "holiest of holy" treasures until such time as peace was achieved between the Church, the state, and the Templars. Sinclair's objective was also to reconcile the chasm between the earth, man, and woman, and between the three prominent world religions: Christianity, Judaism, and Islam (a trinity times three).

The manipulation of the numbers 2 and 3 in terms of anagrams, reflections, and mirror images also goes a long way toward revealing a favorite method of code and concealment by the Templars, including their use of numerology and mathematics. The repeated use of the numbers 14 and 15 results in the notion that a reconciliation of man and woman, or a combination of their two representative forms, is required to receive or ascend to a higher level or spirituality. In simpler terms, by relating this notion back to the shepherdess and her male guardian, we are led back to the point where the spirit of God resides, the Elysian Fields.

BY THE CROSS. Numerous crosses, both symbolically and physically, occur in the Nova Scotia landscape. The settlement of New Ross was once referred to as "The Cross." A Latin Christian cross has been uncovered on Oak Island. A Gothic cross can be applied to the small valley of Green Creek, and both a Templar and a Maltese Cross can be applied to mainland Nova Scotia.

The Sign of the Cross also relates to Saint John the Baptist and his campaign of preparing his flock for the coming of the "chosen one." Prince Henry may indeed have adopted the parable and hidden what he considered to be his "Lambspring of God" in a pool of water, until such time that it was ready to be "reborn."

AND THIS HORSE OF GOD. Not too much explanation has to go into the background of this phrase. It was demonstrated that, by planting a grove of "golden" oaks on the hillside in the shape of a bough or wing, Prince Henry and those before him were confirming that the winged horse Pegasus is not only a sacred symbol of the Templars but is the symbol that helps one slay the daemon guardian of the Holy Spirit.[10] In the Greek myth of Bellerophon, the hero was sent against the Chimaera (a monster with the head of a lion, the body of a goat, and the tail of a dragon), which he slew with the help of the winged horse.

The location of the grove also conjures up the multiple vision of the eagle with a golden wing, the lion with a golden fleece, and the Golden Bough from which the apples of the Hesperides were plucked by Hercules.[11] Practically speaking, the grove of oaks provided Prince Henry with the necessary materials to build his own "golden chariot" upon which he could return to Scotland.

I COMPLETE (or I DESTROY) THIS DAEMON GUARDIAN. This phrase suggests that the monster or serpent that guards the golden apple must first be tamed or destroyed before the treasure may be recovered. In a practical sense, Prince Henry diverted the turbulent red stream of Green Creek to guard the resting place of the treasure. In occult circles, the serpent was tamed by feeding it its own tail and thus, again, "squaring the circle."

In a similar vein, Prince Henry applied the alchemical practice of completing the square by combining a male and female element within a triangle or trinity. What this suggests is that a third element is missing—the Golden Child. Or did Prince Henry reflect the notion that the third element is in fact the spirit of life?

Prince Henry Sinclair and the Templars meant for us to rejoice in the spirit of love, the "miracle" of birth, and the richness of family. Part of the unscrambled message is just this. In fact, if this message is related back to the Cathar belief that Jesus Christ and Mary Magdalene indeed produced a third element, then the remains of the Grail family and/or proof of the Holy Bloodline's genealogy may very well be the treasure that was transported across the Atlantic to the Nova Scotia refuge.

AT MIDDAY BLUE APPLES. This phrase has to be dealt with in a similar manner as to the different levels of meaning that can be interpreted from the four shepherds of Arcadia. There is a wealth of meaning hidden within the last of the enigmatic phrases. For example, the phrase may apply to the three basic degrees of Freemasonry based upon their relative geometric progression. Or the word *at* can be interpreted as *a–t,* the missing *t* being the third element required to form the Triple Tau.

By applying a little of Francis Bacon's philosophy to the phrase "Midday Blue Apples," it may be that the key to finding this lost element is to follow the "midday" sun across the "blue" water to the land of the "apples"—Avalon. Or, by applying the belief in dualism that Prince Henry promoted, then "Midday Blue Apples" becomes "Midnight Red Grapes," or something of a similar notion. Which leads us straight to the Greek myth of Dionysus and the dark secret of human sacrifice and pagan ritual induced by wine.[12] As Bacon must have discovered, the New Temple of Solomon was to be found following the deadly "arc of Diana."

THE SILVER DART

Alexander Graham Bell, the inventor of the telephone, retired to a small retreat called Beinm Bhreagh (pronounced "Bine Bree-ah," from the Gaelic for "beautiful mountain"), located on the island of Cape Breton, on the edge of the Bras d'Or Lake, at a small town called Baddeck. It was here that Bell continued his inventive genius that culminated in the flight of his "Silver Dart" in 1909, the first airplane flight in the British Empire.

On display at the Alexander Graham Bell National Historic Site and Museum in Baddeck are hundreds of original artifacts and photographs that tell the fascinating story of Bell's life from childhood to his death in Baddeck at age 75. Included in these displays are Bell's experiments in the fields of medicine, genetics, and communication, as well as Bell's important work with the deaf. In various exhibits, tribute is also paid to Bell's work in physics, including his pioneering work in optics and light refraction.

In many ways, Alexander Graham Bell could also be considered a modern-day magician. In fact, Scottish tradition maintains that Bell's father, a professor of medicine at the University of Edinburgh, was the role model for Sir Arthur Conan Doyle's Sherlock Holmes, as Doyle was once one of the elder Bell's pupils. Another amazing story is that Bell received the inspiration for transmitting sound currents by studying the sine patterns of the Grand River, which is located next to the original Bell Homestead in Brantford, Ontario. Many others will recognize that it was the Bell family who initiated the development of the National Geographic Society, and its present operation is still overseen by the Bell-Grosvenor family.

But it is with another "Silver Dartt" that this story is concerned, although there are some unnerving similarities to Bell's experiments in the refraction of light. The reason this Dartt is spelled with two *t*'s is that the dart or arrow figuratively belongs to the Christian God and also represents the earlier gods of Apollo/Artemis. As it just so happens, "Dartt" is also one of the more prominent family names still to be found in the Green Oaks area.

It was already demonstrated that following a path through the small communities of Bible Hill, Truro, Hilden, Brookfield, Stewiacke, and Shubenacadie forms a concave arc. A mirror image of this arc may also be developed if one considers that a north–south meridian runs from Bible Hill to Stewiacke. The result is a lens or eyelike image, a symbol suggestive of the "bow" of the gods. Therefore, the arrow or dart must be close by.

At this juncture, the image of the bull's-eye created by the rerouting of the stream should be remembered, since it is at the "oxbow" that the golden apple lies atop the head of the bull. And, if an arrow is fitted to Apollo's/Artemis' bow, the "head" of its shaft points right at the apple (shades of William Tell).

As a result, the feathers of the arrow rest just to the west of Brookfield at the Dartt family cemetery, at the base of the white mountain. Could the Acadian Dartts be the original Knights of the Red Feather who were left behind by Prince Henry Sinclair to protect the Grail? It most certainly appears so.

All of this leads back to the Templars' unique brand of black humor. Were Prince Henry and his men suggesting to those who understood, that "parable has ever been a kind of ark," or, in their interpretation, "parabolic has ever been a kind of arc"? We should not forget the story of Robin Hood, which tells how he was buried where his last shot arrow landed.

On a totally different level, the tools of the archer relate to the astrological sign of Sagittarius, the sign that precedes that of Capricorn. In alchemy, the fiery transformation of the body into a *corpus mundum* supposedly takes place in the sign of Sagittarius, the Archer. The ninth sign of the zodiac is ruled by Jupiter and covers the period from November 23 to December 21, where the Scorpion, or serpent, changes itself into the Archer. Sagittarius, which is traditionally represented by a centaur drawing a bow and aiming at heaven, thus symbolizes this transformation. Could this be another version of the Horse of God?

Prince Henry Sinclair must have related to the attributes of the Archer quite well. The Archer is described as a born explorer and adventurer and, at a moral level, an idealist, constantly pursuing his vision of global love and man's spiritual perfection. To the Archer, the goal is secondary to the movement that brings him toward it; constantly achieving a higher level is its own goal. Thereby, even if in Prince Henry's lifetime world peace was not achieved, the seed was planted.

Throughout this book many other clues were identified concerning the coming together of man and woman and the creation and rebirth of a child or spirit of God. In much the same way, the background story concerning the Merovingian dynasty and its alleged modern-day offshoot, the Priory of Sion, alluded to the continuous planting of seeds and propagation of the descendants of the Holy Bloodline. This accounts for the many references to the growing of grapes, for the winemaker's practice of trimming, grafting, and crossbreeding provides a wonderful analogy to the development of the Grail family tree. In fact, the analogy of planting a seed or acorn can be likened to the fertilization and development of the embryo within the female uterus.

In Prince Henry's case, the fertilized seed was the Holy Grail and the uterus was the valley of Green Creek, with the seed being "impregnated" into the wall of the valley for a gestation period of over six hundred years. If this is indeed the case, Anthony's Nose is positioned directly opposite the tempting sweet smells of the cedar and hemlock that emit from the valley/womb.

To carry this analogy further, the ever-fluctuating red tide that spills from the valley into the Shubenacadie is the cyclical menstrual flow that all women of childbearing age experience. From his eagle's nest atop Green Oaks, Prince Henry Sinclair would surely not have failed to notice that the tides fluctuate with the influences of the moon.

Therefore, it seems that Sinclair prepared his temple to receive the "shaft" of the archer-god, Apollo, and assisted in the ceremony by entombing the fertilized seed in the "uterine" wall. In effect, Sinclair built a "little nest-egg" for himself and his followers.

It is no surprise that a fertilized egg is called a *blastocyst* (from the Greek *blastos*), which means "sprout." The cells of the blastocyst absorb the nutrients of the uterus just as a plant absorbs nourishment from the wet soil. This analogy also gives a totally different perspective to Nova Scotia's possible identification as Vinland. Perhaps the Vikings discovered that the wild grapes of the Annapolis Valley not only fortified them but fortified their women as well.

Prince Henry not only planted a physical seed but a spiritual one. It is as though Prince Henry established his own game of chess and challenged the whole world to "check the mate" of his king. Like the game of chess, knowledge and wisdom is required to not only play the game but understand its meaning. The Templars and the Arabs long before Prince Henry's time recognized chess as an analogy of the quest in very much the same manner that the Money Pit represents the Fool of the tarot. The Fool is overwhelmed by the sweet smell of roses.

A DIFFERENCE OF ONE DEGREE

The secret symbolism of the rose was even carried through to the time of the pirates and corsairs. Many of the earlier pirates named their ships the

"Mary Rose." And many of the same pirates, including the enigmatic Captain Kidd, made Saint Mary's Island, which is located just off of the coast of Madagascar, their center of operations.

Captain Kidd had one of the most appropriate names in all of history. Outwardly portraying the Fool, inwardly the Captain was the ultimate Joker, Trickster or "Kidder." Ironically, he fooled practically everyone, yet he still ended up hanged by a rope. Like the tarot card of the Hanged Man, perhaps Kidd made the ultimate sacrifice, knowing that the secret of the inner circle would not be discovered for a very long time.

According to written histories of the captain's life, at one time he was prepared to disclose where the true treasure lay to several high-ranking Freemasons. During the latter part of his life Kidd had as his privateer partners none other than four of the highest-ranking members of the British aristocracy and Freemasonry, including Richard Coote, Earl of Belmont.

But it is not Kidd's later misadventures that are intriguing in relation to this book's mystery. It is Kidd's life up to the age of thirty that is most fascinating, for nothing really is known of Kidd's early adventures on the high seas. All that really is known of Kidd's childhood and youth is that he probably was born in Greenock (Green Oaks?), Scotland in 1645, and that it is said that he spent most of his life at sea. Only when he was pressed into the Royal Navy in 1673, during the Dutch Wars, is there a consistent record of his activities until his death in 1701.

Two very important pieces of information relating to Kidd and to the area of Nova Scotia attest to the fact that Kidd took to his grave much more than he readily admitted. It is only because no one has been able to properly apply the information that Kidd's involvement in the mystery of Oak Island was considered entirely fictional. The fact that Kidd's name (Kidd with two *d*'s, similar to Dartt with two *t*'s) relates to the name for a young goat, a child, and to tease and jest, as well as meaning "to give birth," must itself mean something more.

Edgar Allen Poe picked up on this hidden meaning when he described in *The Gold Bug* how the image of a kid-goat could be found on the coded parchment in the corner diagonally opposite to the symbol of a skull. Interestingly enough, Poe described the parchment as having one of its corners torn away and the death's-head as a stamp or seal. Did Poe have an inkling as to where Captain Kidd's treasure lay, by positioning the symbol of the goat in a position relative to Oak Island and Green Oaks?

This information starts to become unnerving when it is related to the so-called *Kidd-Wilkins Del Mar map* and several mathematical combinations that were associated with it. One such number sequence is 44106818, which was supposedly on a card that Kidd slipped to his wife just before he was hanged. Unfortunately, these numbers are attributed to one of the more celebrated hoaxes in the history of pirate lore.

Briefly, the practical joke began in 1894 when a Chicago industrialist wrote a pamphlet describing a fanciful lawsuit being filed against descendants of the John Jacob Astor family of New York. The suit alleged that the Astor wealth originated from a Captain Kidd treasure supposedly found and illegally removed from a cave located on Deer Isle, Maine. The invented number code applied to Deer Isle's approximate latitude and longitude: 44° 10' north, 68° 18' west. The elaborate joke was taken seriously by some writers and was often printed as fact in books and magazine articles during the early twentieth century, until a time when its author came forward and confessed to the ruse.

The beauty of the hoax is that there is a legitimate clue within the context of the story. The reader must first remember that an earlier chapter highlighted the order of the Golden Dawn. It was this organization that spawned the offshoot 5 = 6 degrees. Thus, by adding 6 (1 + 5) to the latitude identified in the story, and its opposite, -6 (-5 + -1), to the longitude, then the new coordinates read as 44 + 1 = 45 degrees, 10 + 5 = 15 minutes north and 68 - 5 = 63 degrees, 18 - 1 = 17 degrees west.

Amazingly, these just happen to be the coordinates of the valley of Green Creek: 45° 15' north, 63° 17' west. Furthermore, these are the coordinates of the lost settlement of Shubenacadie shown on the late Acadian map of 1757, if 2 degrees 20 minutes is added to the longitude since it is measured from the Paris Meridian. In turn, the most fascinating thing about the 1757 map is that the lost settlement is positioned at the exact "heart" of Acadie, in the same manner that Old Jerusalem was the heart of Judea.

The question remains as to when Kidd had the opportunity to explore and discover what lay in the heartland of Nova Scotia. The answer to this may lie in notations found upon a rock that still rests at the mouth of the Gaspareau River near modern-day Liscombe, Nova Scotia. Upon the rock are various symbols that are said to represent a boot, a pennant, a staff, and a square, while the name Kidd and the date 1669 can also be seen. Although this rock perplexed the curious for years, it now appears that Kidd was committing to stone, like the Egyptians before him, another clue as to his or someone else's hidden abilities. Like the three Wise Men, Kidd was a trained navigator who naturally fixed his sights on the shining star of the north, better known as the North Star. Kidd might be thought of as another secret agent of the "rose," or inner circle.

Many people forget that the sun is a star. In ancient Egypt, it was the symbol of rebirth and reincarnation. The rose is also identified with the sun and was considered the "heart" of Zoroastrian worship. Since the rose was a symbol of secrecy, particularly a symbol of secret love affairs like those of Apollo and Artemis and, according to Cathar tradition, of Christ and Mary Magdalene, the sun could also be associated with the mysterious love affairs. Is it proof of the latter's love affair that the Rosicrucians and, to this day, the Priory of Sion, perpetuate through reference to the Mysteries of Eleusis? From all the relevant information it appears so.

In light of this, the "Shining Star" appears to represent Christ, who, if not the Son of God, then according to Manichean philosophy was at least the spirit of God. To the Templars, it didn't matter. Christ still represented direct communication with the Almighty. Christ's earlier alleged misadventures also did not bother the Templars. To many of them, including Prince Henry, the notion that there existed direct descendants of Christ only reinforced their belief in God and the ability to create life, particularly if those descendants exhibited a gentleness and kindness reflective of the spirit of God.

There is another aspect to the veneration afforded Christ by the Templars. If the Templars considered themselves to be adepts and possessors of ancient wisdom, then they considered Christ the living body and a continuation of that wisdom. Furthermore, if the Templars possessed written proof of Christ's understanding and knowledge of the ancient mysteries beyond the four gospels, then Christ himself was viewed as a key. *The Little Keys of Solomon,* on one level, may be seen to be the offspring of the House of David.[13]

Regardless of how he was viewed, the Templars believed in one thing: that Jesus Christ walked on the face of this earth and did good. As such, they believed that his example provides the guiding light to the balancing forces of the earth, with the result that a balance is once again achieved between earth, man and woman, the church, the state, and its guardians.

This may appear all too complicated a message but it should be approached in a philosophical manner. Anybody can see meaning where none exists. For all we really know, the medieval Templars were just the greatest bunch of opportunists that the world has ever seen. They may have jumped on every bandwagon going.

The facts show that when the time was opportune the Templars developed liaisons with their enemies. During the Albigensian Crusade, they were perceived as being neutral. Even when October 13, 1307, came about, they sacrificed many of their lower ranks to apparently conceal the holiest of holy treasures. But what if there was no treasure, no direct link to Christ and Mary Magdalene? What if the Knights Templar just executed the greatest sales job ever to the Catholic Church, somehow confirming that something of the greatest magnitude was in their possession? What if there was no master plan?

It would not be the first time that someone attached himself, or herself, to a rising star. But this is the beauty of it all. If $A = B = C = D = E$, does A equal E? It appears within the realm of possibility that the Templars created a quest that had no end, just the beginning to another one. Freemasonry started out with three basic degrees and from these flourished all sorts of branches and offshoots, including the Scottish and York Rites, the Shriners, the Jesters, and the Rosicrucians. Or did the Scottish Rites and the higher levels come first? It really doesn't matter.

What matters is that through the rites of initiation of the various levels, knowledge and understanding is gained. From this knowledge and understanding, wisdom of many things, including our past, is achieved—wisdom that can then be applied to advance oneself. Prince Henry was either one of the biggest fools or one of the greatest geniuses of his time, since he applied an enormous amount of knowledge and understanding to his personal quest. Indeed, Sinclair transcended his human limitations since he accepted the need to sacrifice his life for the rebirth of others.

The spirit exhibited by Sinclair is said to be the aura or halo that everybody carries. There is a long historical tradition that the spiritual body, which in most cultures is assumed to reside within man and to be immortal, is a solar body of light. The Egyptian concept of *ba,* or the soul image of man, was his spiritual double. The *ba* was considered immortal and its hieroglyph was a star. The same notion of an inner spiritual realm in the Greek world was known as the "psyche" and among the Romans as the "genius."

Therefore, the word *baphomet,* a word associated with the Templars' beliefs, may not be interpreted only as Wisdom but as the psyche or genius that is required to apply wisdom.

THE END OF THE JOURNEY

To summarize, this book presents a journey of sorts that is characterized by the tarot sequence of the twenty-two major trumps, the alchemical process of transmutation, and a wild game of chess using central Nova Scotia as the chessboard. This journey, or quest, can also be followed by interpreting the modified zodiac found within the mysterious booklet *Le serpent rouge.* By reading between the lines, the initiate discovers a rather extraordinary journey.

The message found within *Le serpent rouge* could be one big hoax, much like the fairy tales of our youth. If so, as already speculated, the quest is only a "mind-trap" that challenges one to "ascend" to a higher level of personal knowledge. Perhaps the Templars were exercising their warped sense of humor to the fullest by suggesting that the world is only made up of fools. On the other hand, the fact remains that Prince Henry Sinclair dedicated not only his life but also the lives of those around him to a cause. Simple logic tells us that it was for more than just a game.

When the hero, the now-enlightened Fool, appears at the end of the tarot sequence he is depicted as having completed his journey through a world that has been transformed by his own inner transformation. Occult tradition suggests that where once all was discord, all is now harmony; where despair held sway, fulfillment now reigns; where shadows crowded in on every side, every detail of the universe is now radiant with meaningful beauty.

The Fool now ignores the precipice and pit (Oak Island?) beneath his feet because he knows that nothing of value lies at its bottom. As a result, since he no longer identifies himself with his physical body or with his earthly personality, he does not fear for his safety. The dog biting at his thigh, which represents the outmoded thoughts and values of his previous mundane existence, is now ignored as he proceeds along his merry way. The sun above can now be seen to represent the pure light of the spirit shining down on him, and the white roses that grow at his heels now symbolize the fruits of the spirit springing up in his footsteps.

Our hero Prince Henry did not leave the shores of the Shubenacadie River empty-handed. He carried with him an accumulated store of truth and wisdom. As a result, there surely was a slight smile on his lips, to know that the puzzle that he perpetuated would drive men to greater heights (or to their graves) for centuries to come.

At this point, there is a personal satisfaction for those who, knowing that another, higher journey has just begun, aspire to learn more. In other ways, the culmination of the rather eclectic array of esoteric symbolism and knowledge that the Templars exhibited may appeal to more than a few, as it seems to suggest that their general knowledge and bizarre sense of humor knew no bounds.

Saunière may not have been the Fool after all. He may have realized that the time was not right to reveal the inner knowledge that he possessed. On the other hand, maybe Saunière discovered that there was no secret and was blackmailing those who were perpetrating the biggest hoax in the history of mankind.

Bérenger Saunière was born in a narrow, three-storied house with iron verandas overlooking a central square and a curious fountain known as the Fountain of the Tritons. The Tritons were considered to be half-man/half-beast, -mammal, or -fish, much like the Minotaur. Early Renaissance artists portrayed Triton, the son of King Neptune and Queen Amphitrite, as a man down to the waist with the rest of his body being a fish's tail. A statue in the Vatican museum portrays Triton more as a centaur, in the mode of Sagittarius the Archer, with a horse's forelegs and a human torso from the waist up.

Ancient myth placed the home of Triton to the west of the coast of Libya, where he is said to live with his parents, the king and queen, in a spectacular golden palace below the sea. To the west lies Nova Scotia and Oak Island, where the Triton Alliance, the corporate owners of most of the island, believes is the resting place of an enormous treasure hoard. All the evidence suggests, however, that Oak Island is the island of the Fool, the ultimate Fool, who fails to look beyond the obvious. It is the Fool who fails to follow the stars, the sun, and moon. After all, Sol–omon stands for the sun. The Fool also fails to follow the salmon to the stream's source, as the word *salmon* is a derivation of Solomon.

Fittingly, the modern-day Knights Templar recognize in their rituals and beliefs that love, compassion, and kindness allow the individual to ascend to a higher level. In Prince Henry Sinclair's lifetime, these principles, which are embodied within the vision of the Elysian Fields of Arcadia, took on a physical reality at Green Oaks, Nova Scotia.

What may be concluded from all of this? First of all, in the mire of Green Creek there may still lie a physical treasure, which may prove that Christ existed. Whether the treasure is the bones or other relics of the Grail family, a specific genealogy relating back through the Holy Bloodline to the House of David, or a fifth gospel that can be attributed directly to the time that Christ spent on earth, remains to be seen. At the very least, there may remain a metallic treasure that the Templars gained through three centuries of military, political, and religious campaigns. Only time and a well-conducted scientific excavation will tell.

Secondly, the undisturbed site at Green Oaks may yield a remarkable treasure trove of archaeological evidence that answers a number of questions concerning the pre-Columbian exploration and settlement of North America by not only Prince Henry and his men, but by the Vikings, Celts, Phoenicians, Egyptians, Aboriginals, and maybe even perhaps Palaeolithic and Neolithic explorers. Again, only time, public pressure, and government involvement will tell.

Unfortunately, there may be a sad ending to these first two conclusions, since the local, provincial, and federal governments are extremely hesitant to acknowledge any possibility of pre-Columbian exploration in Nova Scotia. The feeling is that "well enough should be left alone."

The third conclusion, in my mind, is the most valuable. It is that the symbolism of the Lost King and the Holy Grail represent the quest for knowledge and understanding, a journey that transcends darkness into light. Beyond the slightest doubt, it is through this quest for knowledge and understanding that modern Freemasonry, though perhaps rather unwittingly, perpetuates the rituals and beliefs of at least the medieval Templars.

Finally, it must now be recognized that the mythological island of Avalon, like the blessed landscape of Arcadia, is a symbol of the spiritual reward of the quest. It should also be realized that on the "island" of Nova Scotia, within Prince Henry Sinclair's New Jerusalem, there lies an unfinished temple. In this unfinished Temple of Solomon lies the Holy Spirit of God—a spirit that reflects the goodness that is found within all humankind.[14] This spirit also reflects the ideal that modern society must return to the ancient beliefs, when Woman and the gifts of Mother Earth were considered to be the real treasure of God. Only then will the labyrinth of the Grail be followed to its source.

Notes

Chapter 1: A Fool's Quest

1. In *Holy Grail Across the Atlantic*, Michael Bradley presented an intriguing theory that the planting of various distinctive varieties of oaks provided future explorers with signposts directing them to a refuge or sanctuary. Through correspondence with another well-known author on the subject of Rennes-le-Château and Oak Island, the Reverend Lionel Fanthorpe of Cardiff, Wales, presented the supporting theory that the planting of red and green oaks may, in fact, be likened to the modern-day traffic light—red means stop and green means go.
2. Throughout this book the reader will recognize that certain periods or dates signaled an increase in discovery or investigation into the mysteries of Rennes-le-Château, the Holy Grail, and Oak Island. The early 1950s appear to be one of the latest periods in which new information surfaced concerning the mystery of Rennes-le-Château both through the Bibliothèque Nationale material and through the discovery of the stone triangle on Oak Island.
3. A great deal of the material used in this book concerning the life of Bérenger Saunière and the mystery of Rennes-le-Château originally derived from Gérard de Sède's *L'Or de Rennes,* but the bulk of the story derived from Baigent, Leigh, and Lincoln's *Holy Blood, Holy Grail*, 24–32.
4. Although the decipherment appeared in many books devoted to the mystery of Rennes-le-Château, including *L'Or de Rennes, Holy Blood, Holy Grail* was the first to present, in English, a summary of the French research into the mystery. Therefore, *Holy Blood, Holy Grail* must receive acknowledgment for the decipherment, as found on page 26 of *Holy Blood, Holy Grail.*
5. Baigent, Leigh, and Lincoln, *Holy Blood, Holy Grail*, 2.
6. Ibid., 30–31.
7. Again, according to several of the French investigators and the three British authors of *Holy Blood, Holy Grail*, the theory is that Godfroi de Bouillon was a direct descendant of Jesus Christ through Mary Magdalene and the Merovingian dynasty. For further background see Baigent, Leigh, and Lincoln, *Holy Blood, Holy Grail*, 111–18.

8. Baigent, Leigh, and Lincoln, *The Messianic Legacy,* xv. In their introduction the British authors speculate that the Priory of Sion was and still is working to some kind of "grand design" or "master plan" for the future of France, for the future of Europe as a whole, and perhaps even beyond.

9. Lincoln, *The Holy Place,* 32. As Lincoln noted, when a magician wishes to raise a spirit, he does so within the protective circle of a pentacle, with a break in the surrounding circle to allow the evil to enter. To Lincoln, this was just one more clue that there remains an undercurrent of symbolism to the imagery presented throughout the many mysteries found in the area of Rennes-le-Château.

10. In a similar manner, the result of David Wood's *Genisis* was the recognition and identification of an immense geometrical figure, which he called the Temple of Rennes. Wood noted that it covers an area of over forty square miles, and every part is marked by a mountaintop, a church, an outstanding rock feature, or some intersection of carefully designed geometry.

    In order to arrive at this figure, Wood employed a photogrammetric system generally referred to as "radial control," which was widely used in World War II for the compilation of maps in areas where insufficient ground control existed to employ standard methods. However, in order to employ his method one must first find the "key." In this case, the key related to definitive angles and distances in order to establish a sequence of positions relative to both angular and ground-position disciplines.

    As Henry Lincoln noted in his foreword to David Wood's book, what Wood developed is truly amazing because it is demonstrable and has a basis in geometry and measure. It is for this reason that I included Wood's book as an essential element in the mystery, and it is for this reason that the results of Lincoln's and Wood's geometric analyses are included in later chapters.

11. Baigent and Leigh, *The Temple and The Lodge,* 27. The authors recognized that, indeed, it was the simplicity and anonymity of the Templar graves that distinguished them from the graves of other nobles, because when one entered the Temple one supposedly gave up his individual identity, effectively becoming just another part of the Order.

12. Ibid., 30–31. For years the Mann family of Norwich, England made annual pilgrimages to the Chapel of Saint Sophia, located in Glendaruel, Argyll, Scotland. Baigent and Leigh noted that in Argyll there appears to be a unique concentration of Masonic graves and anonymous military gravestones.

13. Ibid., 242–43.

14. Ibid., 249.

15. Ibid. Baigent and Leigh presented a great deal of background material concerning the centralization of English Freemasonry, in support of the theory that within the United Grand Lodge there was an "inner core" of other Freemasonic bodies, which originated in Jacobite Freemasonry. Because of this, the English Freemasonry of Grand Lodge was to have an important role in both the French

and American revolutions. For more in-depth information concerning the influence of Freemasonry on eighteenth and nineteenth century societies, *The Temple and The Lodge* is a must-read.

16. Sinclair, *The Sword and The Grail,* 1–7. Unknown to Andrew Sinclair at the time, his identification of these distinct Templar symbols led me to associate the quest of Prince Henry Sinclair with occult symbolism and to examine closely the individual symbols found within the various cards of the tarot. For example, the veil of Saint Veronica is similar to the veil or curtain depicted within several of the major arcana of the tarot.

17. Ibid., 2.

18. Ibid., 2–3. What Andrew Sinclair provided in *The Sword and The Grail* is the most wonderful description of the chapel and other workings at Rosslyn and how sacred geometry and symbolism were applied during their late medieval construction. What he also confirmed, again perhaps unknowingly, is that if Rosslyn provided a resting place for the Holy Grail, then it only served as a temporary depository due to its relative vulnerability to English invasion.

19. Ibid., 5.

20. Ibid., 5.

21. Ibid., 6. The description provided by Andrew Sinclair of the symbolic traditions brought to Scotland by the designer and the masons of the chapel at Rosslyn in itself is a clue as to how the Christian teachings of Masonry overlap and parallel earlier pagan and ancient beliefs. This is a theme that recurs continually throughout *The Knights Templar in the New World* and becomes a primary consideration for solving the mystery of where Prince Henry Sinclair's New Temple lies.

22. Although Bradley's *Holy Grail Across the Atlantic* sometimes reads strangely, the range of content allows the reader to gain a lengthy historical perspective leading up to Sinclair's transatlantic voyages. What Bradley does is tell the story as it became revealed to him; therefore, the connections made are not always readily apparent.

Fortunately, this style of writing reflects how I think. In many ways, I have a strange ability to amalgamate significant amounts of seemingly unrelated material into a cohesive progression of logic and events. This must come, as Michael Bradley himself so aptly demonstrated, from the absorption of numerous books and topics at one time. Bradley rightfully acknowledged this ability by sharing credit for his book through some similarity of content with French-language books published during the 1950s and 1960s, by authors such as Gèrard de Sede, Pierre Duriban, Maurice Magré, Pierre Belperron, and Fernando Neil. Unfortunately, most of these writers are not translated into English, and so, while they had a definite impact on European thinking similar to that of *Holy Blood, Holy Grail,* they are almost unknown to North Americans.

However, with the publishing of *Holy Blood, Holy Grail* in 1982, the stage was set for Bradley's *Holy Grail Across the Atlantic.* Bradley's book was largely based on the research of the French authors referred to above, as well as on some original and very interesting contributions by the three British authors of *Holy Blood, Holy Grail*. But whereas Lincoln, Baigent, and Leigh did not make any mention of the North American chapters of the Holy Bloods' story, Bradley attempted to return King Arthur to his proper place in history as a descendant of the supposed Holy Blood, while emphasizing the North American part of the Holy Blood tale, which was largely ignored by the Europeans.

23. Bradley, *Holy Grail Across the Atlantic*, 45–79. Bradley noted that the ruins at New Ross are generally similar in type of construction and style to the famous Newport Tower in Newport, Rhode Island. However, in mentioning the Newport Tower, Bradley introduced a controversy that crops up throughout his book. The Newport Tower is a structure that apparently stood before Newport was founded in 1639. The problem is that conventional historians are unable to concede that the Newport Tower must have been built prior to any acceptable colonial periods. To the contrary, evidence of pre-colonial European settlement was documented by Barry Fell in his *America B.C.*, as well as in Salvatore Michael Trento's *The Search for Lost America*.

24. Bradley, *Holy Grail Across the Atlantic*, 213. Of equal importance to Bradley is the Gastaldi map, which first appeared in the Venice ptolemy of 1548, three years after the Vopell map, but which may have been drawn as early as 1539. Of interest on this map are the place names "p=refuge," "Larcadia," "Angoulême," "Flora," and "Le Paradis." Bradley logically put the progression of these names together to form the message "the Flower of Angoulême has found a refuge in the Paradise of Arcadia." Of special note is the map's reference to "Norumbega" ("New France"), which calls the region of Nova Scotia "Terra de Norumbega" ("land of Norumbega"). Norumbega will be dealt with in a later chapter; at this point suffice it to say that the land of Norumbega plays an important part not only in the discovery of the New Jerusalem, but in the reasoning that Prince Henry Sinclair was following in his Norman ancestors' footsteps.

25. Ibid., 95. Much of Bradley's general information concerning portolan charts relies heavily on *Maps of the Ancient Sea Kings* by Charles Hapgood. Professor Hapgood arrived at his conclusions after an exhaustive search through hundreds of early maps and replotting the important ones on a modern projection. According to Hapgood, these maps constitute the first hard evidence that advanced peoples preceded all the peoples now known to history.

26. Ibid., 95. Unbelievable as it may appear, Hapgood's evidence indicated that some ancient people explored the coasts of Antarctica when its coasts were free of ice. It is clear, too, that these ancient people had an instrument of navigation that was far superior to anything possessed by the peoples of ancient, medieval, or even modern times.

27. Ibid., 101–5.

28. Bradley, *The Columbus Conspiracy*, 1–15.

29. Of the numerous books and articles written on Oak Island and the Money Pit, three of them are prominent because of their in-depth background to the story and the theories as to the nature of the group of men responsible for the construction of such an impregnable defense.

   In *The Money Pit,* author D'Arcy O'Connor concentrated on Captain William Kidd as the legendary depositor of immense treasure.

   W. S. Crooker, in *The Oak Island Quest,* attributed its building on the same level with the mysteries of Easter Island, the Nazca Plain, and the great pyramids of Egypt. To Crooker, the Money Pit can only be compared with the many strange works found in various parts of the world that apparently originated long before recorded history. But to Crooker, the Money Pit on Oak Island is different in one way. Unlike the other great mysteries of the world, the artifacts or workings cannot be physically viewed and examined because everything is underground. In Crooker's mind, the Money Pit on Oak Island, with its labyrinth of shafts and tunnels, is an inverted Easter Island or great pyramid.

30. Furneaux, *The Money Pit Mystery,* 23–52. The book on this topic that I feel most comfortable with is *The Money Pit Mystery* because of its more logical reasoning, from an engineering viewpoint, as to the identity of the mysterious "Mr. X" who constructed the Money Pit and why he might have done so.

31. Bradley, *Holy Grail Across the Atlantic,* 152.

Chapter 2: Balance of Nature

1. The Pythagorean belief in an ordered world made it possible to investigate qualities, functions, and processes systematically. Pythagoreans believed that logic aided in the understanding of the processes that invest the physical world with "life"—birth, growth, death, and renewal.

   To facilitate this understanding, a system of twelve terms was required; it was this twelve-term system that became the root of Western astrology, with its zodiac of twelve signs. Thus, the meanings ascribed to the various signs of the zodiac and to the planets were dictated by number. The choice of the relative symbols occurred because the given symbol best represented the qualities, functions, and processes inherent in the given numerical position.

2. Astrology is one of the oldest and most widespread of human activities and interests. A recognizable astrology played an integral part in every highly developed civilization of the past—Egyptian, Babylonian, Greek, Indian, Chinese, Muslim, and Mayan.

   Great minds of the past, such as Plato, Pythagoras, Saint Thomas Aquinas, and Johannes Kepler, accepted astrology as a symbolic master plan of the structure and functioning of the universe that satisfied their inner experience. This becomes an important point to remember as the reader follows the series of geometric progressions across mainland Nova Scotia.

3. Gimbutas, *The Language of the Goddess,* 265.
4. Matthews, *The Household of the Grail,* 26.
5. Ibid., 26–27.
6. Pohl, *Prince Henry Sinclair: His Expedition to the New World in 1398,* 140–46, and Bradley, *Holy Grail Across the Atlantic,* 133–36.

Following the reading of *Holy Grail Across the Atlantic,* I could not get out of my mind the idea that the mainland of Nova Scotia held a mystery, a mystery that surrounded the notion that Prince Henry Sinclair, in the guise of Glooscap, established a Templar settlement in pre-Columbian Nova Scotia. And then it struck me! Pohl suggested that Glooscap crossed the Atlantic by first paddling southwest along the Fundy shore to the site of modern Digby. From Digby, he followed the Fundy shore to Annapolis, where he crossed the peninsula through the Lequille River to Liverpool Head Lake and the Mersey River to the site of present day Liverpool, Nova Scotia.

But this is where Pohl and Bradley differed. Pohl suggested that Sinclair returned to the Bay of Fundy by the same route. On the other hand, Bradley suggested that Sinclair traveled westward along the Atlantic coastline to the Lequille–Liverpool Lake–Mersey River route from the Gold–Gaspereau River route, which conveniently passes by the back door of the castle ruins at New Ross.

What stuck me were two things. First of all, the Gold River is not navigable even for the small flat-bottomed boats that Sinclair employed in his explorations. From New Ross to the mouth of the Gold River, where Oak Island is located, there is a drop in elevation of five hundred feet. Surely Glooscap/Sinclair would not have chosen a route with so many rapids and waterfalls.

Second, when Sinclair first reached Parrsboro and the Minas Basin, he would have experienced for the first time the largest tidal rip in the world, which drops in places over sixty feet. To a group of knights in small rowboats, this must have presented a giant obstacle. But to a man-god like Glooscap, why not change an obstacle into opportunity?

From Parrsboro, Glooscap was able to see a great distance in all directions. To his west lay the Bay of Fundy, a very large, open body of water that funnels the tidal turbulence into the Atlantic Ocean. To his east, the Minas Basin narrows considerably and falls gently into the mouth of the Shubenacadie River.

If Sinclair timed it right, he could ride the tides that move up the Shubenacadie across the width of Nova Scotia to Lake William, and from there only have a short and gentle downhill portage to Bedford Basin and the Halifax harbor. From here he could have leisurely made his way westward along the coastline to the site of modern-day Liverpool and connect to the Medway River, as confirmed by both Pohl and Bradley.

7. The earliest indications of any system of measurement come from the ancient Babylonians, or the people who lived before them in the region known as

Babylonia. The Babylonians developed a system of land measurement and their clay tablet records show that they had methods for finding the areas of several simple figures, including the circle.

Most of the ancient records show that definite methods and knowledge of measurement arose in connection with land measurement, building, and astrology. The Babylonians supposed that the heavens revolved around the earth and that the year consisted of 360 days. This led them to divide the circle into 360 parts and thus originated the present-day degree system of angle measure.

8. This work seems to be a copy, with improvements, of an earlier work that dates back about a thousand years. Hence, the earliest written record of definite geometrical knowledge probably dates back to 1700 B.C. and possibly to about 2700 B.C.

9. The fame of the wisdom of the Egyptians spread over all the civilized world of their time, and students and scholars came from other countries to travel and study in Egypt. Among these were the ancient Greeks, who began coming to Egypt about 600 B.C.

10. The Greek scientists determined very closely the earth's size and exact shape. One of the leaders in this work was Eratosthenes, who in later years went to Egypt to teach. He determined the circumference and diameter of the earth to within a few hundred miles, determined almost exactly the length of the year, and suggested the calendar now known as the Julian calendar, which was used until comparatively recent times.

11. Of Euclid, very little is known beyond the fact that he was born about 300 B.C. It is known that he spent most of his life in Alexandria and taught mathematics there at the university and to private students for many years. It is to Euclid that the proverb "there is no royal road to knowledge" is attributed.

Although little is known of Euclid's life, his work fills a large part of the history of mathematics. Euclid's great work is known as the *Elements of Mathematics*. It covered parts of arithmetic, theory of numbers, algebra, and proportion, and all that was then known of geometry. The complete work consisted of thirteen books; of these, seven were devoted to geometry. The books on geometry are usually separated from the others and together are known as Euclid's *Elements of Geometry*, often simply referred to as *The Elements*.

In *The Elements*, Euclid supposed that the reader could use only the ruler and compass and no other instruments. All the drawings, proofs, and solutions are therefore based on and carried out by means of the straight line and circle. The geometry thus developed is called elementary geometry. During and since Euclid's time other methods were developed, but these belong to what is called higher geometry. It is the simpler Euclidean geometry upon which the geometric lessons of Freemasonry are based.

12. In ancient times this mysterious island remained undiscovered because of its distance from the inhabited world. It was discovered at a later period by the

Phoenicians. For purposes of trade, the Phoenicians established colonies through-out Libya and in the eastern parts of Europe. They amassed great wealth and managed to voyage beyond the Pillars of Heracles (Hercules). While exploring the coast outside the Pillars, many of their ships were driven by strong winds a great distance out into the ocean, bringing them to the island.

13. Ashe, *Avalonian Quest,* 175–76, 206.

14. Ibid., 202–11.

15. Ibid., 174–79. Apollo's practice of visiting his Hyperborean friends is also referred to by Hecataeus, though the visits happen less often. Traditionally, at Delos, where Apollo was worshipped jointly with his sister Artemis, gifts supposedly from Hyperboreans were offered. Close to Artemis' temple there was also a tomb where traditional honors were paid to two Hyperborean maidens. It was said that they had come to Delos in the first days of its sacredness and died there, all of which provides the connection between Apollo and tarot card VII, the Chariot.

16. Chadwick, *The Celts,* 17–27.

17. Ibid., 37. In the early years of the third century the Celts were masters of a vast area extending from Galatia in the east to Britain and probably Ireland in the west. The Celts reached the apex of their power later in the fourth century and thereafter entered a period of rapid decline.

18. Ibid., 42. The Welsh poet did not solely think of this place as a land of the dead. One of the titles he gives it is Caer Feddwid, "Court of Intoxication" or "Carousal," and its staple drink is sparkling wine (again, more wine!). It was also named Caer Siddi, meaning "the land of the living." The significant thing is that the poet, while obviously aware of their disparity, saw no inconsistency in conjoining the land of the dead and the land of the living as two aspects of the same otherworld.

19. Ibid., 57. This recalls an episode in Nennius's *Historia Brittonum* that describes how the sons of Mil, having come to Ireland, tried to capture a tower of glass that stood in the middle of the sea. The occupants of the tower, when addressed, made no answer, maintaining the silence that is the specific mark of the dead in Celtic as in other traditions. Quite clearly the glass tower and the glass fortress are one and the same and symbolize the realm of the dead.

20. MacKenzie, *The Royal Masonic Cyclopedia,* 193–95. In many ways, the description of the Eleusian ceremonies that MacKenzie provided resemble, on a much grander scale, the rites of the basic three degrees of Masonry.

In 1866 the English Societas Rosicruciana in Anglia was founded by Robert Wentworth Little on the basis of ancient rituals that he supposedly discovered. Of particular interest is the fact that this body counted among its members Kenneth MacKenzie, the author of *The Royal Masonic Cyclopedia,* who at that time was considered the utmost authority on Masonic symbolism and relation-ship. Had previous ancient societies possessed an understanding of the natural world in some manner beyond today's comprehension? Men such as Kenneth

MacKenzie, who spent all of their lives trying to decipher the countless rituals and symbolism, certainly believed it was so.

21. Baigent, Leigh, and Lincoln, *Holy Blood, Holy Grail,* 60–93. But also see Barber's *The Trial of the Templars* and Upton-Ward's *The Rule of the Templars* for more detail concerning the beliefs and philosophy behind the Order.

22. Baigent, Leigh, and Lincoln, *Holy Blood, Holy Grail,* 69.

23. Ibid., 66.

24. Ibid., 67–68.

25. Ibid., 69.

26. Ibid., 47.

27. Ibid., 48–49. The knowledge that the gnostic sought was direct realization of God. It was a secret knowledge because it could only come as the product of certain personal revelations. The basic gnostic belief was that the human spirit represented the Divine's essence entrapped in matter.

28. Ibid., 50.

29. Ibid., 72–73.

30. Hannon, *The Discoverers,* 27. Folk tales included exaggerated reports of sea monsters and island colonies of Amazons and savages. No doubt fable and folk tale intertwined with fact, as recorded on parchments by monks and scribes of royal households.

31. Ibid., 30–32. Brendan was born on the Dingle Peninsula in Kerry, southwest Ireland, in A.D. 484. Ireland was one of the few sanctuaries of learning in the Dark Ages, and Brendan was fortunate enough to attend school in Limerick, learning Latin, Hebrew, Greek, Gaelic, mathematics, and astronomy. Many of the educated priests sought martyrdom as hermits in crude stone "beehive" huts on sea-swept islets in the Atlantic. Others cast themselves adrift in boats; Brendan is said to have done this in 545 with fourteen other monks, safely reaching the Fortunate Isles, which later became known as St. Brendan's Isle.

    On Martin Behaim's globe, unveiled at Nüremberg in 1492, "Saint Brendan's Isle" was included among the lands west of the Canary Islands. Later on, expeditions were sent to look for it from both Spain and Portugal, but it was never found. Several fifteenth-century maps show a vague but large island called "Antilla" across the western ocean. Brasil, yet another name for the Fortunate Isles, and Atlantis, the land of a forgotten civilization mentioned by Plato, were somewhere in the same far seas to the west, but they too were never discovered.

32. Ibid., 36.

33. Ibid.

34. Ibid., 37–38.

35. Ibid., 39.

36. Ibid., 40. Erik the Red died shortly after the return of the first Vinland expedition and Leif, his son, took his place as leader of the clan. At that time the Greenland settlement included several hundred farmers, hunters, fishermen, and traders. A

Christian church built to the order of Thorhild, Erik's consort, thrived until the settlers reverted to their pagan roots. The island population reached about four thousand at its peak, but many eventually returned to their homeland.

Thorvald, the second son, borrowed Leif's *knorr* and sailed for Vinland in 1004 with a crew of thirty. The saga mentions no incident on a journey direct to the *Leifsbodarna,* Leif's wintering place. The saga says that Thorvald first sent parties to explore "the land to the west" and then he "followed the coast to the northward."

After three years in Vinland, during which a long coastline (perhaps one thousand miles) was thoroughly explored (and mapped?), the settlement broke up and returned to Greenland. One version has it that the men fell to quarreling over the favors of the few women, but most references blame the relentless hostility of the natives.

Chapter 3: The Legend of Glooscap

1. Pohl, *Prince Henry Sinclair: His Expedition to the New World in 1398,* 178–79. Most of the references in this chapter concerning Prince Henry Sinclair originate from Pohl's book, although some sources, with reference to Glooscap, for example, have been independently checked using later sources such as Bradley's *Holy Grail Across the Atlantic,* Hill's *Glooscap and His Magic,* and Sinclair's *The Sword and The Grail.*
2. Pohl, *Prince Henry Sinclair,* 129. It should be noted that many people accepted Pohl's premise that June 2, 1398, was the specific date of Sinclair's landing, and appear to have dismissed the notion that Sinclair and his men made more than one expedition to the New World. I think that several transatlantic journeys were made between the acceptable dates of 1395 and 1403, based upon the extensive research that indicates that they brought with them the necessary provisions, tools, materials, livestock, and personnel to advance a large settlement of farmers and miners.
3. Sinclair, *The Sword and The Grail,* 119–27. But also see Pohl, *Prince Henry Sinclair,* 7–25.
4. Silas Tertius Rand, *Legends of the Micmacs,* 232, as quoted by Pohl, *Prince Henry Sinclair,* 134.
5. It's interesting to note that most children in Nova Scotia, at some time during elementary school, are taught this poem.
6. Quoted from Helen Creighton, *Bluenose Magic,* 97–98. Reprinted by permission of the Helen Creighton Folklore Society, Inc.
7. Bradley, *Holy Grail Across the Atlantic,* 136, as quoted from Pohl, *Prince Henry Sinclair,* 143.
8. Spicer, *Glooscap Legends,* 39–40.
9. Bradley, *Holy Grail Across the Atlantic,* 45–46.
10. Ibid., 59, 292–93. If any of Bradley's theory concerning the Stuart refugees is true, then it is possible that the castle at New Ross sheltered its last refugees in

1653. If the puritan Robert Sedgewick of Massachusetts did not destroy it out of hatred for the Stuarts, then maybe Acadian settlers themselves did what they could to erase obvious signs of the inland haven.

11. Ramsey, *No Longer on the Map,* 173. Although many books present cartographic evidence concerning medieval mapping, this section relies most heavily on Ramsey's in-depth studies of many of the earliest Ptolemaic maps. In distinct contrast to the accuracy demonstrated by the Zeno and the earlier portolan maps, the Ptolemaic maps appear to have been composed more by mariner tales and rumors than by actual discovery and cartographic skills.

12. Ibid., 173.

13. Ibid., 175–76.

14. Ibid., 121–32.

15. Andrew Sinclair, in *The Sword and The Grail,* traced the Saint Clair name back to the More family of Viking and Norman ancestry. According to Sinclair, on the Epte River, Rolf Rognvald of the powerful More family concluded the Treaty of Saint Clair in 911, when King Charles the Simple married his daughter and was converted to Christianity, taking the name of Saint Clair, which means "holy light." The river Epte is found in the north of France in what was once the duchy of Normandy, which also included the southern states of the Lowlands. It is an area that was at one time part of the Merovingian dynasty, a dynasty that could claim as one of its shoots the Byzantine emperors and empresses of the eastern Roman Empire. This means that the Flemish and the Scots, Norse, French, and perhaps even the Holy Roman Empire can lay claim to Sinclair's explorations.

16. A recent book, *The Columbus Myth* by Ian Wilson, supports the claim that Bristol mariners, expelled from Iceland and searching for a new supply of cod, "rediscovered" Newfoundland some twelve years before Columbus. Wilson attempts to demonstrate that Bristol fishermen not only preceded Columbus but also their fellow countryman John Cabot to the shores of America by over a decade. I really cannot comment on Wilson's claim because of the knowledge that *The Knights Templar in the New World* presents. It seems obscure to argue who discovered America around 1492 when all of the evidence points to pre-Christian exploration of North America. What is of importance in relation to Norumbega and the lost Seven Cities is the historical account presented by Wilson of Cabot's supposed voyage(s) that, like Columbus's and Champlain's, are full of suspicion and contradiction.

Of John Cabot's voyage, who under the flag of England's King Henry VII reputedly sailed from the West Country port of Bristol to "discover" North America in 1497, there survives no journal, no biography, not a single document in his handwriting nor even any remotely contemporary portrait. Yet he was hailed as a conquering explorer when, in 1756, the British required a claim to the New World.

17. Bradley, *Holy Grail Across the Atlantic,* 144–46.

18. Pohl, *Prince Henry Sinclair,* 156–58.

19. Rand, *Legends of the Micmacs,* 232, 234, 235, 255–57, but as quoted from Pohl, *Prince Henry Sinclair,* 165–66.

20. What further intrigued me about the story of the Westford knight is the fact that the surname Mann falls within the Gunn clan. I find myself continually going back to the question of how my great-uncle could become privy to certain information developed by a band of medieval Scottish Knights Templar. This question is especially puzzling given that the Manns' ancestral home is in Norwich, England, and knowing that relations between England and Scotland have been, at best, lukewarm for centuries. Did Henry Sinclair not die at the hands of the English in 1400? Or is it just possible that the notion of the brotherhood of Knights Templar being stronger than individual loyalty to one's country is true, especially if one looks back to the creation of the brotherhood?

 Luckily, Michael Baigent and Richard Leigh provided me with the solution to this piece of the riddle through their book, *The Temple and The Lodge.* I just couldn't get over the question, why me? What is it about the Mann family's background that allows me to relate a seemingly simple diagram to a Scottish prince's expedition to Nova Scotia in and around A.D. 1398? The answer just might lie in Baigent and Leigh's explanation of the ties between Scotland, England, and Flanders, knowing that the Mann family is of strong Flemish descent.

 According to the British authors, during the reigns of David I (1124–1153) and Malcolm IV (1153–1165) there was a systematic policy of settling Flemish immigrants in Scotland. As a result, Scottish towns assumed certain distinctly Flemish characteristics, while elements of Scotland's ancient Celtic heritage found their way back to Flanders.

 It is not hard to imagine that old loyalties remained with the class of tradesmen and merchants, many of Flemish origin, who settled throughout the new towns of England and Scotland. Indeed, it was these "middle class" tradesmen and merchants who became the administrators and financiers of the network of Templar holdings and who maintained regular shipping and trading between the larger urban centers throughout Europe. These old loyalties would have also continued throughout the centuries through fraternities such as the Freemasons.

21. Bradley, *Holy Grail Across the Atlantic,* 53–56.

22. Ibid., 207–11.

23. Ibid., 97–109.

24. Bradley, *The Columbus Conspiracy,* 4–16.

25. Ibid., 27–38.

26. Bradley, *Holy Grail Across the Atlantic,* 217–18. Bradley noted that the Flemish could also be considered to be of Norse descent. Interestingly, Chrétien's story of the Grail was dedicated to Philippe d'Alsace, Count of Flanders. The New Ross ruins and Newport Tower discussed earlier have definite Norse characteristics. In

Prince Henry's time (the fourteenth century), the Norse sagas were just being written down in Latin; they formed the nucleus of Scandinavian lore. Earlier stories of the Celtic Avalon must have intertwined with the Norse sagas to produce a blended version of the "Isle to the West."

Chapter 4: Mary, Mary Quite Contrary

1. Baigent, Leigh, and Lincoln, *The Messianic Legacy,* 225.
2. Baigent, Leigh, and Lincoln, *Holy Blood, Holy Grail,* 247.
3. Bradley, *Holy Grail Across the Atlantic,* 176–83.
4. Ibid., 183.
5. Baigent, Leigh, and Lincoln, *Holy Blood, Holy Grail,* 249.
6. Ibid.
7. Ibid., 250. The British authors of *Holy Blood, Holy Grail* seemed to be more surprised by the fact that the Welsh word for "bear" is *arth,* as in "Arthur," rather than by the fact that *ursus,* the Latin word for "bear," is associated with the royal Merovingian line. Whereas Bradley, in *Holy Grail Across the Atlantic,* 301–18, provides sound reasoning that associates the transfer of the Holy Grail from Arthur to the Merovingians circa A.D. 500. Bradley noted that in the fifth century the invasion of the Huns, and more particularly the invasions of the Angles and Saxons and others into Britain, provoked massive migrations of all European tribes, including the Sicambrian ancestors of the Merovingians, into Gaul.
8. Baigent, Leigh, and Lincoln, *Holy Blood, Holy Grail,* 250–51. In the early fifth century, around the same time that the Celts were declining, the Sicambrians moved into Gaul, establishing themselves in what is now the Lowlands of Belgium and northern France. Prior to this, the Sicambrians had maintained close contact with the Romans and had adopted their customs and administration. Following the collapse of the Roman Empire, it was natural that the Sicambrians would assume control of the already existing but vacant administrative structure in a region that came to be called the kingdom of Austrasie. The core of this kingdom is what is now known as Lorraine. Subsequently, the regime of the early Merovingians conformed to the customs and fashions of the old Roman empire.
9. Baigent, Leigh, and Lincoln, *The Messianic Legacy,* 224.
10. Interesting enough, the Ramusio text, *Pella navigationi et viaggi,* and its accompanying map, first published in 1556, illustrates in a classical manner the huntress and a circle of dancing maidens within an idyllic forest setting in the New World.
11. In Roman mythology Diana, who was the counterpart to the Greek Artemis, possessed the same general attributes, yet forever remained a virgin. Artemis, on the other hand, was said to be desired and loved by many but ultimately possessed by none. Knowing this provides an inkling as to the notion of the important women surrounding Jesus being a "virgin" and a "harlot."

12. Just as in the Lovers card of the tarot, Artemis and Hekate are one, a lunar goddess of the life cycle with two aspects. One stands at the beginning of the cycle, the other at the end. One is young, pure, and beautiful, connected with young life, and the other is gruesome, connected with death. In Greek mythology Hekate, whose temples and altars stood at gates, entrances, or in front of houses reminiscent of the gates of hell, is described as traveling above graveyards with her hounds, collecting poison and then mixing potions of death.

13. In another myth, the hunter Aktaeon paid the penalty for spying upon the unclothed Diana as she bathed in the stream of a forest valley. So enraged was Diana at his arrogance that she turned him into a stag and the very dogs with whom he hunted tore him limb from limb.

14. Delos, the birthplace of Artemis, has always been considered the most sacred place of ancient Greece. No one knows why, but to Maurice Chatelain, author of *Our Ancestors Came from Outer Space,* the only logical explanation for this belief is that Delos is the geometric center of a Maltese cross of majestic proportions that extends hundreds of miles over the Aegean Sea, Greece, and Turkey.

    When, using Delos as his center point, he connects by a simple circle thirteen geographical sites that have always been sacred places marked by temple ruins, he arrives at a magnificent Maltese cross visible only to those high up in the air. The giant geometric figure passes in succession through sites that relate to major Greek/Roman mythology, such as Delphi in Greece, the island of Psathura in the northern Sporades, Antandrus and Sardis in Anatolia, Cairus on Rhodes, and Akkra and Araden of Crete.

15. According to Greek mythology, Persephone was abducted from the garden of earth and thrown into a chariot by Pluto and carried off into the earth's labyrinth, leaving Demeter, her mother, to grieve over her death.

16. Frazer, *The Golden Bough,* 161–67.

17. Ibid., 149–56.

18. Ibid., 280–81.

19. Ibid., 265.

20. Ibid.

21. Robinson, *Born in Blood,* 201–10, 231–34.

22. Ibid., 255–68.

Chapter 5: Peace 681

1. The majority of the references and conclusions found in this chapter are based on interpretations of the Rennes Parchments first presented by Henry Lincoln in *The Holy Place* and further deciphered by myself. Although some of the original deciphers were presented in Gèrard de Sede's *L'Or de Rennes,* I first learned of the decoding through *The Holy Place* and Baigent, Leigh, and Lincoln's *Holy Blood, Holy Grail,* 24–40. Therefore, most of the following notes and references identify

these two sources as the origin of my investigation, although my conclusions deviate from those of the British authors.

2. Lincoln, *The Holy Place,* 16–32.

3. Ibid., 22–23.

4. Ibid., 23.

5. Ibid.

6. Ibid., 25.

7. Ibid., 27.

8. Baigent, Lincoln, and Leigh, *Holy Blood, Holy Grail,* 138–44. Lincoln found yet another password. There are further dropped letters that spell "bread and salt," possibly connoting the mixing of water and wine, or the body and blood of Christ, during the celebration of the Eucharist.

9. Ibid., 264–65.

10. Lincoln, *The Holy Place,* 51.

11. Baigent, Leigh, and Lincoln, *Holy Blood, Holy Grail,* 34 and 91.

12. Fanthorpe and Fanthorpe, *Rennes-le-Château,* 91.

13. Baigent, Leigh, and Lincoln, *Holy Blood, Holy Grail,* 133.

14. Quoted from *Holy Blood, Holy Grail,* 133.

15. Ibid., 444–45.

16. Ibid., 445.

17. Ibid., 446.

18. Ibid.

19. Ibid., 140–44. René d'Anjou's other particular interests included chivalry and the Arthurian and Grail romances.

20. Ibid., 142–43.

21. Ibid., 143.

22. Perhaps Leonardo's *Mona Lisa* also reflects the knowledge that, as Grand Master of the Priory of Sion, he knew where the treasure of the Templars was hidden. If one examines the background of his most famous painting carefully, one will notice that a red serpentine avenue or stream leads from what appears to be an underground cave, through a mountainous and deserted landscape, to the breast of what may well be an androgynous figure of the Goddess and Leonardo himself.

23. Fanthorpe and Fanthorpe, *Rennes-le-Château,* 59–64. The Fanthorpes uncovered a very mysterious subplot of misinformation concerning the number of paintings completed by Poussin on the *Shepherds of Arcadia* theme. Not surprisingly, the trail leads back to Shugborough Hall, Staffordshire and the home of the Shepherd Monument.

24. Ibid., 63.

25. Lincoln, *The Holy Place,* 62.

26. Ibid., 63.

27. Ibid., 64.

28. Ibid.
29. Ibid.

Chapter 6: The Temptation of St. Anthony

1. Butler, *Butler's Lives of the Saints,* 15–16. In about the year A.D. 285, at the age of thirty-five, Saint Anthony crossed the eastern branch of the Nile and took up residence in some ruins on the top of a mountain. Here he lived almost twenty years in solitude. To satisfy his ever-growing group of followers, he eventually came down from the mountain and founded his first monastery. But he chose for the most part to shut himself up in his cell upon the mountain until his death.

2. In Sassetta's famous painting (circa A.D. 1440), *The Meeting of Saint Anthony and Saint Paul,* three scenes in one are presented. In the first scene, Anthony is shown setting out across the desert to find his companion, Saint Paul. In the second scene, he blesses the centaur, a symbol of the pagan world, in a manner suggesting that the Christian church adopted many symbols from its pagan roots. The third scene is where Saint Anthony finally meets with Saint Paul (bringing together the two rings of light that surround them in a symbolism reminiscent of the vesica pisces!). All of this takes place in a landscape dense with woods, under a horizon high above the airy hills. In scene three, though, instead of sky there is an abstract gold ground that seems to emphasize a gold-rich land where simple objects and events are treated with preciousness. Could this be another sly reference to the blessed land of Arcadia?

    What is missing within these enchanting scenes from the life of Saint Anthony is the completion of his task, the completion of the fourth scene: Saint Anthony burying Saint Paul within the cave with the help of the two lions. This omission has provoked a flood of literature and arguments with respect to the overall concept of the series of events. Is one to conclude that the Christian church was not founded upon the rock of Saint Paul but upon the pagan symbolism that came before it, and that the church's sanctity is tainted by its demand for riches? In the eleventh to fifteenth centuries, these were part of the secret teachings of the Cathars and the Knights Templar. Could Saint Anthony the Hermit's deeds be seen as the true path to Christendom? The Knights Templar certainly believed that in order to seek the light, one had to retreat into the desert or the wilderness.

3. Saint Anthony was also known as the patron saint of skin diseases, in particular ergotism, or "Saint Anthony's fire." He had a reputation as a healer in general and for this reason was the object of much devotion in the Middle Ages and during the Crusades.

4. Charroux, *Treasures of the World,* 23–24. To date, there have been many possible explanations as to what the Holy Grail was. Other possibilities still remain: some as wildly far-fetched as the two cruets containing the blood and sweat of Christ to the bones and relics of Joseph of Arimathea, Saint Anthony

the Hermit, or Saint Paul. The one sure fact is that whatever Saunière discovered, whether it was treasure or the keys to the treasure, it caused him to forego his religious beliefs for something far more valuable.

A strong contender for the source of his wealth lies within the ancient and medieval history of Europe, more particularly the intertwining of the history of the Knights Templar and Rennes-le-Château. According to one popular explanation, the coded messages led Saunière to a cache of Visigoth gold, silver, and jewels hidden below the ancient church. An elaboration on this theory traced the treasure back to Solomon and the Treasure of Zion in the Holy Land. Other historians suggested that the Jewish treasure was taken to Rome by Titus and looted from the Roman treasury by Alaric, the Visigoth, in A.D. 410. This is supported by the knowledge that what is now the tiny village of Rennes-le-Château was once a major Visigothic center, and substantially fortified.

Another theory suggested that Saunière actually discovered several ancient tombs in which it was customary for the nobility to be buried in all their finery, complete with jewels and golden ornaments. Others suggested that Saunière found the sacred chalice Jesus once used at the Last Supper with his disciples or the lance once buried in the side of Christ at the moment of his death. Any such Christian relic would have accounted for Saunière's apparent unlimited supply of wealth.

But the fact is that modern-day politico-religious societies such as the Priory of Sion and the Knights Templar continue to search for the "holy treasure" or links that confirm Jesus Christ as the rightful Messiah and provide direct proof of God's presence on earth.

It would seem that the greatest treasure of symbolic and literary relevance to Western religious tradition and the Knights Templar included the legendary treasure of the Temple of Jerusalem. This would warrant the references to "Sion" within the Rennes Parchments, the contents of the holy of holies included the immense gold seven-branched candelabrum so sacred to Judaism, and possibly the reference to the Ark of the Covenant as well.

5. Quoted from Charroux, *Treasures of the World*, 22.
6. Ibid., 31.
7. Butler, *Butler's Lives of the Saints*, 197–98.
8. Ibid., 25.
9. The twin pillars found at the main entrance of Solomon's temple also have similarities to traditional Canaanite fertility symbols. The temples dedicated to the Goddess in Tyre are said to have featured stone pillars of phallic design at their entrances; these pillars were the focus of fertility rites performed in honor of Astarte at her special festivals. Connections have also been made between these pillars and the monoliths used by Lamech and his sons to preserve their ancient knowledge within the hieroglyphic symbols carved on their surfaces.

According to Canaanite beliefs, a pre-Flood patriarch named Lamech, who had three sons (the three apprentices), was the first to invent geometry. It is said that the first son taught geometry, another was supposedly the first mason, and the third was a blacksmith who was supposedly the first human to work with precious metals. Similar to the story of Noah, Canaanite tradition maintained that Lamech was warned by Jehovah of the impending Flood, caused by the wickedness of humanity. Consequently, Lamech and his sons decided to preserve their knowledge in two hollow stone pillars so that future generations would discover it.

One of these pillars was apparently discovered by Hermes Trismegistus or Thrice Greatest, known to the Greeks as the god Hermes and to the ancient Egyptians as Thoth. According to occult sources, the Emerald Tablet of Hermes is said to contain the essence of the lost wisdom from before the days of the biblical Flood. It is said that the mystic Apollonius of Tyana discovered this tablet in a cave. The first published version of the Emerald Tablet dates from an Arabic source of the eighth century A.D. and it was not translated into Latin in Europe until the thirteenth century.

It has even been suggested that it was the legendary Emerald Tablet that eventually found its way to Rennes-le-Château, and was ultimately discovered by Bérenger Saunière.

10. The question as to who was the original author and when the fourth gospel was first written remains one of the paramount enigmas for any Testament scholar. If the gospel was written toward the end of the disciple's life, then this would place it at the end of the first century.

11. Ancient legends tell of the removal of Saint Andrew's relics from Patras in Achaia, an ancient district in southern Greece, where he was supposedly crucified, to Scotland in the eighth century. At a place in Fife, now called Saint Andrew's, the relics were supposedly enclosed within a church, which eventually became a center for pilgrimage. It is that Andrew was chosen as the patron saint of Scotland that Prince Henry would have recognized the need to sanctify a new church with the (re)consecration of certain relics.

12. Butler, *Butler's Lives of Patron Saints*, 272–73.

13. Ibid., 274. There is a stranger legend concerning Saint Joseph that has found its way into the traditions of the metals trade of the western counties of Britain. Local folklore says that Joseph of Arimathea was once a metal merchant who visited Britain in search of tin and lead long before he came back to settle there. The story tells that on one of these visits he brought the young Jesus with him.

14. Saint Catherine's vision supposedly occurred during the time of Constantine the Great, who was originally a worshipper of the sun god but one day apparently had a vision of his own. King Constantine professed to have seen Christ in a dream and it was Christ who instructed Constatine to conquer his enemies using the sign of the cross. Following these instructions, it is said that, at the Battle of the Milvian Bridge in A.D. 312, Constantine's soldiers bore the Christian symbol on their shields, and when the battle was won Constantine devoted his remaining years to the development of Christianity.

15. Sinclair, *The Sword and The Grail,* 138.
16. Baigent, Leigh, and Lincoln, *Holy Blood, Holy Grail,* 113–14.
17. In the early 17th century, Charles I commissioned a painting which depicts himself as Apollo, the patron of the arts, and his Queen as Diana, overseeing the seven Liberal Arts. Among the arts, the Duke and Duchess of Buckingham are shown to represent Hermes (music) and poetry respectively. What Charles I was obviously trying to convey in an allegorical manner was that by Divine Right he saw himself as the stewart (or Stuart) of knowledge and promoter of understanding, and therefore, protector of the hidden treasure—wisdom.
18. Sir Arthur Conan Doyle, in his *Memoir of Sherlock Holmes,* wrote of "The Greek Interpreter." It is a story of an interpreter who is forced to act as a go-between during a meeting between a Greek gentleman and his sister. Unfortunately, the lady fell in with two unscrupulous scoundrels who tried to force the brother, through torture and starvation, to sign over his own and his sister's property. But the Greek interpreter devises a second underlying code based on simple arithmetic that allows the brother to convey his message of alarm. Holmes is summoned by the interpreter and intervenes only to find that the two villains have escaped with the girl and that the brother was murdered. Is it just possible that Doyle knew that clues to the interpretation of the Holy Grail mystery lie within Greek allegory? One might suspect that Doyle understood, in a manner similar to Poussin, an interpretation of the Bible not normally preached by the Roman Catholic Church.
19. MacKenzie, *The Royal Masonic Cyclopedia,* 374–79, 715.
20. Ibid., 635–37.
21. Sinclair, *The Sword and The Grail,* 89–107.

Chapter 7: The Keys

1. MacKenzie, *The Royal Masonic Cyclopedia,* 254–56.
2. Both sexes were eligible for initiation into the Zoroastrian religion at the age of fifteen. One of the main symbols of initiation was a special cord that the candidate wore. Every day the initiate was required to untie the cord and then to replace it while reciting prayers. This was the forerunner to the Catholic rosary. In a similar manner, the cord is very much like the one worn by present-day Catholic priests. In other ways, the cord resembles the girdle described within the Arthurian romances that secured the sword Excalibur.
3. The deciphered Rennes-le-Château parchments indicate that if you find the individual that holds the "key," then you will find the treasure. To accomplish this is not as simple as it first appears. The original keys supposedly were given to Saint Peter. But from the information presented, it is apparent that there are many keys intermixed throughout all ancient religions and myths.

   The next question appears to be: who possesses the keys to this day? Do the Church, the Priory of Sion, or the Freemasons possess the keys that unlock the highest orders of the ancient mysteries? Or can the key be discovered by any individual who has an inkling as to how the cord can be unraveled?

4. Within all secret mysteries lie the key elements of death, rebirth, and fertility. These elements are central to any understanding of the pagan origins of the myths of Osiris, Dionysus, Adonis/Tammuc, and even Freemasonry.

5. The key to the pagan origins of Freemasonry lies in the symbolic story of Hiram Abiff and the association or adoption of ancient initiation rites into the three basic degrees of Masonry. In Masonic lore the basis of the legend of Hiram Abiff is the semimythical story of the construction of King Solomon's temple in Jerusalem. This building is regarded as the repository of ancient occult wisdom and symbolism by both the modern-day Freemasons and the Knights Templar.

6. Kabbalistic traditions suggest that during the building of Solomon's temple, the craftsmen who came from Tyre with Hiram were paid in corn, wine, and oil. These specific sacrificial offerings were associated with the fertility cults of the dying gods, such as Osiris and Adonis. (Of note is the fact that the same offerings would have been available to Prince Henry Sinclair and his men during their stay in Nova Scotia.)

    The same kabbalistic traditions tell of how Solomon supposedly carried King Hiram of Tyre off to hell by evoking a demon. However, this was not an act of vengeance. The story goes that when the King of Tyre returned from the depths, he told Solomon of all that he had seen and learned in the infernal kingdom. According to the Kabbalah, this was the true source of Solomon's wisdom. What this suggests is that Solomon was in actual fact a student of Hiram and was instructed by him in the pagan mysteries of the goddess Ishtar or Astarte and her story of the underworld. It was even suggested that Solomon and Hiram communicated in coded form and that this may be the basis for the coding of the Rennes-le-Château parchments.

7. The reader may now begin to see the association that the Templars developed in relation to the Ark of the Covenant. The Templars, for all intents and purposes, probably assumed that they were in fact the substitute guardians of an "ark" of the Cathars, which allowed for direct communication with God. This may explain the positioning of the angelic nymphs or winged messengers on either side of the Ark of the Covenant, which is displayed on the Golden Arms of the Antient Grand Lodge, as discussed in chapter 11.

8. MacKenzie, *The Royal Masonic Cyclopedia*, 357–86.

9. In a dualistic nature, the tail or vulnerable part of the crab is positioned to allow penetration at Green Oaks. In alchemy, this point is identified as the point where the "virgin's milk" fuses with the child, or the lunar sea. On another level this is known as the "nurturing of the philosopher's stone." A strange variation on the theme is the suckling of the toad on the breast of the Dual Mother so that she may die as the toad grows big with her milk. Can this have anything to do with the fact that the Merovingians revered the symbol of the toad or the frog?

10. Remember that the deity Baphomet was not only seen as an androgynous, dual nature symbol but also possesses a number of elements of the Goat. Therefore,

through a rather loose interpretation, the Templars may have been worshipping the essence of Jesus Christ when they worshipped Baphomet. This may explain why it was said that both the Templars and the Cathars spat and stomped on replicas of the Cross, the object of Christ's crucifixion.

11. The number 666 was also identified as a beast, half-man and half-god, that possessed intellect and understanding. This relates back to the tale of King Merovee being the offspring of his mother and two fathers, King Clovis of the Merovingians and a sea creature of Neptune. It also suggests ancient memories of Goddess worship through the myth of the she-demon that inspires sexual desires in men by sending them erotic dreams. Like Venus in her *femme fatale* or enchantress form, this aspect of the feminine was transformed into a demonic symbol.

12. Fell, *America B.C.*, 253–76 and Bradley, *Holy Grail Across the Atlantic*, 160–62.

13. Fell, *America B.C.*, pages 250, 283–85.

14. In support of this intriguing notion is the fact that many other place- names throughout Nova Scotia, through minor alterations to their spelling or obvious relationship to the landscape, can relate to the known story of the Holy Grail/Jesus Christ. For instance, the community name of Lantz could possibly relate to the lance that pierced Christ's side. "Walden" could relate to Christ's tomb that was located in the wall or cliff face of a mountain, similar to a bear's den. And "Marie Joseph" obviously relates to Christ's parents.

   Other place names have a distinct relationship to the Masonic allegory of Hiram Abiff. There is Acaciaville, Head of St. Margaret's Bay, and Hillgrove. Still others relate to the background history of the Templars themselves. There is St. Margaret's Bay, Elmsdale (the cutting of the Elm at Gisors), Old Barns, Lyons Brook, Minasville, and the ever-present Anthony, St. Paul, St. Mary, and St. Peter.

15. Wood, *Genisis, The First Book of Revelations*, 65.

16. General references for this section concerning prehistoric monuments and ancient ruins mainly come from E. C. Krupp's, *In Search of Ancient Astronomies*.

17. Krupp, *In Search of Ancient Astronomies*, 67–68.

18. Ibid., 56–76.

19. Goode, *Goode's World Atlas*, 66–67.

20. There are two more numerical oddities that relate the numbers 666 and 72 back to what we now know of *The Little Keys of Solomon*. The first relates to the mapping of the world using the azimuthal equidistant projection and the Seal of Solomon. From Green Oaks to Alexandria there is a distance of 4,801.5 miles on a bearing of 66.6 degrees. The number 4,801.5 when divided by 66.6, equals 72.09. When the number 4,801.5 is divided by the key of fusion, 1746, it equals 2.75, the number generally associated with the megalithic yard. When 4,801.5 is divided by the number of ancient poles in a mile, 320, the result is 15, the number assigned to man and the reciprocal of 666—the sign of the

beast. One last relationship before this gets really crazy: 4,801.5 divided by 2775 (the sum of the numbers 1 to 74) equals the approximate numerical value of a cubit, 1.72.

The second relates to the notion that a snake's (666 again?) movement reflects a sine wave or motion curve. It just so happens that the first two angles derived from a sine curve are 72 and 66.6 degrees. Anyone who has ever been graded on a bell curve will appreciate that being located between these two angles in relation to the class average is like taking a free ride to the next station. Therefore, the two symbols of the snake and bell must somehow provide a key to the location of the deity, as do the equilateral triangle and the pentagram.

21. Baigent, Leigh, and Lincoln, *Holy Blood, Holy Grail,* 190–92.

22. Quoted from *Holy Blood, Holy Grail,* page 190 although the original quote appears in S. Erdeswick's *A Survey of Staffordshire.*

23. Quoted from *Holy Blood, Holy Grail,* 192.

24. Daraul, *Secret Societies, Yesterday and Today,* 220–26.

25. Ibid., 227.

26. Lord Anson is of general interest because of his many victories over Spain and the amount of money that he personally gained from these endeavors. It almost appears that Anson acted more like a pirate than lord admiral of the British fleet. It also appears that George III, the reigning monarch during Anson's conquests, and his contemporaries, Sir George Pocock (1706–1792), Lieutenant-General George Keppel (1724–1772), and Sir Jeffrey Amherst (1717–1797), Commander in Chief of the Army in North America, financially shared in Lord Anson's personal endeavors.

In 1762, just before his death, Lord Anson, as First Lord of the Admiralty, was instrumental in the capture and surrender of Havana. The plunder amounted to approximately one million pounds of gold and silver, according to the official records of the time. Yet perhaps there was something more valuable than gold and silver among the many Catholic churches of Havana. Perhaps one more key to the never-ending mystery was obtained.

Chapter 8: La Val d'Or

1. Before the discovery of the New World, gold was extremely scarce in Europe, Asia, and Africa. Yet, according to biblical sources, in order to build his temple Solomon exchanged twenty-five cities for 4,400 pounds of gold from Hiram, King of Tyre. However, Hiram Abiff, Solomon's architect, was still forced to send several expeditions to the Ophir mines in order to meet a gold shortfall. Although these expeditions left from the gulf of Aqaba in the Red Sea, their ultimate destination has never been determined.

2. Charroux, *Treasures of the World,* 60–70.

3. Fell, *America B.C.,* 1–13.

4. Ibid., 93–111.

5. Trento, *The Search for Lost America,* 190–93. Mystery Hill is one of the better-known sites of ancient travelers to America. But a lesser-known area quite close to Nova Scotia yielded some very interesting artifacts that link the Phoenicians to the New World. On Manana Island, which is located off the larger Monhegan Island of Maine, inscriptions identified by Barry Fell as a Celtic script known as Hinge-Ogam were found. The pointed runic characters differ from the seventy well-known varieties of Irish Ogam in that they lack symbols for vowels. Past epigraphers apparently failed to understand these differences and therefore always considered the runes to be marks created by natural erosion. Barry Fell, in essence, cracked the code of a previously unknown writing system.

Evidence of an active sea trade between North America and the Mediterranean over two thousand years ago was found in the bay at Castine, which is located about fifty miles northeast of Monhegan Island along the Maine coast. In 1921, at about forty feet below the water's surface and stuck in the mud, two ceramic amphorae dating back to ancient Phoenicia were found. These led to the theory that thriving seaports grew in ancient times all along the eastern seaboard of the New World.

6. Grant, *Myths of the Greeks and Romans,* 338.
7. Ibid., 339.
8. Ibid., 32.
9. There is speculation among many historians that the famous Ugarit poems are indications that an earlier enlightened civilization existed before the Flood and from this civilization evolved the varying dialects and customs of Arcadia.
10. Grant, *Myths of the Greeks and Romans,* 44.
11. Ibid.
12. It is possible that Ugarit and Phoenician sailors encountered bears, wolves, and other wild animals during their trading journeys to the New World.
13. Baigent, Leigh, and Lincoln, *Holy Blood, Holy Grail,* 287.
14. Ibid., 287–88. After their war against the other eleven tribes of Israel, the Benjamites fled westward toward the Phoenician coast, since the Phoenicians were their allies. They too worshipped the Mother Goddess—Astarte, Queen of Heaven.

Prince Henry Sinclair would surely have recognized the similarities to his own exodus to the west.

15. Grant, *Myths of the Greeks and Romans,* 247. The Minotaur, the product of the love between the bull and Pasiphaë, is only one of a series of monsters that appeared on Cretan seals. On some of the seals, a man's face and head are covered by a bull's mask, reflecting the Celtic theme of the man in the mask.
16. Leonardo da Vinci recognized that over time stories that became myths and customs of one country are adopted by other civilizations. In fact, this knowledge was considered by Leonardo to be the thread that held civilization together. In his painting *The School of Athens,* Leonardo depicted himself as Plato carrying

the *Timaeus* while a second figure appears anxious. While the second figure is painted to reflect what Christ is generally known to have looked like, he is wrapped in Greek dress. Curiously, the outer toga displays a golden border that wraps itself around the Christlike figure while Plato appears to be reassuring the other figure that, given time, the thread will lead to the knowledge contained within the temple's pillar or to heaven itself.

Knowing that many levels of symbolism are found throughout all of Leonardo's work, what may be suggested is that through the patience and wisdom gained through one's lifetime, a series of relationships from ancient time to Christianity will become evident. Leonardo may also be suggesting that this wisdom will lead to an increased understanding of the true relationship of heaven and earth, as well as a specific location on earth where this wisdom may be obtained.

Leonardo gave an additional clue in his drawing titled *Val d'Arno*, which sounds very similar to *Val d'Or*. The drawing is in fact one of the most important documents of Leonardo's early work. It shows him already master of an original technique in which the effects of light are achieved with a directness only gained through quick broken stokes of the pen and flicks of golden paint from the brush. But what is most significant in terms of providing further clues to the mirror image of the Valley of Gold is the composition of the landscape. The landscape is full of movement, with water flowing over the side of a hill, cascading into a dark pool and running through a cultivated valley to a distant shoreline. The background shows mist-enclosed hills and a castle located on an adjacent precipice. If one looks closely enough, the face of a lion or bear can be seen in the rock edge next to the golden waterfall or cascade. It appears that Leonardo knew that the Valley of Gold was light itself or that only through knowledge and understanding of the ancients would one find the true Val d'Or.

17. Alchemy is extremely complicated and the initiate is not expected to understand the principles and perform successful transmutations at an early stage. In many ways, this reflects the appeal of any secret society. Only through the wisdom and understanding gained through a succession of steps or rituals can the student hope to achieve an enlightened state.

18. Alchemy is a combination of those skills developed by the early metal workers and craftsmen, with Greek philosophy, Eastern mystic cults, earth science, numerology, astronomy, and sacred geometry—everything the well-intentioned Templar of the fourteenth century needed to establish a mining and agricultural community in the New World. But Prince Henry Sinclair possessed something else, the wisdom to understand that what many considered to be magic were simply the forces of nature. On the other hand, he understood that if certain natural forces could be attributed to magic, then he would appear to be a magician to those of a lesser light. Therefore, no one would dare enter the magician's Valley of Gold.

19. Baigent, Leigh, and Lincoln, *Holy Blood, Holy Grail*, 455.

20. According to legend, Arthur's Stone, the stone from which Excalibur was drawn, is located on a ridge overlooking the Golden Valley in Hereford, England. Excalibur is said to be cast away in at least five different places within southern England, and the best known is Dozmary Pool, on Bodmin Moor. The likeliest derivation of the name Excalibur is from the Latin *chalybs,* which means steel; in English, *steel* can poetically mean a sword. It was said that Arthur's sword was forged at a smithy of the fairy-folk on the island of Avalon.

21. Baigent, Leigh, and Lincoln, *Holy Blood, Holy Grail,* 237–44.

22. Ibid., illustration 27.

23. Rutherford, *Celtic Lore,* 146. The notion of turning a "blind eye" to what may appear apparent to most can be found in the Norse and Celtic myths of Woden and Lugh. Odin, the son of Woden, is blind in one eye, as is Cu Chulainn, the son of Lugh. This brings to mind the notion of an all-seeing third eye being present in everyone, but not everyone has the ability to "see" with it.

24. The skull and crossbones was associated with both the Templars and the murdered Master, Hiram Abiff. During the seventeenth and eight- eenth centuries, in Masonic ritual, the skull and crossbones denoted Hiram's grave or the grave of any Master Mason. Legend has it that even Bruce was buried with his leg bones crossed beneath his skull. The skull and crossbones is also an important symbol within the modern-day Knights Templar, and it figures prominently among the ancient Knights Templar graves discovered by Baigent and Leigh at Kilmartin, Scotland.

25. Fanthorpe and Fanthorpe, *Rennes-le-Château,* 100–102 and Crooker, *Oak Island Gold,* 146–49.

26. Grant, *Myths of the Greeks and Romans,* 13–44.

27. Quoted from Binns, *Ovid.*

28. Frazer, *The Golden Bough,* 163, 701–14.

Chapter 9: The Fortress of Glass

1. Ashe, *Avalonian Quest,* 13–20.

2. Ibid., 202–221.

3. Matthews, *The Voices of the Wells,* 1–40.

4. One conclusion that can be made rather quickly is that there remain certain common elements that can be applied to the location and character of the Fortress of Glass. Another conclusion is that the concept of the Grail castle survived from pagan and Celtic mythology. The Grail castle was originally an earthworks, cave, or simple stone dwelling, which protected the inhabitants from the elements and provided burial chambers for the dead. These simple dwellings soon gave way to the thatch huts of the peasants and hermits and by the time of the creation of the Celtic Elysium had become the courts and halls of the kings and knights.

5. Sinclair, *The Sword and The Grail,* 32–33.

6. Quoted from Pohl, *Prince Henry Sinclair,* 208.

7. Fanthorpe and Fanthorpe, *Rennes-le-Château,* 12–13.

8. Ibid., 12.

9. Baigent, Leigh, and Lincoln, *Holy Blood, Holy Grail,* 105–6, 121, 170.

10. Ibid., 170.

11. Ibid., 106.

12. Ibid., 145 and 178. Once again, Baigent, Leigh, and Lincoln, through some remarkable research, flagged a key to the seemingly unrelated manipulations behind European politics of the sixteenth and seventeenth centuries which appear to have originated from the ancient Ardennes town of Stenay.

   Most significant concerning the layout of this village stronghold is the fact that apart from the historical perspective, it appears to provide architectural components for Poussin's many classical landscapes. For example, in Poussin's two paintings *Landscape with a Man Killed by a Snake* and *Landscape with Pyramus and Thisbe* the castles that are situated on the hilltop found in each painting display distinct architectural elements resembling those found at the Castle of Gisors. In Poussin's *The Exposition of Moses,* a lady in blue points to a distinctive octagonal tower found in the left background while cautioning her fellow accomplice to be silent.

   If one compares this to Poussin's later series *The Four Seasons* it is interesting that the castles depicted in both *Summer* and *Fall* take on a lighter, more whiter, appearance as they seem to be bathed in a bright light. Poussin's earlier castles always seemed to be situated in the shadows. Was Poussin hinting at God's presence, which appears to emerge from the shadows during times of classical revival?

13. From the earliest times, Judaism and Islam recognized geometry as the actualization and application of God's word. Therefore, by adopting the practice of building architectural structures based on sacred geometry, later medieval Christianity was, in effect, searching for God's presence or essence on earth. What this also does, perhaps inadvertently, is support the earliest beliefs of the Goddess as the temple.

14. Holroyd and Powell, *Mysteries of Magic,* 180–83.

15. Baigent, Leigh, and Lincoln, *Holy Blood, Holy Grail,* 362–66, 424. There may be another solution as to what happened to the holiest of holy treasures of the temple. The priests of the temple may have hidden the items relating to the House of David and the rightful king of Israel, Jesus Christ, in the catacombs of the temple in what had been Christ's sepulcher.

   A non-Canonical saying of Jesus states: "He who is near unto me is near unto the fire." In simpler terms, the fire of life is essential to the achievement of wholeness. The alchemists supposedly conceived their *aqua vitae* or water of life to be *ignis* (fire). Apparently, the all-dissolving *aqua vitae* is a basic ingredient in the production of the Stone of the Wise, which confers immortality upon those who possess it.

16. MacKenzie, *The Royal Masonic Cyclopedia,* 195.

17. In Poussin's painting *The Deluge* there is a background silhouette of Noah's ark sailing toward the setting sun, which is positioned between two faint pillars or towers. Unfortunately, as with the sanctuaries of the Templars, one cannot see what is occurring within the ark. One could speculate, however, that Poussin was suggesting that the Ark of the Covenant, with its true word of God, could be found in the land to the west. In both esoteric and Templar circles, the symbolism of the circle with two bars through its middle was known to be a code meaning "to the west." Perhaps the pillars represent the Strait of Gibraltar, otherwise known as the Pillars of Hercules. Or they could represent the staggering cliffs of the Bay of Fundy that Prince Henry Sinclair, the Celts, Jason and the Argonauts, and only God knows who else, appear to have passed through en route to the new Temple of Solomon.

18. Unlike the Roman Catholic Church, which remained fixated on the concepts of the devil and hell as all-encompassing, supreme forms of evil, the Cathars/Templars thought that they knew the true nature of the devil. This statement may appear blasphemous from a Christian point of view but it can be argued that the devil is only a symbol created by the Church of Rome. On the other hand, the Cathars/Templars were eliminated as an outward force because of their inability to adapt to the orthodox teachings of their day. The confusion may lie in the Church's direct association of Satan with the devil and all that is evil. The Cathars/Templars considered all created matter the work of Rex Mundi/Satan and, as flesh, Jesus could only be so related. What this implied was that we are all descendants of Satan and that the true House of God could be the House of Satan the Good, or Lucifer.

   In the Jewish *Targusm Sammael,* the birth of Cain is ascribed to a union of Satan and Eve. Hiram Abiff supposedly descended from the line of Cain through Tubal-Cain who, with his son, was said to be the only survivor of the superior race after the Flood. Masonic tradition also tells us that this race was created by the Elohim, "the serpent people," those of the fire snake.

   Looking back at Poussin's painting *The Shepherds of Arcadia,* the Christ figure is associated with winter, due to a number of clues including his snow-white garment, laurel wreath, and the reasoning that Christ was born around the winter solstice. Relating this information to Poussin's series of paintings, *The Four Seasons,* we see that winter is represented by a flood and referred to as *The Deluge.* In the foreground, opposite the only people that appear to be saved, is a serpent with its head pointed in the direction of these people. Is this another of Poussin's hidden references to the serpent people?

19. The Tower is number sixteen in the tarot sequence. The number 16, if made up of 1 and 6, reduces to 7, which is a solar number designating power and positive action. The lightning flash (the bolt of Jove) depicted within The Tower was one of the attributes of Jupiter and the Norse god Thor and also figures promi-

nently in Mahayana and Tantric Buddhism as a symbol of the overpowering light of truth in which all falsehood, and ultimately all duality, is destroyed. According to occult lore, it is the flash of inner illumination that brings the freedom of enlightenment.

In the tarot card, the top of the tower is seen to have been struck off by a fiery bolt from heaven. Symbolically, the crown or point of a monument frequently represents the peak of consciousness, revealing that in its flashing descent the lightning of pure selfhood, the primal energy of the psyche, strikes aside and rends all structures of the ego. Thus, having accepted the true nature of the devil, Prince Henry can be seen to have symbolically transformed into Lucifer, who embodies the purity of divine Truth.

Chapter 10: Out of the Shadows

1. One of the most stately and dignified of all the temples of Egypt is that at Dendera. An earlier temple must have stood on the site, for the Ptolemies built only on sites that were already holy and sanctified by shrines. The entrance portico of the great Temple of Hathor in Dendera is singularly impressive because of its gigantic pillars.
2. Krupp, *In Search of Ancient Astronomies,* 198–200.
3. Ibid., 207–9.
4. As this appears to be a parallel to the story of the Westford Knight, perhaps the death of Kuhkw was viewed by Prince Henry Sinclair and his men as a necessary sacrifice.
5. Krupp, *In Search of Ancient Astronomies,* 215–18.
6. Rock-cut temples normally began as natural caves but were scarce in Egypt for the simple reason that the cliffs were positioned so far away from the Nile River, then the natural highway and life-support of the Egyptian people. However, one of the most magnificent temples or tombs found in Egypt, which also rivals the Great Pyramids, is the great temple built by Rameses II at Abu Simbel in Nubia. The temple at Abu Simbel was designed to face the sunrise and contains four deities to whom the temple was dedicated. The temple was designed so that as the sun rises the rays strike right through the temple and fall on the four enshrined figures.
7. Stone "doors" with large copper handles block access to the new chamber. This brings to mind the most famous fairy tale of all, the Cinderella tale, where two elder stepsisters jealous of the youngest enslave her within an inner chamber of a castle. This fairy tale was told through the *Cabinet de Fées* of Charles Perrault (1628–1703), but Apuleius's work *The Golden Ass* had already given us a version in Cupid and Psyche where "Once upon a time there lived a king and queen who had three very beautiful daughters." Remarkably, this relates back to the story of Dagobert II and his Celtic queen, Mathilde, who bore him three daughters but no son and heir. A son and heir was only produced after Dagobert's subsequent marriage to the Merovingian princess, Giselle.

8. Krupp, *In Search of Ancient Astronomies,* 187–215. During the period of development of the Egyptian calendar, which was later adopted and modified by the Greeks and Romans, the star Sirius rose helically at the same time each year that the Nile overflowed its banks. This annual nourishing of the rich farmland adjacent the Nile coincided, approximately, with the summer solstice and thus the most northerly sunrise came to assume a more dominant tradition than Sirius.

9. Among the animals considered to be sacred to Apollo were the wolf, the dolphin, and the white trumpeter swan. As a symbol of a prophet, Apollo was known to have assumed the shape of a hawk, a raven, a crow, or a snake. Of the numerous objects or symbols attached to Apollo, the most common were the lyre and the bow. Of further significance, in his role as the Pythian Apollo, the god was portrayed with the tripod, which was also the favorite offering at his altars.

10. The theory that subterranean regions lie below the earth's oceans is an old one and at times resurfaces in the context of the Hollow Earth theory. The Hollow Earth theory suggests that we live inside a spherical cosmos in the center of which are the sun, moon and planets, and that there are openings at the north and south poles through which we can pass to an inner world. According to the theory of John Cleves Symmes in the early part of the nineteenth century, in the inner world there lies a Utopian society.

In Jules Verne's *A Journey to the Center of the Earth*, the heroes climb into an extinct volcano and descend to the interior of the earth. Verne's interest in volcanoes stemmed from his friendship with the noted geographer Charles Saint-Claire Deville. Deville had explored volcanoes all over the world and had even descended into the temporarily dormant crater of Stromboli, a famous volcano in the Mediterranean.

In his discussions with Deville, Verne learned that hundreds of active volcanoes and thousands of dormant or extinct ones are distributed over the earth's surface. At that time, no one knew what caused volcanic activity, even though scientists had realized that many volcanoes occur in well-defined belts, or chains. One such chain runs through the Mediterranean region and includes Stromboli, Vesuvius, and Etna. Another chain runs northward through the Atlantic Ocean and includes volcanoes in the Canary Islands, the Azores, and Iceland. According to one past theory, different volcanoes were connected by deep subterranean tunnels or passages, and were fed from the same fiery source inside the earth.

Along these very same lines, many of the critical points determined through the manipulation of a Star of David across a map of the world, employing an azimuthal equidistant projection, fall on known volcanic regions. Even Nova Scotia exhibits certain physiography, including the "smoking hill" at Stellarton, which relates to volcanic activity. As the reader will remember, Glooscap's "right-hand man," Kuhkw, had the ability to travel under the earth.

11. Hill, *Glooscap and His Magic, Legends of the Wabanaki Indians,* 100–107.

12. Ibid., 161–70.

13. Crooker, *Oak Island Gold,* 48.

14. Ibid.

15. Bradley, *Holy Grail Across the Atlantic,* 159–60, 311. The skull and cross-bones symbol seems to have been adopted, or openly adopted, by the pirates around the year 1704. Tradition has it that around this time the pirate John Quelch was one of the first pirates to fly the Jolly Roger, or black jack. The earliest record of a Jolly Roger occurs in 1700, when a French pirate flew "a sable ensign with cross-bones, a death's head and an hourglass" during an engagement with an English man-of-war off Jamaica. Interestingly enough, all three of these elements relate back to the story of the Knights Templar and the Priory of Sion.

16. Ross and Deveau, *The Acadians of Nova Scotia: Past and Present,* 25.

17. Clarke, *The Acadians,* 47–53.

18. The unsettling aspect to come out of all the manipulations between the French and English during the mid-eighteenth century is that during this time major manipulations were also occurring in Europe and, more specifically, within the realm of Freemasonry. For example, the Freemasonry of Grand Lodge had by 1755 infused itself into every aspect of English society and the majority of British officers stationed in North America were affiliates of the English Grand Lodge. But the ill-fated 1745 Scottish rebellion must surely have exposed the same high-ranking English officers to further traditions and secrets of Scottish Freemasonry. Therefore, one may never be sure as to who was ultimately responsible for the expulsion of the Acadians since, indeed, it is known that the Grand Lodge had absorbed the objectives and principles of the Jacobite cause.

Chapter 11: Into the Light

1. It must be noted that in all of the stories in which the Grail appears, whether they be the earlier Irish and Welsh myths or the later French and English versions, there remains one constant element: all of the Grail-bearers are maidens.

2. Fanthorpe and Fanthorpe, *Rennes-le-Château,* 88.

3. Among others who claimed that they had arrived at their scientific theories by studying the secret writings of the ancient Egyptians, including the hidden works of Thoth, were Copernicus, the renaissance astronomer, and the seventeenth-century mathematician Kepler.

4. Many so-called new age authors have tried to make the definitive connection between Saint John's Gospel and earlier rituals such as those of the Egyptians and, more particularly, the Celts. For example, one of the strongest aspects of both John of the New Testament and Celtic lore is the principle of rebirth and, more specifically, its association with the rite of baptism through immersion in water. The sacrifice of victims during pagan times by drowning is somewhat analogous to both the druid ceremony of initiation and the later practice of baptism conferred through Saint John the Baptist.

5. Kujawski, Pedro de Salles P., "In Service to the Psyche, The Grail Legend in C.G. Jung's Individuation Process," In: *The Household of The Grail* edited by John Matthews, 185–97.

6. This recalls the rather cryptic message that Michael Bradley interpreted from the original Gastaldi map in the Venice Ptolemy of 1548. In Bradley's case, the word *flora* was meant to be interpreted as "the flower." However, as we have seen, there is no reason why the same word or phrase cannot be interpreted on many different levels.

7. Kujawski, Pedro de Salles P., "In Service to the Psyche, The Grail Legend in C.G. Jung's Individuation Process," In: *The Household of The Grail* edited by John Matthews, 190–91. Perceval, in his quest for the Grail, is shown on one level to be concerned with the problem of finding the form or essence in which the spirit of Christ exists in the heart of man.

8. This same principle can be applied to Prince Henry's reconstruction of the labyrinth of the Grail across mainland Nova Scotia.

9. MacNulty, *Freemasonry—A Journey through Ritual and Symbol,* 16.

10. Scholasticism was the intellectual framework for medieval Christianity that supported the early establishment of the Latin Church and reconciled the classical philosophers with the teachings of Christianity; whereas, Humanism examined the ancient philosophers for their individual and scientific thought, regardless of whether or not it supported the Church and its doctrine.

11. Fanthorpe and Fanthorpe, *Rennes-le-Château,* 13–16.

12. Ibid., 17, 40–41. The gnosticism and hermeticism that grew out of southern France were based in part on Manichanism, which is a branch of theology that is mainly concerned with the teachings of Mani, a mystic who lived in the third century A.D. According to the principles espoused by Mani, the human soul originated in the Kingdom of Light, to which it is continually trying to return. Hence, the human body was seen as the Kingdom of Darkness.

    This supports gnostic, Neoplatonist, and hermetic thought that spirit is good and matter is evil. In a sense, this principle may be interpreted as an attempt to weld the classical patterns of reincarnation onto the teachings of Christ whereby if a person can acquire the necessary inner spiritual knowledge, he or she can escape from the prison of matter which is the body.

13. It is interesting that the *Hermetica* sporadically remained to a certain extent approved by the Church of Rome even during the Renaissance and the Reformation. In fact, in the enthusiasm for new learning and the rediscovery of antiquity that was an integral part of the Renaissance, the figure of Hermes Trismegistus and the *Hermetica* occupied a privileged position. One of the results of the revival of Hermes in the Renaissance was the commitment to scientific experimentation, even if it was magical or alchemical experimentation.

14. Cavendish, *Encyclopedia of the Unexplained,* 110–13.

15. Ibid., 112.

16. Nicolas Poussin's painting *La Peste D'Azoth,* completed by the artist in 1632, shows the Ark of the Covenant between the two pillars of a temple on top of a stone plinth that can be likened to the cornerstone of the temple. Strangely, a figure clad in white resembling the perceived image of Christ is located to the right of the Ark and appears to be conveying to the crowd the notion that something is concealed in the hollow left-hand column. Other clues in the painting lead to the conclusion that the Ark may be found in a "land of the dead."

One of the most interesting clues lies in the fact that within the foreground there lies a young child who appears to be providing a foundation for the rest of the painting and its story. This may relate to the common ancient practice of sacrificing a small or newborn child beneath the initial foundation stone of a proposed building in order to ensure its architectural strength and "oneness" with the earth.

17. Hutchinson, *The Spirit of Masonry,* 82–109.

18. Ibid., 110–11.

19. Ibid., 82–109.

20. Glastonbury is probably the best-known site suspected of having its landscape altered in order to reflect celestial or spiritual beliefs and to accommodate pagan rituals. Some researchers believe they have found similar sculpting of the natural landscape at Kings-upon-Thames, Edinburgh, and Glasgow. There is also the recent theory that the three Great Pyramids reflect the history of man.

21. The idea that a continuation or record of time and belief may be constructed out of earth and stone continued into the masons' guilds of the fifteenth century. Rosslyn Chapel is perhaps the best known example and it is speculated that the chapel is built on the site of at least three earlier sacred enclosures.

22. Fanthorpe and Fanthorpe, *Rennes-le-Château,* 35–46.

23. Hill, *More Glooscap Stories: Legends of the Wabanaki Indians,* 168–78.

24. MacNulty, *Freemasonry,* 20–32.

25. Ibid., 19, 50.

26. Relating the story of Prometheus to the actions of Prince Henry Sinclair, we remember that the sculpted eagle in the landscape appears to be devouring the red serpent (stream). Could it not be perceived that the eagle is feasting upon the blood-rich liver of Prometheus? If this is the case, then it may shed some light on where the "entombed god lies," because the waterfall that originates from a spring on top of the hill at Green Oaks follows a narrow crevice in the rocks into a pool of mire in the valley below.

27. Certain pagan cults worshiped the sun as a deity under the name Sol Invictus, the "Invincible Sun." Even Constantine was hailed by his contemporaries as a "Sun Emperor," and Sol Invictus figured in every aspect of society. At the appropriate time, Jesus Christ and thus all of Christianity assumed many of the Sun cult's attributes and tolerances.

The emphasis on the sun as a deity draws an interesting parallel with the very foundations of the Christian Church. In Poussin's painting *The Deluge,* the setting sun in the west is split by two parallel, horizontal bars. This symbolism may represent the twinning of Saint John the Baptist and Saint John the Evangelist, two significant figures in the formation of the Christian Church as we know it today. Or it may be confirming the parallel that is becoming increasingly apparent between ancient pagan practices and early Christian philosophy.

28. Francis Bacon's *The New Atlantis* as contained within Warhart, *Francis Bacon: A Selection of His Works,* 448.

29. The notion conveyed by the walled garden supports the Masonic tradition that walls or hollow pillars are where tokens, or emblems, of their builders were deposited. It was assumed that these symbols would be safe because very few men would take the time and expense of digging to the very cornerstone or foundation of such buildings. The "angle-stone" is another name for the finished cornerstone, which usually formed a perfect cube.

    Perhaps it is a rough cornerstone upon which the fourth figure in Poussin's *The Shepherds of Arcadia* has placed his foot. This appears to suggest that the stone has not as yet been shaped. Could this also be another suggestion as to "the completion of the square"? This perhaps sheds further light on Prince Henry's task. Perhaps his objective was to hide a holy treasure within a new yet unfinished Temple of Solomon until such time as the world was prepared to rebuild the temple. What this suggests is widely supported by the ever-increasing awareness that many of today's churches have been built on older medieval and pagan foundations. One prime example is Saunière's Rennes-le-Château Chapel, which was dedicated to Saint Mary Magdalene.

Chapter 12: On A Golden Wing

1. Frazer, *The Golden Bough,* 14–15, 163–67. Sacred groves were common among the ancient Germans, Greeks, and Romans, as well as the Celts. The oak worship of the druids is familiar to everyone in one form or another, as there are still annual gatherings within sacred groves and woodland glades around the world.

2. Ibid., 711.

3. Although Frazer's *The Golden Bough* is the primary source of reference here as it relates to interpretation of classical myth, I have always been struck by the similarities between these classics and Masonic ritual. Of course, one of the strongest similarities is between the story of Orestes and the death of the architect, Hiram Abiff. In many ways, it is suggested that ancient secrets are only avaliable to the true initiate, and that earlier practices have been hidden within the temple, and not at its doorsteps.

4. Frazer, *The Golden Bough,* 14–15. The flight of Orestes and his combat with the priest was reminiscent of the human sacrifices once offered to the Tauric Diana. This became the rule of the sanctuary. A candidate for the priesthood

could only succeed to office by slaying the priest, and having slain him, he retained office until he or she was in turn slain by a stronger or craftier foe. In many ways, this suggests that it was absolutely necessary for Prince Henry Sinclair to defeat the Sorceress of the Atlantic before he could hold the position of master, magician, and priest.

5. Ibid., 3–5, 8. At Rome and in other Latin cities, history tells that there was a priest called the Sacrificial King or King of the Sacred Rites. His wife was therefore traditionally called the Queen of the Sacred Rites. In republican Athens and many other Greek states, there also existed titular kings whose duties appear to have been solely priestly in nature. During the later Roman period, after the abolition of the monarchy, the Sacrificial King-cum-priest was appointed to offer the sacrifices that before had been offered by the stately kings.

6. It is disappointing to learn that after all the solemnity attached to the original use of magical powers, the object of the ritual may turn out to be only the concealment of treasure, the persecution of an enemy, and/or the conquest of a woman. Or maybe it isn't. Perhaps the Templars and Prince Henry Sinclair applied these objectives for a higher level of purpose.

7. Baigent, Leigh, and Lincoln, *Holy Blood, Holy Grail*, 209–44.

8. Frazer suggested that the ancients and mystics set great store on the magical qualities of precious stones and natural and carved rocks. Indeed, natural stones were used as talismans, and carved stones were used as ornaments. Prehistoric people and pagans alike worshipped naturally shaped or slightly modified stones in many different ways. During the time of the Greeks, the name of "tree agate" was even given to a stone that exhibited treelike markings. Reminiscent of the power of the King of the Wood and his Queen, early Greek farmers believed that if two of these gems were tied to the horns or necks of the plough oxen, a bountiful crop would be ensured.

    The Greeks also believed that a certain stone could cure snakebites, and hence named it the "snake stone." Remember that the Westford Knight supposedly died of snakebite and was subsequently "immortalized" by carving his effigy in stone. Another rather remarkable association between Prince Henry Sinclair and the ancient beliefs can be found in the Greek belief that the wine-colored amethyst, which in Greek means "not drunken," can keep its wearer sober. Again, this relates back to the legend of Glooscap, whose magic supposedly came from the amethyst stone set in his belt and whose first attribute was that he was "sober and grave."

9. Graves, *The White Goddess*, 17–27.

10. Ashe, *Mythology of the British Isles*, 244–49. The two main concepts of Arthur's survival, the Avalon legend and the cave legend, both derive from the Celtic myth of the banished god, Cronus, who sleeps in a cave on a western island until the dawning of a new Golden Age.

    A similar version of the cave legend is still part of the Arthurian lore of Glastonbury and Cadbury-Camelot. The legends tell of a king that sleeps in a cave whose doors or gates occasionally open so that the unsuspecting may catch a glimpse of him.

From all accounts, it is because of Arthur's fall at the hands of his son, Mordred, that the Golden Age perished. However, because of the belief in Arthur's immortality, the ideal of the Golden Age is not lost. In many parts of rural Britain, there exists a deep-rooted belief that King Arthur lies in his cave, awaiting discovery. Thus, the archetypal pattern reflected by the Lost King has maintained a real influence on past and present religious and political movements, as well as mythology and tourism.

11. Fanthorpe and Fanthorpe, *Rennes-le-Château*, 127–28. Although several books present the notion that many famous writers had an inkling as to the true story behind the Grail mystique, it is Lionel and Patricia Fanthorpe who most clearly and concisely (in my mind at least) capture the essence of the underlying mystery and its relationship to Rennes-le-Château. Although I have independently checked some sources and other references, all references in this chapter originate from the Fanthorpes, since I consider them to be most expert in relation to Tolkien's and many of his contemporaries' works, as well as with the life and times of Francis Bacon.

12. Ibid., 92–96, 100–2, 118–21. One point that the reader will now have determined is that this book, along with most other books, based its contents and conclusions not on a glorious flash of original thought but on extensive and well-documented research and association, mingled with some intuitive and determined insight. Fortunately, other authors such as the Fanthorpes provided much of the in-depth research in such disparate topics as "inklings" and Francis Bacon, which has allowed the intuition to come much faster. Therefore, to disguise the debt that I owe to authors such as Henry Lincoln, Michael Bradley, and the Fanthorpes, as well as to Andrew Sinclair, would be unfair. Thus, I must once again acknowledge that most of the background pertaining to Francis Bacon and his use of watermarks comes directly from the Fanthorpes' work on Rennes-le-Château.

13. Not so curiously, the mass production of paper and the dissemination of "secret" information coincided with a time when occult beliefs were first experiencing a revival of sorts, during the late sixteenth century, Queen Elizabeth I's "golden age of revival."

14. For a far more extensive and illustrative look at the subject of these curious watermarks, please refer to the Fanthorpes' *Rennes-le-Château*, 92–96, and also Higenbottam's, *Codes and Ciphers*.

15. Fanthorpe and Fanthorpe, *Rennes-le-Château*, 94. It was Lionel Fanthorpe who unsuspectingly confirmed that a deeper mystery lies within the use of watermarks by the secret societies of the sixteenth century. I must say that for an ordained Anglican priest, Reverend Fanthorpe possesses a remarkable ability to look beyond the formal teachings of the church.

16. Ibid., 95. The reason for quoting the dates of the watermarks that derive from the Fanthorpes' research is to identify that "inklings" of Prince Henry's endeavors in the New World, circa 1398, may have been disseminated immediately after the fact. This raises some very interesting questions as to whether the full story had indeed been lost or was suppressed by those who knew.

17. Bradley, *Holy Grail Across the Atlantic,* 221–58. Here I change wheels, so to speak, and follow Michael Bradley's notion that Champlain explored Nova Scotia in search of Sinclair's lost settlement and perhaps even dissuaded his fellow explorers by falsifying his maps and reports. Although I have deviated slightly from Bradley's conclusions pertaining to Champlain, nevertheless Bradley's examination of the intricacies of Champlain's motives and actions are in far greater detail than I could ever have determined on my own.

18. Ibid., 223.

19. Ibid., 235. Michael Bradley noted the fact that Champlain is as silent about the Minas Basin and Cape d'Or as he is about Mahone Bay. Unfortunately, Bradley failed to pursue this line of questioning and concentrated instead on the idea that Mahone Bay acted as a port of "refuge" to those in on the secret.

20. Quoted from William Hutchinson, *The Spirit of Masonry,* 79–80.

21. Fanthorpe and Fanthorpe, *Rennes-le-Château,* 55–73. If the reader is interested, the Fanthorpes provided a wonderful account of the many significant aspects of the Paris Meridian as it is located throughout France.

22. The experience of the Grail journey and its initiation sequence, like that of the tarot cards, provides an increasingly complex connection with those sacred mysteries that were designed to induce transformation or show the path to a higher consciousness. The Kabbalah and kabbalistic thought is another such ritual.

23. Baigent, Leigh, and Lincoln, *Holy Blood, Holy Grail,* 318–19.

24. Ibid., 319.

Chapter 13: A Fool's Discovery

1. Baigent, Leigh, and Lincoln, *The Messianic Legacy,* 445.

2. Baigent, Leigh, and Lincoln, *Holy Blood, Holy Grail,* 423–24.

3. Ibid., 426. If events had turned out differently, current descendants of some of the most prominent European families could still claim the throne of the Kingdom of Jerusalem.

4. Ibid., 344.

5. Ibid., 345.

6. Ibid. Another striking coincidence (?) to emerge from all of the seemingly unrelated evidence found within the ancient and pagan mysteries and the later Testaments is that a great deal of the material apparently originated in the vicinity of the Greek city of Ephesus. What strikes me is that if one substitutes the letter *j* for the root word *Ephe,* one arrives at the Lost King's first name, Jesus. The British authors of *Holy Blood, Holy Grail,* 342, supported the notion that "Jesus

the Messiah" actually derived from the Greek mysteries of Ephesus. In simpler terms, the word *Ephe* (meaning "short-lasting" in Greek) was replaced by Jesus, the son of God (Jehovah), a forever-lasting concept and symbol of the Almighty.

7. Francis Bacon's *The Wisdom of the Ancients* as contained within Warhart, *Francis Bacon: A Selection of His Works,* 274–77.

8. Ibid., 278.

9. Once again, this supports the idea that additional knowledge was derived from that which was already known and passed on through classic myth and allegory.

10. In *The Sword and The Grail,* Andrew Sinclair highlighted the notion that the winged horse Pegasus was but one symbol that allowed the Templars to associate their Christian activities with the more ancient pagan and Greek myths.

11. One connection between the earliest pirates and the medieval Templars appears to be that they both considered themselves to be somewhat super-human, molded in the image of Hercules and bound to the notion that they, too, could accomplish over time the twelve feats of Hercules. Though Hercules was sometimes worshipped as a god, he was considered to be more of a man-hero who always chose the hard path of right action in preference to a life of ease.

12. In Greek religion, as described in the "Orphic holy books," from which Plato quoted verses, there are the accounts of the life, death, and miracles of Orpheus, the supreme singer and patron of poetry. What the Orphics did was to combine all of Apollo's and Dionysus's "good" tendencies into the myth of Orpheus, while Dionysus and Apollo themselves retained all of their darker secrets and habits. Once again, we are struck with the notion of a fusion of ancient traditions, folktales, romances, and, perhaps, semihistorical memories. Plato, in turn, saw the stories of Orpheus as one way for the common folk to escape everyday tedium and to provide temporary absences of the soul from its human frame— in other words, to allow the oppressed a moment of relief and to daydream.

13. Francis Bacon's *The Wisdom of the Ancients* as contained within Warhart, *Francis Bacon: A Selection of His Works,* 431–42.

14. Catholic Bible Press, *The Holy Bible Containing the Old and New Testaments. New Revised Standard Version (Catholic edition).* Perhaps it is most fitting to end this book by referring one more time to the building of Solomon's temple and to the knowledge that Solomon possessed. According to Proverbs 9:1: "Wisdom, and wisdom alone, built her house"; and, according to Proverbs 25:2, "it is the glory of God to conceal a thing: but the honour of kings is to search out a matter." What this means, I think, is that the seeker of wisdom, no matter who that may be, is immeasurably the richer, for he or she follows in the footsteps of the ancient kings.

Bibliography

Andersen, Hans Christian. *The Complete Fairy Tales and Stories*. Translated by E.C. Haugaard. New York: Anchor Press/Doubleday, 1974.

Ashe, Geoffrey. *Avalonian Quest*. London: Collins, 1986.

———. *King Arthur's Avalon*. Rev. ed. London: Collins, 1966.

———. *Land to the West*. London: Methuen, 1986.

———. *Mythology of the British Isles*. London: Methuen, 1990.

———, ed. *The Quest for America*. New York: Praeger Publishers, 1971.

———, ed. *The Quest For Arthur's Britain*. London: Granada, 1968.

Baigent, Michael, and Richard Leigh. *The Dead Sea Scrolls Deception*. London: Corgi Books, 1991.

———. *The Temple and The Lodge*. London: Jonathan Cape, 1989.

Baigent, Michael, Richard Leigh, and Henry Lincoln. *Holy Blood, Holy Grail*. London: Corgi Books, 1991.

———. *The Messianic Legacy*. London: Jonathan Cape, 1986.

Barber, Malcolm. *The Trial of the Templars*. Cambridge, England: Cambridge University Press, 1993.

Bennett, John G. *Gurdjieff, the Making of a New World*. London: Turnstone Books, 1973.

Binns, J. W., ed. *Ovid*. London: Routledge & Kegan Paul, 1973.

Bird, Will R. *Off-Trail in Nova Scotia*. Toronto: The Ryerson Press, 1956.

Birks, Walter, and R.A. Gilbert. *The Treasure of Montségur*. London: Thorsons, 1987.

Bord, Janet and Colin. *Mysterious Britain*. London: Granada, 1974.

Boudet, H. *La vraie langue celtique et le cromleck de Rennes-les-Bains*. Nice: Belisane, 1984. Facsimile of 1886 original.

Bowen, Catherine Drinker. *Francis Bacon: The Temper of a Man*. Boston: Little, Brown, 1963.

Bradley, Michael. *The Columbus Conspiracy*. Willowdale, ON: Hounslow Press, 1991.

———. *Grail Knights of North America*. Toronto: Hounslow Press, 1998.

———. *Holy Grail Across the Atlantic*. Willowdale, ON: Hounslow Press, 1988.

Budge, E.A. Wallis. *The Egyptian Book of The Dead*. New York: Dover, 1967.

———. *An Egyptian Hieroglyphic Dictionary*. 2 vols. New York: Dover Publications, 1978.

———. *The Gods of The Egyptians*. 2 vols. New York: Dover Publications, 1969.

———. *Osiris and The Egyptian Resurrection*. 2 vols. New York: Dover Publications, 1973.

Butler, Alban. *Butler's Lives of the Saints*. San Francisco: HarperSanFrancisco, 1991.

———. *Butler's Lives of Patron Saints*. San Francisco: Harper & Row, 1987.

Canada Department of Mines and Resources. *Geology and Economic Minerals of Canada*. Ottawa, 1947.

Canada Department of Tourism and Culture. *Nova Scotia Travel Guide*. Halifax, NS: 1993

Cathlolic Bible Press. *The Holy Bible Containing the Old and New Testaments, New Revised Standard Version* (Catholic edition), 1993.

Cavendish, Richard, ed. *Encyclopedia of the Unexplained*. London: Arkana, 1989.

Chadwick, Nora. *The Celts*. Harmondsworth, England: Penguin, Pelican Books, 1971.

Champlain, Samuel de. *The Works of Samuel De Champlain*. 6 Vols & Folio. Ed. H.P. Biggar. Toronto: University of Toronto Press, 1971.

Charroux, Robert. *Treasures of the World*. London: Frederick Muller Limited, 1966.

Chatelain, Maurice. *Our Ancestors Came From Outer Space*. London: Pan, 1980.

Clark, Andrew Hill. *Acadia: The Geography of Early Nova Scotia to 1760*. Madison: The University of Wisconsin Press, 1968.

Clark, Kenneth. *Leonardo Da Vinci*. London: Penguin, 1959.

Clarke, George Frederick. *Expulsion of the Acadians: The True Story*. Fredericton, NB: Brunswick Press, 1980.

Creighton, Helen. *Bluenose Ghosts*. Toronto: McGraw-Hill Ryerson, 1957.

———. *Bluenose Magic*. Toronto: McGraw-Hill Ryerson, 1968.

———. *Folklore of Lunenburg County, Nova Scotia*. Toronto: McGraw-Hill Ryerson, 1976.

Crooker, William S. *The Oak Island Quest*. Windsor, NS: Lancelot Press, 1978.

———. *Oak Island Gold*. Halifax, NS: Nimbus, 1993.

Daraul, Arkon. *Secret Societies, Yesterday and Today*. London: Frederick Muller, 1961.

Delaney, F. *The Celts*. London: Grafton, 1989.

Doyle, Sir Arthur Conan. *Sherlock Holmes: The Complete Novels and Stories*. 2 vols. Toronto and New York: Bantam Books, 1986.

Duriez, C. *The C.S. Lewis Handbook*. Essex, England: Monarch, 1990.

Eco, U. *Foucault's Pendulum*. London: Picador, 1990.

———. *The Name of the Rose*. London: Picador, 1984.

Encyclopedia Britannica. Fourteenth edition, volume 1 s.v. "Francis Bacon," 1952.

Erdeswick, S. *A Survey of Staffordshire*. London: JB Nichols, 1844.

Eschenbach, Wolfram von. *Parzival.* Translated by Helen M. Mustard and Charles E. Passage. New York: Vintage, 1961.

Fabricius, Johannes. *Alchemy.* Northamshire, England: The Aquarian Press, 1976.

Fanthorpe, Patricia, and Lionel Fanthorpe. *The Holy Grail Revealed.* North Hollywood, Calif.: Newcastle Press, 1982.

———. *The Oak Island Mystery: The Secret of the World's Greatest Treasure Hunt.* Toronto: Hounslow Press, 1995.

———. *Rennes-le-Château.* Middlesex, England: Bellevue Books, 1991.

Farmer, D. H. *The Oxford Dictionary of Saints.* Oxford: Oxford University Press, 1982.

Fell, Barry. *America B.C.* New York: Pocket Books, 1979.

———. *Bronze Age America.* Toronto: Little, Brown, 1982.

Feugere, Pierre, Louis Saint Maxent, and Gaston de Koker. *Le serpent rouge.* SRES Vérités Anciennes, 1981.

Fraser, Mary L. *Folklore of Nova Scotia.* Antigonish, NS: Formac, 1928.

Frazer, James G. *The Golden Bough.* New York: Macmillan, 1923.

———. *Magic and Religion.* London: Watts, 1944.

Furneaux, Rupert. *The Money Pit Mystery.* New York: Fontana/Collins, 1976.

Ganong, William Francis. *Crucial Maps.* Toronto: University of Toronto Press, 1964.

Geoffrey of Monmouth. *History of the Kings of Britain.* Edited and translated by Lewis Thorpe. Harmondsworth, England: Penguin, 1966.

Gimbutas, Maria A. *The Language of the Goddess.* San Francisco: HarperSanFrancisco, 1991.

Goode, J. Paul. *Goode's World Atlas.* New York: Rand McNally & Co., 1991.

Goodrich, Norma Lorre. *King Arthur.* Danbury, Conn.: Franklin Watts, 1986.

Goss, John. *The Mapping of North America.* Secaucus, N.J.: The Wellfleet Press, 1990.

Grant, Michael. *Myths of the Greeks and Romans.* New York: New American Library, 1962.

Graves, Robert. *The White Goddess.* London: Faber and Faber, 1961.

Guirdham, A. *Catharism, The Medieval Resurgence of Primitive Christianity.* Paris: St. Helier, 1969.

———. *The Cathars and Reincarnation.* London: Neville Spearman, 1976.

Hancock, Graham. *The Sign and The Seal - The Quest for the Lost Ark of the Covenant.* Toronto: Doubleday Canada, 1992.

Hannan, Leslie F. *The Discoverers.* New York: Random House, 1983.

Hapgood, Charles. *Maps of the Ancient Sea-Kings.* Philadelphia: Chilton Books, 1966.

Harris, Reginald V. *The Oak Island Mystery.* Toronto: The Ryerson Press, 1967.

Hawkins, Gerald S. *Stonehenge Decoded.* New York: Doubleday, 1965.

Heindenreich, C. E. *Cartographica - Explorations and Mapping of Samuel de Champlain, 1603-1632.* Toronto: University of Toronto Press, 1976.

Higenbottam, Frank. *Codes and Ciphers.* London: English Universities Press, 1973.

Hill, Kay. *Glooscap and His Magic: Legends of the Wabanaki Indians.* Toronto: McClelland and Stewart, 1963.

———. *More Glooscap Stories: Legends of the Wabanaki Indians.* Toronto: McClelland and Stewart, 1988.

Hitchcock, Henry Russell. *In the Nature of Materials - the Buildings of Frank Lloyd Wright - 1887–1941.* New York: Da Capo Press, 1975.

Holroyd, Stuart and Neil Powell. *Mysteries of Magic.* London: Bloomsbury Books, 1991.

Hutchinson, William. *The Spirit of Masonry.* New York: The Aquarian Press, 1987.

Israel, Gerald, and Jacques Lebar. *When Jerusalem Burned.* New York: William Morrow, 1973.

Jung, C. G. *Collected Works.* (London: Routledge; Princeton, N.J.: Princeton University Press.) Volumes include:

Archetypes and the Collective Unconscious, 1959

The Interpretation of Nature and the Psyche, 1955

Mysterium Coniunctionis, 1963

Psychology and Alchemy, 1953

The Structure and Dynamics of the Psyche, 1969

Jung, C. G. *Memories, Dreams, Reflections.* London: Fontana, 1972.

———. *Synchronicity.* London: Routledge, 1972.

Kerr, D. G. G. *Historical Atlas of Canada.* 3rd Rev. ed. Don Mills, ON: Thomas Nelson & Sons (Canada) Limited, 1975.

Knight, G. *The Secret Tradition in Arthurian Legend.* Wellingborough, England: Aquarian Press, 1983.

Krupp, E. C., ed. *In Search of Ancient Astronomies.* New York: Penguin, 1984.

Lescarbot, Marc. *History of New France.* Vol. 2. Translated by W. L. Grant. Toronto: The Champlain Society, 1911.

Levi, Eliphas. *History of Magic.* London: Rider, 1968 reprint; New York: Weiser, 1969, paperback.

———. *The Key of the Mysteries.* London: Rider, 1968 reprint; Hackensack, N.J.: Wehman, and New York: Weiser, 1970, paperback.

———.*Transcendental Magic: Its Doctrine and Ritual.* London: Rider, 1962 reprint; Hackensack, N.J.: Wehman, 1962; New York; 1970, paperback.

Lincoln, Henry. *The Holy Place.* London: Jonathan Cape, 1991.

Loomis, Roger Sherman. *The Grail - From Celtic Myth To Christian Symbol.* Princeton, N.J.: Princeton University Press, 1991.

MacKenzie, Kenneth. *The Royal Masonic Cyclopedia.* Wellingborough, England: The Aquarian Press, 1987.

MacNulty, W. Kirk. *Freemasonry—A Journey Through Ritual and Symbol.* London: Thames and Hudson Ltd., 1991.

Mathers, S. Liddell MacGregor. *The Kabbalah Unveiled.* New York: Weiser, 1970.

———. *The Key of Solomon the King.* London: George Redway, 1888.

Mathews, John, ed. *The Household of the Grail*. Wellingborough, England: The Aquarian Press, 1990.

McGhee, Robert. *Canada Rediscovered*. Ottawa: Canadian Museum of Civilization, 1991.

Merot, Alain. *Nicholas Poussin*. New York: Abbeville Press Publishers, 1990.

Moncrieffe, Iain. *The Highland Clans*. New York: Clarkson N. Potter, 1967.

Mouni, Sadhu. *The Tarot*. London: Allen & Unwin, 1962. Hackensack, N.J.: Wehman, 1962.

Mowat, Farley. *West Viking*. Toronto: McClelland and Stewart, 1995.

Munro, R. W. *Highland Clans and Tartans*. London: Peerage Books, 1987.

Murray, Margaret A. *The Divine King in England*. London: Faber, 1954.

O'Connor, D'Arcy. *The Big Dig*. New York: Ballantyne, 1988.

———. *The Money Pit*. New York: Coward, McCann & Geoghegan, 1976.

Philip, J. A. *Pythagoras and Early Pythagoreanism*. Toronto: University of Toronto Press, 1966.

Poe, Edgar Allan. *The Complete Tales and Poems of Edgar Allan Poe*. Toronto: Vintage, 1975.

Pohl, Frederick. *The Lost Discovery*. New York: W. W. Norton, 1952.

———. *Prince Henry Sinclair*. New York: Clarkson N. Potter, 1974.

Quarrell, Charles. *Buried Treasure*. London: MacDonald & Evans, 1955.

Ramsey, Raymond H. *No Longer on the Map*. New York: Viking, 1972.

Rand, Silas Tertius. *Legends of the Micmacs*. New York: Longmans, Green & Co, 1894.

Regardie, Israel. *The Golden Dawn*. 3rd ed. St. Paul, Minn.: Llewellyn, 1970.

———. *Roll Away the Stone*. St. Paul, Minn.: Llewellyn, 1968.

———. *The Tree of Life*. 2nd ed. New York: Weiser, 1969.

Robinson, John J. *Born in Blood*. New York: M. Evans, 1989.

Ross, Sally and Alphonse Deveau. *The Acadians of Nova Scotia: Past and Present*. Halifax, NS: Nimbus, 1992.

Rutherford, Ward. *Celtic Lore*. London: The Aquarian Press, 1993.

Sadler, Henry. *Masonic Facts and Fictions*. Wellingborough, England: The Aquarian Press, 1985.

Schwartz, Lillian. "Leonardo's Mona Lisa." *Art and Antiques*. January 1987.

Sède, Gérard de. *L'Or de Rennes*. Paris: J'ai Lu, 1967.

Sinclair, Andrew. *The Sword and The Grail*. New York: Crown, 1992.

Spicer, Stanley T. *Glooscap Legends*. Hantsport, NS: Lancelot, 1991.

Sumption, Jonathan. *The Albigensian Crusade*. London: Faber and Faber, 1978.

Taylor, F. S. *The Alchemists*. New York: Schuman, 1949.

Temple, Robert, K. G. *The Sirius Mystery*. London: Futura, 1976.

Tennyson, Lord Alfred. *The Holy Grail, and Other Poems*. London: Strahan and Co., 1870.

———. *Idylls of the Kings*. London: Penguin, 1961.

Tompkins, Peter. *Secrets of the Great Pyramids*. New York: Harper & Row, 1971.

Trento, Salvatore Michael. *The Search for Lost America*. Chicago: Contemporary Books, 1978.

Upton-Ward, J. M. *The Rule of the Templars*. Woodbridge, England: The Boydell Press, 1992.

Vermaseren, M. J. *Mithras, the Secret God*. London: Chatto, 1959; New York: Barnes & Noble, 1963.

Vermes, Geza. *The Dead Sea Scrolls in English*. Harmondsworth, England: Pelican, 1962.

Verne, Jules. *Journey to the Center of the Earth*. London: Penguin, 1965.

Warhart, Sidney, ed. *Francis Bacon: A Selection of His Works*. Toronto: MacMillan of Canada, 1965.

Whyte, Jack. *The Sky Stone*. Toronto: Viking, 1992.

Wilkins, Harold T. *Captain Kidd and His Skeleton Island*. New York: Liveright, 1937.

Williamson, Hugh Ross. *The Arrow and The Sword*. London: Faber, 1947; New York: Fernhill, 1955.

Wilson, Colin. *The Occult*. London: Hodder, 1971; New York: Random House, 1971.

Wilson, Ian. *The Columbus Myth*. Toronto: Simon and Schuster, 1991.

Wilson, John A. *The Culture of Ancient Egypt*. Chicago: University of Chicago Press, 1951.

Wind, E. *Pagan Mysteries in the Renaissance*. London: Peregrine, 1967.

Wood, David. *Genisis*. Tunbridge Wells, England: The Baton Press, 1985.

Yates, F. A. *The Art of Memory*. London: Routledge, 1966.

———. *Giordano Bruno and the Hermetic Tradition*. London: Routledge, 1964; Chicago: University of Chicago Press, 1964; New York: Random House, 1969, paperback.

———. *The Rosicrucian Enlightenment*. London: Routledge, 1972.

Young, G. *Ancient Peoples and Modern Ghosts*. Queensland, NS: self-published, 1980.

About the Author

————⟫◆⟪————

William F. Mann is an urban planner who specializes in new town planning and urban design. He is a registered landscape architect, forester, and professional planner, with a Bachelor of Science in Forestry degree from the University of Toronto and a Master of Landscape Architecture degree from the University of Guelph.

Following in the footsteps of his great-uncle, Frederic George Mann, past Supreme Grand Master of the Knights Templar of Canada, he has recently become a member of Oakville Lodge No. 400, White Oak Chapter No. 104, and Godfrey de Bouillon Preceptory No. 3, under the Sovereign Great Priory of Canada of the United Orders of Malta and of the Temple.

Bill maintains a wide range of interests, including a love of what he terms "hidden history." He lives in Oakville, Ontario, Canada, with his wife, Marie, their two children, William III and Thomas, and their golden retriever, Merlin.

Index

Books of Related Interest

The Lost Treasure of the Knights Templar
Solving the Oak Island Mystery
by Steven Sora

Secret Societies of America's Elite
From the Knights Templar to Skull and Bones
by Steven Sora

The Templars and the Assassins
The Militia of Heaven
by James Wasserman

The Templars
Knights of God
by Edward Burman

The Templar Treasure at Gisors
by Jean Markale

Montségur and the Mystery of the Cathars
by Jean Markale

The Church of Mary Magdalene
The Sacred Feminine and the Treasure of Rennes-le-Château
by Jean Markale

The Woman with the Alabaster Jar
Mary Magdalen and the Holy Grail
by Margaret Starbird

Inner Traditions • Bear & Company
P.O. Box 388
Rochester, VT 05767
1-800-246-8648
www.InnerTraditions.com

Or contact your local bookseller